When Franz Kafka died in 1924, his loyal champion Max Brod could not bring himself to fulfil his friend's last instruction to burn his remaining manuscripts. Instead, Brod devoted the rest of his life to editing, publishing and canonizing Kafka's work. By betraying his friend's last wish, Brod twice rescued his legacy – first from physical destruction, and then from obscurity. But that betrayal was also eventually to lead to an international legal battle: as a writer in German, should Kafka's papers come to rest in Germany, where his three sisters died as victims of the Holocaust? Or, as a Jewish writer, should his work be considered as a cultural inheritance of Israel, a state that did not exist at the time of his death?

Alongside an acutely observed portrait of Kafka, Benjamin Balint traces the journey of the manuscripts Brod had rescued when he fled from Prague to Palestine in 1939 and offers a gripping account of the Israeli court case that determined their fate. He tells of a wrenching escape from the Nazi invaders of Czechoslovakia; of a love affair between exiles stranded in Tel Aviv; and of two countries whose national obsessions with the past eventually faced off in the courts. Benjamin Balint invites us to consider Kafka's remarkable legacy and to question whether that legacy belongs by right to the country of his language, that of his birth, or that of his cultural affinities – but also whether any nation state can lay claim to ownership of a writer's work at all.

KAFKA'S LAST TRIAL

KAFKA'S
LAST TRIAL

The Case of a Literary Legacy

BENJAMIN BALINT

PICADOR

First published 2018 by W. W. Norton & Company, New York

First published in the UK in paperback 2018 by Picador

This edition first published 2019 by Picador
an imprint of Pan Macmillan
20 New Wharf Road, London N1 9RR
Associated companies throughout the world
www.panmacmillan.com

ISBN 978-1-5098-3671-0

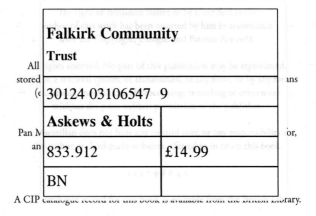

Falkirk Community Trust	
30124 03106547 9	
Askews & Holts	
833.912	£14.99
BN	

Printed and bound by CPI Group (UK) Ltd, Croydon, CR0 4YY

Visit **www.picador.com** to read more about all our books
and to buy them. You will also find features, author interviews and
news of any author events, and you can sign up for e-newsletters
so that you're always first to hear about our new releases.

For Karina

Contents

1 The Last Appeal   3

2 "Fanatical Veneration": The First to Fall under Kafka's Spell   16

3 The First Trial   32

4 Flirting with the Promised Land   49

5 First and Second Judgments   70

6 Last Son of the Diaspora: Kafka's Jewish Afterlife   85

7 The Last Ingathering: Kafka in Israel   101

8 Kafka's Last Wish, Brod's First Betrayal   121

9 Kafka's Creator   132

10 The Last Train: From Prague to Palestine   142

11 The Last Tightrope Dancer: Kafka in Germany   155

12 Laurel & Hardy   173

13 Brod's Last Love   189

14 The Last Heiress: Selling Kafka   202

15 The Last Judgment   209

Epilogue   222

Acknowledgments   229

Notes   231

Bibliography   253

Index   267

KAFKA'S LAST TRIAL

The Last Appeal

Supreme Court of Israel, Shaarei Mishpat Street 1, Jerusalem
June 27, 2016

The word *sein* means two things in German: *being* and *belonging-to-him.*

—Franz Kafka, *Meditation*, aphorism 46

One summer morning in Jerusalem, Eva Hoffe, eighty-two, sat with her hands clasped on a polished curved wood bench in an alcove of the Israeli Supreme Court's high-ceilinged lobby. To pass the time before her hearing, a friend who had come to lend support leafed through a copy of the daily newspaper *Maariv*. On the whole, Eva avoided the press; she resented the farrago of lies generated by journalists bent on portraying her as an eccentric cat-lady, an opportunist looking to make a fast buck on cultural treasures too important to remain in private hands. A headline inked in large red letters on the front page caught Eva's eye. "They're even putting David Bowie's lock of hair up for auction," she said with a hint of indignation. "Yes, as if it were a religious relic," the friend replied.

The fate of another kind of relic would be decided on this day. Three months earlier, on March 30, 2016, Eva had learned that the Supreme Court had agreed to hear her case, "given its public significance." Oddly, Eva's case did not appear on the court's public agenda alongside the others listed for the day. A digital screen in the Supreme Court entrance hall announced her hearing only as Anonymous v. Anonymous.

Eva had arrived almost an hour early; perhaps she had missed the screen on her way in. Today, in any case, anonymity would elude her, no matter how devoutly she wished for its comforts. An eight-year custody battle of sorts was reaching its climax. Earlier stages of the trial—dense with dilemmas legal, ethical, and political—had been covered in the Israeli and international press as the hearings wound their way through the Tel Aviv Family Court (September 2007 to October 2012) and the Tel Aviv District Court (November 2012 to June 2015). From the outset, the contest had pitted private property rights against the public interests of two countries: Does the estate of the German-speaking Prague writer Max Brod (1884–1968) belong to Eva Hoffe or the National Library of Israel, or would it be best housed at the German Literature Archive in Marbach, Germany? At stake was more than the estate of Max Brod, a once acclaimed figure in Central European cultural life. Brod was the friend, editor, and literary executor of another Prague writer, whose name stands for modern literature per se: Franz Kafka.

Brod's estate included not only his own manuscripts, but also sheafs of Kafka's papers, as brittle as autumnal leaves. Ninety-two years after Kafka's death, these manuscripts held out the promise of shedding new light on the uncanny world of the writer who coined an inimitable, immediately recognizable style of surreal realism and etched the twentieth century's most indelible fables of disorientation, absurdity, and faceless tyranny—the rare writer whose name became an adjective. The unlikely story of how Kafka's manuscripts came into the hands of the Hoffe family involved a then-unrecognized writer, endowed with genius, whose last wish was betrayed by his closest friend; a wrenching escape from Nazi invaders as the gates of Europe closed; a love affair between exiles stranded in Tel Aviv; and two countries whose obsessions with overcoming the traumas of the past came to a head in the Supreme Court on this day. Above all, the trial opened up another, highly charged question: Who owns Kafka?

Eva, who now found herself in the eye of the storm, was born in Prague on April 30, 1934, a decade after Kafka was buried in the city's Jewish cemetery. She was five years old when she fled the Nazi-occupied city together with her parents, Esther (Ilse) and Otto Hoffe, and her older sister Ruth. She showed me photos of her mother Esther as a young beauty in Prague with her pet dog, a Great Dane named Tasso, after the sixteenth-century Italian poet best known for his poem *La Gerusalemme liberata* (Jerusalem Delivered, 1581). "I named one of my cats Tasso too," Eva said.

On arriving in Palestine, Eva attended school in Gan Shmuel, a kibbutz near the northern town of Hadera, and then studied until age fifteen at the agricultural boarding school at the Ben Shemen Youth Village in central Israel. Her favorite teacher there, the artist Naomi Smilansky (1916–2016), took Eva under her wing. But Eva's time at Ben Shemen was occluded by loneliness. "I suffered from terrible homesickness there and cried almost every night," she said. At the outbreak of Israel's War of Independence in 1948, with Ben Shemen besieged by forces of the Arab Legion, Eva and the others were evacuated in armored buses. Eva completed her education at Tichon Hadash, Tel Aviv's elite and progressive high school. Here she flourished under the close attention of the German-born principal Toni Halle (1890–1964), a friend of Gershom Scholem since their university days.

After the war, Eva served in a Nahal unit of the Israel Defense Forces (such units, under the command of the Education and Youth Corps, combine social volunteerism, community organizing, agriculture, and military service). On completing her service, she opted to study musicology in Zürich. Before completing her studies, however, she returned to Israel in 1966, in part to soothe her father Otto's anxieties of imminent hostilities between Israel and its neighboring Arab states. "He suffered from a terrible fear of war," she said. "He feared they would slaughter us."

The Six-Day War broke out in the summer of 1967. Every day for six days, Eva walked to Cafe Kassit on Tel Aviv's Dizengoff Street, where she sipped espresso at one of the tiny tables spilling out onto the sidewalk, beneath the six panels of marionette-like harlequins and musicians Yosl Bergner had painted for the café wall facing the street. The café served as a gathering place and gossip mill for long-haired bohemians, down-at-heel intellectuals, hucksters, and the army's top brass, including Moshe Dayan. (Major Ariel Sharon, later prime minister, once chastised a noncommissioned officer: "You spend your time at Kassit and you chat away, talking about our operations to *Haolam Hazeh* [a weekly magazine published by Uri Avnery] journalists.") Anyone who was anyone, said Uri Avnery, one of the café's habitués, "rubbed shoulders with one another, and in friction itself there is inspiration." And every day, Eva brought home snatches of overheard conversations, updates on the progress of the war. Her father greeted her reports of Israeli victories with disbelief.

After the Six-Day War, Eva taught music and rhythm to first- and second-grade children, delighting in their improvisations. The next year, however, Eva suffered a double loss: her father and the writer Max Brod, a Prague émigré and a father figure to her, died in the space of five months. She found she could no longer take pleasure in either playing or teaching music.

As Eva grieved, the Israeli poet and songwriter Haim Hefer, another denizen of Cafe Kassit, recommended her for a job at El Al, the Israeli airline. She served as a member of the ground staff for the next three decades. "I didn't want to be an air-stewardess," she said, "because I wanted to be close to my mother." Instead, she took an almost childlike glee in listening to the roar of a plane's engines, in watching the ground mashallers, with their reflecting safety vests and acoustic earmuffs, wave their illuminated wands and guide an arriving plane to its gate. She retired in 1999, at age sixty-five.

In all her years at El Al, Eva never felt like flying to Germany. "I couldn't forgive," she said. Nor in all those years did she marry. "When

I heard how scathingly Felix Weltsch [a friend of Kafka who fled from Prague to Palestine with Max Brod] talked about his wife Irma, I knew I didn't want to get married." Reconciling herself to childlessness, she preferred to live in a kind of symbiosis with her mother Esther—and their cats—in their cramped apartment on Tel Aviv's Spinoza Street.

———

Eva Hoffe moved in Tel Aviv's intellectual circles—counting the Berlin-born Hebrew poet Natan Zach and the artist Menashe Kadishman among her friends—but she did not pretend to be an intellectual herself. She conceded to me that she had not read many of Brod's books. Eva had no children; she took her nourishment from a circle of devoted friends who doted on her. Three of them huddled with her now in a nook of the Supreme Court lobby, waiting for the hearing to begin. "Whatever happens," the one carrying the newspaper cautioned her, "don't utter a word; no outbursts." She nodded and put her frustration in someone else's words. "If Max Brod were still alive," she said in ventriloquy, "he would come to court and say, *jetzt Schluss damit* (enough already)!"

An Israeli novelist once told me she thought of Eva Hoffe as "the widow of Kafka's ghost." Eva, haunted by the prospect of disinheritance, had acquired something of the ghost's despair at the opacity of justice. In Kafka's unfinished novel *The Trial*, edited and posthumously published by Brod, Joseph K.'s uncle tells him: "A trial like this is always lost from the start." Today Eva communicated that she was bowed under the weight of a similar despair. "If this were a tug-of-war contest, I'd have no chance," she said. "I'm up against immensely powerful opponents, immensely." She was referring to the State of Israel, which claimed that the manuscripts her mother had inherited from Kafka's closest friend belonged not to her but to the National Library in Jerusalem.

The clamor of the previous hearing was quieting down. It was time for Eva, her face sallow but alert, to enter the chamber. "As far as I'm concerned," Eva said as she pressed through the heavy doors leading from the lobby into the courtroom, "the words justice and fairness have been erased from the lexicon."

In *The Trial*, legal chambers are dimly lit. The Jerusalem chamber, by contrast, resembles a high-ceilinged chapel, its unadorned white walls suffused with natural light. There is no glitz or gilding here. The angular building, commissioned by the London-based philanthropist Dorothy de Rothschild, is sheathed in Jerusalem stone. It is capped by a copper-clad pyramid inspired by the ancient tomb of the prophet Zechariah, the monument hewn out of the solid rock of the Kidron Valley on Jerusalem's eastern flank.

Nine lawyers in black robes sat at a semicircular table. They were there to give voice to the three not necessarily equal parties to this dispute: the National Library of Israel (which enjoyed the home-court advantage, so to speak, since the proceedings played out on Israeli turf); the German Literature Archive in Marbach (which had the advantage of financial resources of a magnitude not available to the other two parties); and Eva Hoffe (who, at least for the time being, had physical possession of the prize sought by the others). Each of the parties engaged in polemic by legal means, and each (and in turn, the judges) fluctuated between two rhetorical registers: the legal and the symbolic. The legal proceedings promised to throw light on questions of enduring significance for Israel, Germany, and the still fraught relationship between them. Both Marbach and the National Library brought to the courtroom a concern about their respective national pasts (albeit in very different ways); both sought to use Kafka as a trophy to honor those pasts, as though the writer was an instrument of national prestige.

The lawyers, their backs to the rows of spectators, faced a panel of three justices on the raised dais: Yoram Danziger (formerly a leading commercial lawyer) to the left, Elyakim Rubinstein (a former attorney general) in the center, and Zvi Zylbertal (formerly of the Jerusalem

District Court) to the right. These were the men tasked with measuring the legitimacy of each claim against the limits of that legitimacy.

Eva seated herself alone in the front row. Months earlier, I had chanced to see her on Tel Aviv's Ibn Gvirol Street, not far from her apartment; she seemed to be wandering, forlorn and companionless. Today, the expression on her face, mottled with melanin spots, was one of unmixed attention and lucidity. She took a seat just behind her lawyer, Eli Zohar, a well-connected hot-shot litigator who represented executives, high-ranking Israeli army officers, power-players in the Israel Military Industries and the Shabak (Israel's internal security service), and, somewhat less successfully, Israel's former prime minister, Ehud Olmert. (Olmert, convicted of breach of trust in 2012, and of bribery in 2014, began serving a nineteen-month prison sentence in February 2016.) Eva had switched lawyers several times in the last eight years: before settling on Zohar, she had been represented at various stages by Yeshayahu Etgar, Oded Cohen, and Uri Zfat. Eva told me she had given a lien on her apartment to Zohar to ensure he'd be paid in the event she died before the proceedings concluded.

Zohar, his thinning hair slewed to one side, his black robe perfectly perpendicular to the polished floor, cleared his throat and spoke with remote courtesy—straightforward, not showy. In a firm baritone, he opened by saying that the court need not render a decision. The judgment had, in effect, been handed down four decades earlier. When Franz Kafka died of tuberculosis in 1924, a month short of his forty-first birthday, his close friend and champion Max Brod—a prolific and acclaimed author in his own right—balked at Kafka's last instruction: to burn his remaining manuscripts, diaries, and letters unread. Instead, Brod rescued the manuscripts and devoted the rest of his life to canonizing Kafka as the most prescient—and most disquieting—chronicler of the twentieth century. When Brod died in Tel Aviv in 1968, these manuscripts passed to his secretary and confidante Esther Hoffe, Eva's mother.

In 1973, five years after Brod's death, Zohar continued, the State of Israel sued Esther Hoffe for possession of the Kafka manuscripts she had inherited. The case was brought before Judge Yitzhak Shilo of the Tel Aviv District Court. In January 1974, Judge Shilo ruled that Brod's last will "allows Mrs. Hoffe to do with his estate as she pleases during her lifetime."

Invoking this precedent, Zohar argued before the justices that with all due respect the present proceedings were unnecessary; there was no need to relitigate a case that had given Esther the right to what she already had.

The argument did not cut much ice with Justice Rubinstein. With a schoolmaster's manner, and with an air of omnicompetence about him, the judge gave Zohar short shrift. "The gentleman will please take the bull by the horns. We cannot devote too much time to Judge Shilo's ruling, which we have read. The gentleman will proceed."

Unrattled, Zohar tried another tack: why, he asked, should the Kafka and Brod estates be transferred to the National Library of Israel, an institution that manifestly lacks the experts capable of discernment in German literature?

The issue, Justice Zylbertal interjected from the right side of the dais, is not so much whether the library can furnish experts, but whether it can house material and make it accessible to scholars who wish to consult it.

Attorney Yossi Ashkenazi, court-appointed deputy executor of Max Brod's estate, rose, younger and less smooth in his manner than Zohar, and less convoluted in style. Brod had granted Esther Hoffe the choice of how and to whom to give the manuscripts, he argued, but not the right to pass that choice on to her heirs. Brod "did not want her daughters to deal with the matter."

Eva lowered her blue eyes and shook her head, her long hair swaying slightly. But she suppressed any other signs of distemper.

Polished to a high sheen, the bald cannonball head of attorney Meir Heller now came into view from the right corner. Heller, who represented the National Library of Israel throughout the eight-year legal battle, came out swinging. He blamed Esther Hoffe for preventing researchers access to the manuscripts she kept locked away for decades, and counseled the court to put an end to that untenable situation. Hundreds of researchers come to the National Library annually to consult the thousand personal archives of Jewish writers it holds, he said, and he expressed the hope that Kafka's papers, rescued by Brod, would soon find their rightful place among them. The undercurrent of his argument was unmistakable: Kafka, a writer of Jewish literature in a non-Jewish language, belongs in the Jewish state.

"The attempt to portray Kafka as a Jewish writer is ridiculous," Eva once told me. "He did not love his Jewishness. He wrote from his heart, inwardly. He didn't have a dialogue with God." But even those who do consider him a Jewish writer, she said, cannot justifiably deduce from that anything about "the proper home" of his literary legacy. "Natan Alterman's archives are in London, Yehuda Amichai's are in New Haven," she said, referring to two of Israel's most beloved poets. "By what law must a Jewish writer's archives stay in Israel?" As she spoke, I noticed the shift of registers between "love" and "law."*

Of course, Amichai had the luxury of deciding in his lifetime where his papers should go; Brod can no longer tell us about his own preferences. The posthumous handling of literary estates (*Nachlässe* in German) is not the same as the acquisition of papers from living authors (*Vorlässe*). But Hoffe's point did have parallels elsewhere. The British novelist Kingsley Amis (1922–95), for instance, once remarked that

* The acquisition of Yehuda Amichai's archives by Yale's Beinecke Rare Book and Manuscript Library, authorized in 1998 by Israel's state archivist, Evyatar Friesel, created a storm of indignation in Israel when the sale became public after Amichai's death in 2000. "What people in the world can give up cultural assets like this?" Israeli poet Natan Yonatan said. Rafi Weiser, then director of the manuscripts department of the National Library in Jerusalem, said: "We could probably have prevented the deal by leaking Amichai's intention to the media. The public pressure would certainly have sabotaged the sale. But we decided to respect his wish and keep things quiet."

he had little patience for the view that manuscripts by British authors should stay in Britain. Nor did he entertain qualms about his own papers leaving England:

> I will sell any of my manuscripts to the highest bidder, assuming such bidder to be of reputable standing, and I have no feeling one way or the other about such bidder's country of origin. It seems to me no more incongruous that the Tate Gallery should have a large collection of Monets (say) than that Buffalo University should have a collection of [the English poet and novelist] Robert Graves manuscripts (say).

In 1969, Amis sold one-and-a-half boxes' worth of manuscripts to the Harry Ransom Humanities Center in Texas.* Fifteen years later, he sold the remainder of his papers and rights to all future papers to the Huntington Library in San Marino, California (which also happens to house one of the world's finest collections of early editions of another English writer: Shakespeare).

Four days before the Supreme Court hearing in Jerusalem, Germany's parliament in Berlin offered an example of how European countries were seeking to clamp down on such sales. On June 23, 2016, the Bundestag adopted a controversial cultural heritage protection law aimed at keeping works in Germany that are considered "national treasures" (defined as "national cultural property of outstanding significance for the nation" whose removal would cause a "significant loss"). "The cultural nation of Germany," Culture Minister Monika Grütters said, "is obligated to collect and preserve its cultural property." Grütters dismissed concerns that the law would be used to "nationalize" German art and artifacts owned by private citizens. "Protection is not, in my eyes, expropriation."

---

* In 2014, the Ransom Center at the University of Texas at Austin—which holds papers of British authors Doris Lessing and Graham Greene—acquired the archives of Man Booker prize-winning British author Ian McEwan for $2 million.

As the lawyers in the Israeli courtroom debated where protection ends and expropriation begins, it became clear that the Israeli effort to claim Kafka for the Jewish state depended not only on positive assertions about his Jewishness but also on defining him by what he is not—in other words, *not* a German national treasure.

Meir Heller took his seat, and attorney Sa'ar Plinner addressed the court in a clipped cadence. His client, the German Literature Archive in Marbach, headed by Ulrich Raulff, wished to add the Kafka and Brod collections to its world-class holdings of literary estates of prominent writers. But as Plinner told me later, he was constrained by precise instructions from Raulff about what to say and not to say in supporting Hoffe's right to sell the estate to the Germans. All along, the German Literature Archive had implied that in Germany, Kafka would be read universally (from an objective "view from nowhere," if such a thing were possible), and in Israel, where some are tempted to reduce Kafka to being a Jewish author, he would be read in more parochial and idiosyncratic ways.

Now, aware that they had made some tactless moves in earlier stages of the trial, the directors of the German Literature Archive wished at this crucial juncture to keep a lower profile, to tread more lightly. Accordingly, as he says he was instructed to do, Plinner merely stressed that because of the abundance of material, previous attempts to inventory Max Brod's estate were incomplete. "At present, I don't think anyone knows what's there," he said.

Before an hour has elapsed, Justice Rubinstein brought the proceedings to a close. He and his two colleagues retired to their chambers. Eva and her friends milled about anxiously in the lobby. "When will the verdict come down?" one asked. One of Eli Zohar's aides replied by citing the medieval biblical commentator Rashi on the verse, "And it shall be when your son asks you tomorrow . . ." (Exodus 13:14). "There's a tomorrow that means tomorrow, Rashi explained, and there's a tomorrow that means in the world to come."

Not one to be deferential, Eva remarked that Eli Zohar seemed to be suffering from a summer cold. "He was not at the top of his game," she said. But she seemed to signal that she could withstand the pressure, that she was made of sterner stuff. As she left the lobby and headed toward the footbridge that connects the Supreme Court compound with a garish mall across the street, she said: "Still, I hope against hope. My name is Hoffe [German for 'I hope'], after all."

As she walked away, I thought of Kafka's subversion of that old Latin motto of obstinacy, *dum spiro spero*—"While I breathe, I hope." In his biography of Kafka, Max Brod reports a conversation in which Kafka suggested that human beings may be nothing more than nihilistic thoughts in God's mind. Then is there any hope? Brod asked. "There is plenty of hope," Kafka replied, "an infinite amount of hope—only not for us." And as Eva's small figure receded, I wondered whether Kafka—with his "passion for making himself insignificant," as the German-language Jewish writer Elias Canetti put it—would shudder from the possessiveness the trial laid bare. Would he remind us that we can be intoxicated by what we possess, but even more intoxicated by what we don't?

Eva Hoffe at Max Brod's graveside, Tel Aviv, January 2017. (photo: Tomer Appelbaum)

2

"Fanatical Veneration": The First to Fall under Kafka's Spell

Charles University, Prague
October 23, 1902

A book must be the axe for the frozen sea inside us.
—Franz Kafka, 1904

Where faith is lacking, everything seems bare and frigid.
—Max Brod, 1920

Burning to impress, Max Brod, eighteen, a first-year law student at Charles University in Prague, had just wrapped up a talk on the philosopher Arthur Schopenhauer in the second-floor club room of the German Students' Union on Ferdinandstrasse. On a sideboard next to the heavy drapes, thickly buttered slices of bread rested on trays next to newspapers from throughout Europe. For two years, Brod had been obsessed with the works of Schopenhauer. He could recite entire passages from memory. "When I was finished with volume six [of his complete works]," Brod recalled, "I immediately turned again to volume one."

From behind the lectern, Brod's disproportionately large head was visible atop a stocky torso. Although you wouldn't have guessed it now, a deformation of the spine (or kyphosis), diagnosed when he was four years old, had forced him to wear an iron corset and neck brace for part of his childhood.

Max Brod was born in 1884, the eldest of three children of a Jewish middle-class family that traced its presence in Prague back to the seventeenth century. As an infant, he had suffered measles, scarlet fever, and a near-fatal bout of diphtheria. Max's father Adolf, deputy director of the United Bohemian Bank, was temperate, easy-going, and urbane; his mother Fanny (née Rosenfeld), was a volcano of unbridled emotions. In his digressive autobiography, *A Contentious Life* (*Streitbares Leben*), Brod writes: "In my brother [Otto] as in my sister [Sophia], my mother's energy was joined with my father's nobility and kindness to form a well-rounded character, whereas in me much remained unstable and I always had to struggle to maintain a semblance of inner balance."

Brod's gregariousness seemed at variance with his small stature, and in conversation one quickly forgot about the geometry of his figure. His friend the Austrian-Jewish writer Stefan Zweig described Brod as a student: "I still remember him as I beheld him for the first time, a twenty-year-old youth, small, slim, and of boundless modesty.... Thus was he then, this young poet entirely devoted to everything which seemed great to him, to the strange, to the sublime, to the wonderful in every shape and form."

As the audience dispersed, a lanky, six-foot-tall, fastidiously dressed student one year his senior approached the lectern with a loping gait. His tie was perfectly knotted; his ears pointed. Brod had never seen him before. Franz Kafka introduced himself and offered to walk Brod home. "Even his elegant, usually dark-blue, suits were inconspicuous and reserved like him," Brod recalled. "At that time, however, something seems to have attracted him to me; he was more open than usual, filling the endless walk home by disagreeing strongly with my all too rough formulations." When they arrived at Schallengasse 1, where Brod lived with his parents, the conversation was still in full swing. With

Brod struggling to keep pace, they walked to Zeltnergasse, where Franz Kafka lived with his parents and sisters, and then back again. Along the way, the two students spoke about Nietzsche's attacks on Schopenhauer, about Schopenhauer's ideal of renouncing the self, and about his definition of genius: "Genius," the philosopher wrote, "is the ability to leave entirely out of sight our own interest, our willing, and our aims, and consequently to discard entirely our own personality for a time, in order to remain pure knowing subject, the clear eye of the world." Brod noticed the color of Kafka's eyes, "a keen, sparkling gray," as he put it. As Kafka showed neither aptitude nor appetite for abstract philosophizing, the conversation soon took a literary turn. With disarming simplicity, Kafka preferred to talk about the Austrian writer, ten years their senior, Hugo von Hofmannsthal. (One of the first gifts Kafka gave to Brod was a special edition, with embossed binding, of Hofmannsthal's *Das Kleine Welttheater*, The Small World-Theater [1897].)

The pair began to meet daily, sometimes twice a day. Brod became attracted to Kafka's gentle serenity, to the "sweet aura of certainty," as he put it, and the "unusual aura of power" he radiated. He seemed to Brod both wise and childlike. In his memoirs, Brod would describe the "collision of souls" as they read together Plato's *Protagoras* in Greek, and Flaubert's *Sentimental Education* (1869) and *The Temptation of Saint Anthony* (1874) in French. (Among many other gifts, Kafka would give Brod a book about Flaubert by René Dumesnil.) "We completed each other," Brod writes, "and had so much to give one another." More mundanely, Kafka depended on Brod to help him pass one of the oral examinations for his law degree. "Only your notes saved me," he told Brod.

The two young men would spend the occasional evening together at the cinema or the cabaret Chat Noir. Although they conversed exclusively in German, they would chuckle at certain Czech figures of speech, like *člobrdo* ("poor little chap"). They enjoyed conversations about the new stereoscopic slide shows called Kaiserpanorama. They often hiked together on Sundays, and took day trips to Karlštejn Castle, a Gothic keep southwest of Prague that had held the Czech crown jewels, sacred relics, and the most valuable documents of the state archive. They discussed the differences between novels and theater as they strolled among promenading couples along the tree-hemmed paths of the Baumgarten, the park known as "the Prater of Prague." Kafka would amuse Brod by imitating the way in which other saunterers handled their walking sticks. They went swimming in the Moldau River, and loafed under chestnut trees after a dip in Prague's open-air bath. "Kafka and I held the strange belief that one has not taken possession of a landscape until a swim in its streaming bodies of water establishes a physical connection," Brod said.

When Kafka and Brod visited Lake Maggiore, Kafka biographer Reiner Stach reports, they began with a swim and "embraced while standing in the water—which must have looked quite odd especially because of the difference in their heights." The pair also vacationed together in Riva on Lake Garda, on the Austria–Italy border; visited Goethe's house in Weimar; and stayed together at the Hotel Belvédère au Lac in Lugano, Switzerland.* In 1909, they attended the air show at the Montichiari airfield near Brescia, in northern Italy. They exchanged their travel diaries. They twice traveled to Paris together: in October 1910, and again at the end of an extended summer trip in 1911. During that trip, Kafka and Brod thought up a new kind of travel guide. "It would be called *Billig* (*On the Cheap*)," Brod said. "Franz was tireless and got a childlike pleasure out of elaborating all the principles down to the least detail for this new type of guide, which was supposed to make us millionaires." Their motto for the series: *Just Dare.*

As wifely and solicitous as he could be, Brod did sometimes tire of what he called "Kafka's hopelessness." "It is pretty clear to me," Brod writes in his diary in 1911, "that . . . Kafka is suffering from an obsessional neurosis." But such reservations did not long interfere with Brod's growing admiration. "Never in my life," Brod wrote, "have I been so

---

* Brod wrote a poem about their time together in Lugano in early September 1911, and later published it with the dedication "To my friend Franz Kafka."

serenely cheerful as during weeks of holiday spent with Kafka. All my cares, all my peevishness stayed behind in Prague. We turned into merry children, we came up with the most outlandish, cutest jokes—it was a great stroke of luck for me to live close to Kafka and enjoy first-hand hearing him spouting his animated ideas (even his hypochondria was inventive and entertaining)."

Even when they were apart, Brod said, "I knew exactly what he would have said in this or that situation." When Brod vacationed without Kafka, he often sent postcards. He once sent Kafka a postcard from Venice, for instance, featuring Bellini's painting of Venus, goddess of love. "For a brief time," writes Reiner Stach, Kafka "even contemplated starting a new private notebook devoted exclusively to his relationship with Brod."

———

And yet the contrasts between the two young men—one as exuberant and outgoing as the other was inward-looking—were evident for all to see. Brod, with his joie de vivre, alive with surplus energies, radiated a verve, vitality, and communion with human life lacking in Kafka. Brod, of a sunnier temperament, less divided against himself, seemed free of the kind of self-doubt that accompanied Kafka's pitiless self-scrutiny. If Kafka could not bring himself to care much about worldly success, Brod (in the words of Arthur Schnitzler) was "consumed with his own ambition, jumping headlong into opportunities that come along like an enthusiast."

Kafka tended to husband his energies inward. His obsession with writing conferred on him a capacity for asceticism wholly lacking in Brod. "When it became clear in my organism that writing was the most productive direction for my being to take," Kafka wrote in 1912, "everything rushed in that direction and left empty all those abilities which were directed toward the joys of sex, eating, drinking, philosophical reflection, and above all music." In a diary entry from August 1914, he put it in another way: "My penchant for portraying my dreamlike inner life has rendered everything else inconsequential; my life has atrophied terribly, and does not stop atrophying." "I am made of literature," Kafka wrote in 1913. "I am nothing else and cannot be anything else." "I hate everything that does not relate to literature," he admitted the same year.

There were other telling contrasts. An accomplished composer and pianist, Brod had a delicate discrimination and refined taste in matters of music. He set texts by Heine, Schiller, Flaubert, and Goethe to music. (He had studied musical composition with Adolf Schreiber, a student of Antonín Dvořák, and was proud of a distant relative, Henri Brod, a famous French oboist.) Stefan Zweig remembered how "his small, girlish hands strayed gently over the keys of a piano." One evening in 1912, when Albert Einstein was teaching in Prague, Brod and the physicist played a violin sonata together. Leon Botstein, the American conductor and president of Bard College, speculates that for Brod, "music facilitated what seemed impossible in politics: the forging of communication between the Czech and the German."

Kafka, by contrast, admitted his "inability to enjoy music cohesively." He never indulged in opera or classical concerts. He admitted to Brod that he wouldn't be able to distinguish a piece by Franz Lehár, a composer of light operettas, from one by Richard Wagner, the composer who gave voice to the Dionysian passions of German myth. (Brod greatly admired Wagner's music, and claimed never to have read the composer's anti-Semitic screeds.)

Certainly, music features in Kafka's fiction. In Kafka's novella "The Metamorphosis" [*Die Verwandlung*], for example, Gregor Samsa, transformed into a repulsive insect, scuttles out of his room toward the vibrating sounds of his sister Grete's violin. "Was he a beast, if music could move him so?" he asks himself. "It seemed to him to open a way toward that unknown nourishment he so longed for . . . No one here would appreciate her music as much as he." In Kafka's first novel, *Amerika*,

Karl expresses an immigrant's longing with his amateurish renditions of a soldier's song from the old country. In the short story "Investigations of a Dog," the canine narrator devotes his life to a scientific study of the riddle of seven dancing "musical dogs" (*Musikerhunde*) whose melodies overwhelm him and in the end restore him to the canine community.

And yet Samsa's creator pronounced himself "completely detached from music," a detachment that overwhelmed him with "a quiet bitter-sweet mourning." "Music is for me like the ocean," Kafka said. "I am overpowered, and transported to a state of wonderment. I am enthusiastic but also anxious when faced with endlessness. I am, as is evident, a poor sailor. Max Brod is the exact opposite. He rushes headlong into the waves of sound. Now that's a champion swimmer."

Nor could Kafka match the erotic passions that Brod expressed in life and literature alike. Together they visited brothels in Prague, Milan, Leipzig, and Paris. Brod, a regular at Prague's upscale brothels like Salon Goldschmied, "would go into raptures in his diary over the perky breasts of a young prostitute," Reiner Stach writes. Not so Kafka, who on visiting one of Prague's thirty-five brothels confessed to Brod that he felt "desperately in need of just a simple caress." Brod, a self-confessed ladies' man and worshiper of women, spoke with Kafka of "my natural disposition to women, my feeling of being utterly abandoned to them." Brod would go to the Cafe Arco and pore over Aubrey Beardsley's erotic illustrations or read, "with inflamed fervor," Casanova's memoirs, with their accounts of his adventures with women. (Kafka "found them boring," Brod writes.) "For me," Brod told Kafka, "the world takes on meaning only through the medium of a woman." Kafka may have had Brod in mind when he wrote that "men seeking salvation always throw themselves at women."

Yet to Brod, sex—and the redemptive power of women—was serious business. "Of all God's messengers," Brod wrote, "Eros speaks to us most forcefully. It drags man most speedily before the glory of God." In contrast with Christianity, which Brod says turns "a sour face" to the carnal, Judaism harnesses its power. "The prodigious achievement of Judaism," Brod writes in his brambly 650-page philosophical treatise *Paganism, Christianity, Judaism* (1921), "radiating down the millennia, is to have recognized the earthly miracle, the purest form of this divine grace, 'God's flame,' in love—not in any diluted spiritual form of love, but in the direct erotic rapture of man and woman."*

Much of Brod's overwrought fiction similarly hinges on eros. His short novel *A Czech Servant Girl* (*Ein tschechisches Dienstmädchen*, 1909), features a Vienna-born German named William Schurhaft—the Prague-born linguist Pavel Eisner calls him "a symbolic figure of the Jewish intellectual from the Prague bourgeoisie." William falls in love with a married Czech country girl who works as a maid in his hotel. He receives from the maid "the sweet sense of true existence." The literary critic Leo Hermann, then chairman of Prague's Bar Kochba Association, quipped that "the young author apparently believes that national problems can be solved in bed." (When he read Hermann's remark, Brod reported, "I jumped up in fury.") In 1913, Viennese writer Leopold Lieger accused Brod of composing his love poems in bed.

Brod's novel *Three Loves* (*Die Frau Nach der Man Sich Sehnt*, literally *The Woman One Longs For*, 1927), can be read as an allusion to the tragic relationship between Kafka and Milena Jesenská, his married Czech translator and lover. Milena became preoccupied both with her fidelity to Kafka's prose, and with her husband's infidelity to her. Brod's narrator finds pure love in Stasha, "a sacred ecstasy engendered by woman," and "a call from the eternal celestial home of our hearts." Stasha, like Milena, cannot and will not leave her husband, despite his affairs. (Brod had known Milena's husband, Ernst Pollak, from the Prague literary scene. Brod may have taken his character's name from one of Milena's closest friends, the translator Staša Jílovská.) In 1929, Brod's novel would be made into a silent film starring Marlene Dietrich as Stasha.

Kafka, by contrast, asked himself in his diary in 1922: "What have

---

* Brod's friend Thomas Mann charitably called the book, which Kafka had read in manuscript, "rich in striking generalizations."

you done with your gift of sex? It was a failure, in the end that is all that they will say." Kafka also noted that several of the literary forebears he admired most—Kleist, Kierkegaard, Flaubert—were lifelong bachelors. "You avoid women," Brod told Kafka, "you try to live without them. And that doesn't work." (He would level the same criticism at some of Kafka's fictional creations. Brod charged Joseph K. in *The Trial*, for instance, with *Lieblosigkeit*, the inability to love.)

Still, Brod often sought Kafka's advice about the vagaries of young love. In 1913, Brod became engaged to Elsa Taussig, who would become a translator from Russian and Czech into German. Kafka noted, "I strongly encouraged Max and may even have helped to make up his mind." And yet after the engagement party Kafka said: "When all is said and done, he is actually being separated from me."

This was no mere friendship, then, but a literary entanglement between two very different types—between a writer of genius and a writer of taste who recognized genius but could not partake of it. The entanglement raised a number of questions: How did Kafka inhabit Brod's fiction? Was Brod an accidental companion to Kafka's writing, or was he somehow internal to its motions?

———

In more than one sense, Brod considered himself a "*Zwischenmensch*," a between-man, precariously perched between German, Czech, and Jewish cultures, and therefore attuned to each. "Where three cultures came together," he would say, "a precocious awareness arises." At a time when Prague, in Anthony Grafton's phrase, was "Europe's capital of cosmopolitan dreams," Brod carved out a place as a *litterateur* in the enclave of cultural ferment known as the Prague Circle. ("For every ten Germans [in Prague]," Prague-born culture critic Emil Faktor quipped, "there are twelve literary talents.") Already a published *Wunderkind* while in his teens, Brod's early reputation as a versatile poet, novelist, and critic—not to mention enterprising networker—launched a career that would gain him recognition as the most successful Prague writer of his generation. Reiner Stach notes that by age twenty-five, Brod was corresponding with Hermann Hesse, Hugo von Hofmannsthal, Thomas and Heinrich Mann, Rainer Maria Rilke, and other leading literary lights. In 1912, a twenty-seven-year-old literary journalist from Prague named Egon Erwin Kisch visited a café in London's East End frequented by Yiddish speakers:

> A nineteen-year-old lad has run away from the Lodz *yeshiva* [Talmudic academy]; he doesn't want to be a "*bocher*" [religious student] and doesn't want to become a rabbi. Instead, he wants to create, to conquer the world, to write books, to "become a second Max Brod."

Brod would prove as prolific (to the point of graphomania) as Kafka was not. His published work would run to almost ninety titles—twenty novels, poetry collections, religious treatises, polemical broadsides (not pugnacious by nature, he called himself a "reluctant polemicist"), plays (including on the biblical heroes Queen Esther and King Saul), essays, translations, librettos, compositions for the piano, and biographies. Read together, they amount to a surpassingly rich literary curriculum vitae. (Of these many works, only seven have been published in English translation.)

Brod, a man inclined to search out greatness in others, was the first to fall under the spell of Kafka's idiosyncratic fiction, the first witness to the range and richness of his friend's imagination. On hearing Kafka read aloud from his early stories "Description of a Struggle" and "Wedding Preparations in the Country," Brod writes: "I got the impression immediately that here was no ordinary talent speaking, but a genius." (With great reverence, Brod read a draft of "Wedding Preparations" to his future wife, Elsa.) After Kafka read him two draft chapters of his novel-in-progress *The Trial* in 1915, Brod effused in his diary: "He is the greatest writer of our time." On reading Kafka's drafts, Brod did not feel that he was encountering a type of writing for the first time, but that he had somehow always known it. He did not imitate Kafka's writing, but he was changed by it. From now on, Brod treated Kafka with what he conceded was a "fanatical veneration." "He stood by my side like a savior," Brod writes in his memoir.

Kafka also served as Brod's first audience, and often looked to Brod's writing for solace. In 1908, he read Brod's first large-scale work, the *avant-garde* novel *Nornepygge Castle: Novel of the Indifferent Man.* "Only your book," Kafka wrote, "which I am at last reading straight through, does me good." A couple of years later, Brod submitted to Kafka's scrutiny a draft of his poems, collected under the title *Diary in Verse* (*Tagebuch in Versen*, 1910). Kafka recommended discarding about sixty poems.

Kafka's admiration for Brod's energy and initiative grew in equal measure to his distrust of himself. Take, for instance, Kafka's diary entry for January 17, 1911, when he was twenty-seven years old.

> Max read me the first act of *Abschied von der Jugend* [*Farewell to Youth: A Romantic Comedy in Three Acts*, one of Brod's early works]. How can I, as I am today, come up to it? I should have to look for a year before I found a true emotion in me.

That fall, Kafka and Brod began a joint novel, to be called *Richard and Samuel.*[*] They published a first chapter in the Prague magazine *Herder-Blätter*, edited by their friend Willy Haas, before aborting the project. "Max and I must be fundamentally different," Kafka noted in his diary. "Much as I admire his work . . . still every sentence he writes for *Richard and Samuel* involves reluctant concessions on my part

---

[*] On May 26, 2018, the original six-page introduction to the novel, which had been in the hands of a private collector from Switzerland since 1983, was sold for €150,000 (nearly $175,000) at the Christian Hesse auction house in Hamburg. The eventual buyer: the German Literature Archive in Marbach.

which I feel in the very depths of my being." Three years later, Kafka wrote: "Max does not understand me, and when he thinks he does, he is wrong."

Did Brod ever read one of Kafka's drafts and wish that he had been its author? Brod suspected that for all his prolific production, he may have been bestowed with the gifts of taste and discernment but not the ability to create a truly original work of art. As a spectator of Kafka's genius, he had to depend on something other than himself.

Perhaps nonartists try to possess materially the art they cannot possess genuinely. Brod, as we'll see, obsessively collected anything that Kafka put his hand to. Kafka, in contrast, felt the impulse to shed everything. "He was impervious to the joys of collecting things," writes Reiner Stach.

———

Before long, Brod began to fictionalize his friendship with Kafka. The main character of his 1912 novel *Arnold Beer* is a dilettante who cajoles his friends to write in the same tonalities as Brod used with Kafka. "Arnold simply demanded that work should go on all around him; as though dimly aware that for his part he was too fragmented to leave behind anything worth mentioning, he sought to make his energy operate through the medium of other people's brains." After reading the novel, Kafka told Brod: "Your book has given me such pleasure. . . . I give you a hearty kiss."

Brod's best-known novel, *The Redemption of Tycho Brahe* (published in a printing of one hundred thousand copies by Kurt Wolff in 1916, and in English translation by Knopf in 1928), tells the story of the relationship between the great Danish astronomer Tycho Brahe (1546–1601) and the intellectually superior German astronomer Johannes Kepler (1571–1630). Kepler, devoted to discovering the laws of planetary motion, refuses to publish anything that falls short of perfection. The fictional Tycho describes Kepler as an enigmatic man in single-minded pursuit of "immaculate purity." The more versatile Brahe, living in exile in Prague, does not know what to make of Kepler's self-doubt, his disinclination to publish, or his declaration "I am not happy and have never been happy . . . and I don't even want to be happy." Kepler's discoveries render Tycho's obsolete. Yet Brahe self-effacingly overcomes his vanity and puts his own work second to Kepler's. Brod dedicated the book to Kafka. "Do you know what such a dedication implies?" Kafka writes to Brod in February 1914. "That I am raised to the same level as Tycho, who is so much more vital than I. . . . How small I shall be, orbiting this story! But how glad I shall be to have a semblance of property rights in it. As always, Max, you are good to me beyond what I deserve."*

Acknowledging Kafka's incapacity for self-promotion, the well-connected Brod came to serve as his friend's advocate, herald, and literary agent. "I wanted to prove to him that his fears of literary barrenness were unfounded," Brod wrote. He gave Kafka favorable mention in the Berlin weekly *Die Gegenwart* before Kafka had published a single line.

Brod waged an uphill battle against Kafka's sense of his own inadequacy. "The core of all my misery remains: I cannot write," Kafka confessed to Brod in 1910. "I haven't managed a single line I'd care to acknowledge; on the contrary, I threw out everything—it wasn't much—that I had written since Paris. My whole body warns me of

---

* *The Redemption of Tycho Brahe*, writes Peter Fenves, professor of literature at Northwestern University, "can be read as a semi-repressed reflection on what would happen to his own literary legacy if Kafka outlived him." The *New York Times* considered the novel "a penetrating study in contrasting genius, taken from historical sources and wrought into a novel of such depth and distinction that it has something of a classical air." Albert Einstein remarked: "It is without a doubt interestingly written by a man who knows the cliffs of the human soul." In a November 1913 letter to Martin Buber, Brod explained the novel's significance: "From the very beginning of my literary development I had before my mind the appeasement of the rational and the irrational, no merger, of course, but the coming together of the two ideals brought to their culmination, therefore my *Tycho*."

every word, and every word first looks around in all directions before it lets itself be written down by me. The sentences literally crumble in my hands; I see their insides and have to stop quickly."

In a letter to another friend, Kafka spoke of his "fear of attracting the gods' attention." Undeterred, and devoid of envy, Brod interceded on Kafka's behalf with editors and publishers. Brod served as the liaison between Kafka and the journal *Hyperion*, edited by Franz Blei, where Kafka's byline first appeared in print. Brod wrote to Martin Buber in 1916: "If you only knew his substantial, though unfortunately incomplete novels, which he sometimes reads to me at odd hours. What I wouldn't do to make him more active!"

In the summer of 1912, Brod brought Kafka to Leipzig, then the hub of the German book business, and introduced Kafka to the young publisher Kurt Wolff. "I promptly had the impression," Wolff recalled, "which I could never afterwards efface, that the impresario was presenting the star he had discovered." At the end of that year, Brod and Wolff arranged for Kafka's first book to be published by Rowohlt Verlag in an edition of eight hundred copies. The ninety-nine-page volume, called *Meditation* (*Betrachtung*) was a collection of eighteen "prose poems." The publisher's advertisement remarked that the author's "idiosyncratic need to polish works of literature again and again has so far held him back from publishing books." Kafka dedicated the book to Brod, who in turn would publish a rave review in the Munich journal *März*:

> I could easily imagine someone getting hold of this book and finding his whole life altered from that moment on, and realizing he would become a new person. That is how much absoluteness and sweet energy emanates from these few short prose pieces. . . . It is the love of the divine, of the absolute that comes through in every line, with such a natural quality that not a single word is squandered in this fundamental morality.

Kafka was mortified. "I could have used a hole to hide in." When the review came out, he wrote to his fiancée Felice Bauer:

> Just because the friendship he feels for me in its most human element has its roots far deeper than those of literature and therefore comes into play before literature even has a chance, he overestimates me in a manner that embarrasses me and makes me vain and arrogant. . . . If I myself were working and were in the flow of work and carried along by it, I wouldn't dwell on the review; in my mind I could kiss Max for his love, and the review itself would not affect me in the slightest! But as things stand . . .

In 1913, Brod published Kafka's breakthrough story "The Judgment" in his anthology, *Arkadia*.* (Kafka acknowledged that "The Judgment," dedicated to "Felice B.," drew on some motifs in Brod's 1912 novel *Arnold Beer*.) In 1921, Brod talked up his friend in a long essay called "Franz Kafka the Writer" (published in *Die neue Rundschau*).

"I wrested from Kafka nearly everything he published either by persuasion or by guile," Brod recalled.

> At times I stood over him like a rod, drove him and forced him . . . again and again by new means and new tricks. . . . There were times when he thanked me for doing so. But often I was a burden to him with my prodding and he wished it to the devil, as his diary informs one. I felt that, too, but it didn't matter to me. What mattered to me was the thing itself, the helping of a friend even against the wish of the friend.

---

* Brod intended *Arkadia*, published by Kurt Wolff, to be an annual journal; his intentions were cut short by the outbreak of World War I, and the 241-page 1913 issue, with its twenty-three contributions, was to be the first and last edition. Its contributors included Robert Walser, Franz Werfel, Oskar Baum, Kurt Tucholsky, and two pieces by Brod himself.

Franz Kafka, Prague, 1917.

3

The First Trial

Tel Aviv Family Court, Ben-Gurion Avenue 38, Ramat Gan
September 2007

> What is intended to be actively destroyed must first of all have
> been firmly grasped.
>
> —Kafka, *The Blue Octavo Notebooks*

In September 2007, having filed a routine request for the probate of
her mother's will, Eva Hoffe's grief was rudely interrupted.

After Esther Hoffe's death, Eva's sister Ruth assembled the necessary
forms and dropped them off herself at the Israeli Inheritance Registrar's office on Tel Aviv's Ha'Arbaa Street. Eva remained skeptical that
the probate of the will would come off without a hitch. Their mother's
will, she told Ruth, "is like a fire in a thorn-field." But she deferred to
her older sister.

According to Israel's Succession Law of 1965, one may bring about
the execution of a will only by obtaining a "probate order" from the
Israeli Inheritance Registrar. The request for such an order includes an
affidavit signed by the petitioner and verified by a notary, an original

death certificate, the original will, and notifications to any other heirs or beneficiaries of the probate request. (Israel does not impose estate taxes on its residents.) In order to allow for objections to the will to be made, requests for a probate order are publicized, usually in the form of newspaper advertisements. The registrar furnishes a copy of the petition to the administrator general at the Ministry of Justice, who has the discretion to intervene if a matter of public interest is at stake. Once obtained, a probate order carries the same binding legal status as a court verdict.

"My [law] partner happened to be walking through the library one day when this old guy came up and gave him this file full of papers," Meir Heller, the National Library's lawyer told the *Sunday Times*. "And there among them was Max Brod's will. When I looked at it, I could see straight away that Brod intended Esther to have the papers in his lifetime. Then, when he was dead, they should go to a public archive. I checked on the internet and saw that a court hearing was taking place in two days to discuss probating Esther's will." Less than forty-eight hours later, Heller made his dramatic entrance. "I busted into the court and said, 'Stop! There is another will—the will of Max Brod!'"

The Family Court occupied a couple of floors in a drab office building on the main boulevard of Ramat Gan, a Tel Aviv suburb. The recessed ground-floor entrance was framed by red-tiled columns. To the right, lawyers and their clients sat on orange plastic chairs at a sandwich, falafel, and shakshuka kiosk. Eva and her sister Ruth had arrived at the court alone that morning in September 2007; Ruth had understood that there was no cause for worry and no need to bring along a lawyer. Heller's appearance came as a shock, a sudden baring of the iron machinery of the state's legal apparatus. "It was an ambush," Eva said. "We were ensnared."

As a result of Heller's intervention, the State of Israel—represented in the Tel Aviv Family Court by the state custodian (*apotropos*), the National Library, and a court-appointed executor of the Brod estate—objected to the probate and filed to contest Esther Hoffe's will. For the next five years, until it concluded in October 2012, the case would be heard before Judge Talia Kopelman Pardo, a specialist in inheritance law, in a cramped room in the Family Court.

Heller contended that Brod had left the Kafka papers to Esther Hoffe as an executor rather than as a beneficiary. The manuscripts were never hers to give, and thus she could not now pass them on to her daughters, Eva and Ruth. Esther Hoffe had betrayed Brod's will, Heller claimed, much as Brod had betrayed Kafka's.

After Esther's death, Heller maintained, Kafka's manuscripts reverted to the Brod estate, which in accordance with his 1961 will should now be bequeathed, not sold, to the National Library of Israel—without a shekel of compensation to the Hoffes. In that will, Brod asked that his literary estate be placed, at Esther's discretion, "with the library of the Hebrew University of Jerusalem [since renamed the National Library of Israel], the Municipal Library in Tel Aviv, or another public archive in Israel or abroad." The National Library was eager to add the Kafka collection to a long list of the papers of German-Jewish writers it already preserved, including those from the "Prague Circle."

Meir Heller submitted to Judge Kopelman Pardo's court the testimony of his star witness, Margot Cohen. Born in 1922 in Alsace, in eastern France, Cohen was awarded the French Legion of Honor medal for rescuing Jewish children in the Holocaust through a clandestine network headed by Georges Garel. She immigrated to Israel in 1952, served as the philosopher Martin Buber's secretary from 1958 until his death in 1965, and then as archivist of his papers at the National Library in Jerusalem.

Cohen told the court that a few months before his death in 1968, Brod visited the National Library with Esther Hoffe. "Brod's intention was first and foremost to deposit the archive in the library in Jerusalem, where the archives of his close friends are located," Cohen testified. "From my conversation with Brod it was entirely clear to me that he had already decided earlier to deposit his archive in the library. . . . His visit to the department was meant to take care of the technical details involved in the proper handling of the archive." "All during Brod's visit to us [at the National Library]," Cohen later told Israeli journalist Zvi Harel, "Mrs. Hoffe never left him for a second. I tried to explain to Brod how I organized Buber's archive. She never let Brod speak at all." As to why Brod stipulated in his will that his literary estate be given to Esther Hoffe, Cohen suggested to Harel that Brod "was very weak when it came to women. That was his weakness."

After Brod's death, the National Library entered into negotiations with Esther Hoffe. In return for the Brod estate and Kafka manuscripts, it pledged to fund scholars researching Brod, to mount an exhibition to mark the centennial of Brod's birth in 1984, and to host an international symposium on his work. But she remained uncooperative.

In a last-ditch effort, in 1982 the National Library had sent the head of its manuscript and archives department, Mordechai Nadav (1920–2011), and his assistant, Margot Cohen, to meet with Esther Hoffe. They visited her ground-story flat in a squat apartment building covered with pinkish stucco at Spinoza Street 20. "We told her how important it was to give the manuscripts of Brod and Kafka to the library," Cohen recalled. "We told her that they would be available to the public and that this would continue the intellectual lives of Brod and his friends from Prague."

Cohen described to the court the disarray in the home Esther shared with Eva. "I was astonished to discover that there were piles of papers and files of documents in the apartment," she said of the 1982 visit. "On almost every pile sat one of the many cats who wandered around the apartment. There was no place to sit and it was hard to breathe. My impression was that Mrs. Hoffe was not really interested in transferring the archive to the library, and in the end she didn't transfer the writings . . . and didn't carry out what Brod wanted her to do."

Here Eva objected that Margot Cohen could not possibly have seen cats clambering over manuscripts because the cats, which belonged to Eva, were not allowed in Esther's room, where the papers were kept.

In a February 2011 hearing before Judge Kopelman Pardo, Eva

Hoffe's attorney cross-examined Margot Cohen. He asked whether she could recall the color of the bookshelf in the Hoffe apartment on Spinoza Street.

"No."

If she could not remember the color of the bookshelf, he pressed, how could she remember the disorder and the cats so vividly?

A bookshelf, she said, "is common among *yekkes* [Jews of German descent], and it did not attract my attention. But I was not accustomed to seeing the cats and the piles of paper."

A month later, Cohen was called again to testify on the question of whether Brod had given his Kafka manuscripts to Hoffe.

> Cohen: "That he was giving her gifts I knew. It wasn't a secret."
> Judge Kopelman Pardo: "That he was giving her gifts?"
> Cohen: "Gifts of books, of manuscripts."

Shmulik Cassouto, court-appointed lawyer for the Esther Hoffe estate, argued that if the National Library had seen itself at the time as the eventual heir of those neglected piles of manuscripts, Margot Cohen should have applied to the court to order the preservation of the materials that were intended for the library. He further reminded the court that Cohen, who met with Brod only once, might not be in the best position to testify about his wishes. Cohen, he said, had been unwittingly put "in the unpleasant position of apparently being used as an (ill-fitted) tool to rewrite Dr. Brod's will." "There is a new Germany and Max Brod was one of the first to recognize that," the attorney said. "There is indeed a new Germany," Cohen replied with a certain sharpness, "but that does not mean that Brod would have thought of sending his archive there."

By June 1983, it was clear that the protracted discussions between Esther and the National Library had run aground. The German literary scholar Paul Raabe, a former director of the library at the Marbach archive who had known Brod, wrote to Esther in exasperation:

It seems that things are as I feared: you are incapable of deciding to do for Max Brod not only what his friends expect, but what should have been self-evident even to you. If you do not reach an agreement now with the National Library concerning the estate of Max Brod, his hundredth birthday will have passed, and you will have done Max Brod the worst disservice anyone could do this good man. As much as I can understand your thousand hesitations and doubts, I must tell you to put them aside in the best interests of Max Brod. . . . It moved us [Raabe and his wife] to see you again in Tel Aviv. I also felt your helplessness, and thus spontaneously offered you my services . . . I would have loved to work with you again, and to stand at your side during your difficulties. But if you antagonize everyone you will soon stand alone. That would be not only grievous for you but also catastrophic for the commemoration of Max Brod and Kafka. I'm sorry to have to write you—and to have to write you so openly—but as one of Max Brod's admirers I must share my disappointment with you and we, dear Mrs. Hoffe, have always been in a close personal relationship.

In a second letter, later that month, Raabe writes:

I see now that the negotiations have failed, and I wish to tell you how saddened I am on that score. You've lost the last chance in your lifetime to accommodate the papers of Max Brod in the way he surely would have wished but unfortunately did not express clearly in his will. Now these papers—like Kafka's—will one day become the plaything of personal interests, a fate your dear good Max Brod does not deserve.

It is common enough for literary executors "to frustrate as utterly as possible the post-mortem exploiter," as Henry James said to his nephew. But in Raabe's view, Esther had betrayed her duties as gatekeeper to Brod's memory and work. Like T. S. Eliot's widow, Valerie, who had been the poet's secretary for eight years before their marriage, and like Ted Hughes, literary executor of Sylvia Plath after her suicide in 1963, Esther had abused her right of veto, her power to fend off biographers and scholars. In her jealous, proprietorial anxiety, she threatened to damage the very memory she had been entrusted with guarding. So, at least, in the eyes of Raabe.

Was this true? Did Esther's possessiveness suppress scholarship? Eva insists that her mother *did* allow leading Kafka scholars to consult the material in the late 1970s and 1980s. "The claim that we didn't allow researchers to access the material is a lie," she tells me. It is true that Esther contracted with the legendary publisher Siegfried Unseld, the patriarch of Suhrkamp Verlag, for rights to use Kafka's manuscript of "Description of a Struggle."* She also sold S. Fischer Verlag the rights to use photocopies of *The Trial*, Kafka's letters to Brod, and the travel diaries of Kafka and Brod for the German critical edition being edited by Malcolm Pasley of Oxford. For the latter, Esther received a payment of 100,000 Swiss francs and five sets of the first printing of the critical edition. Esther must also have allowed access to the German editors of Walter Benjamin's collected works; the originals of several of Benjamin's letters to Brod, published in the collected works, were later found in Esther's estate.

In his definitive three-volume biography of Kafka, Reiner Stach, echoing Raabe, remarks on his frustration with the "unsatisfactory situation" which "would improve greatly if the literary estate of [Kafka's] longtime friend Max Brod were finally made available to researchers. This first-rate resource would contribute valuable insights to our understanding of the literary and historical issues concerning Kafka and the period as a whole." I asked Stach to elaborate.

---

* That contract specified that Unseld would transfer the payment to the bank accounts of Esther Hoffe and her two daughters; each received a third. Unseld also committed to making the manuscript available to the editors of the German critical edition of Kafka's writings.

In the 1970s, Esther Hoffe showed the papers in her flat to some researchers, including Margarita Pazi [a scholar of German-Jewish literature who wrote on Brod] and Paul Raabe, but they had no opportunity to work with it "systematically." This is the reason why they never quoted anything of it in their articles and books. The only exception (as far as I know) was Joachim Unseld [son of Siegfried Unseld]: he bought a Kafka manuscript and was then allowed to copy some of Max Brod's letters.

Malcolm Pasley got access to the safes, because the S. Fischer publishing house paid a lot of money for copies of the Kafka manuscripts, which they needed for the Critical Edition. He got *no* access to the papers in the flat, although this would have been very important for the commentary.

Hans-Gerd Koch, who was and still is busy with the commentary since about 1990, *never* got access to the papers in the flat, although for him and the edition, too, it would have been very important.

Stach wrote his volume on Kafka's fledgling years last, though in chronology it is the first, for just this reason. As his translator Shelley Frisch explains:

This order of publication, which may appear counterintuitive—even fittingly "Kafkaesque"—was dictated by years of high-profile legal wrangling for control of the Max Brod literary estate in Israel, during which access to the materials it contained, many of which bore directly on Kafka's formative years, was barred to scholars.

In 2013, when Stach was researching his *Kafka: The Early Years*, he says he "asked Eva Hoffe in a detailed letter to show me just some of Brod's early notebooks." She refused. Eva confirmed this to me. "I told him that my hands are tied," she said, "and that I no longer have the keys to the safe deposit boxes."

From the outset, Heller's legal arguments in the case became entangled with ideological considerations, and were joined by a chorus of Israeli figures who contended that Kafka's rightful place was in an Israeli public institution. Kafka scholar Mark Gelber, for instance, a professor at Ben-Gurion University, told the *New York Times* that the writer's "intimate connections to Zionism and Jews" lent weight to the claim that his lost writings should remain in Israel.

———

The Israeli decision to contest the validity of Esther Hoffe's will left observers in Germany as stunned as it did Eva. The German Literature Archive (Deutsches Literaturarchiv) in Marbach, had been in negotiations to buy the Brod estate—including the Kafka material—from the Hoffes. The German archive successfully applied to the court as an interested party, and weighed in to support Hoffe's right to the manuscripts. The institute in Marbach, the world's largest archive of modern German literature, is more or less to Germany what the National Library is to Israel. It is financed by the state of Baden-Württemberg and the Bund (the German state), with third-party funds from the German Research Foundation (or Deutsche Forschungsgemeinschaft, which in turn receives the majority of its funds from the federal government).

Unlike the Israelis, Marbach did not claim legal ownership of the manuscripts; it simply wished to be granted the right to bid for them. Marbach, in other words, regarded the Israeli claim as a desperate if cunning maneuver. If commerce were allowed to take its natural course, Marbach argued, Hoffe would sell the manuscripts to Germany.

As tensions mounted, Ulrich Raulff, director of the Marbach archive, wrote a letter to Eva Hoffe attesting that her mother Esther had "expressed her intention on a number of occasions to convey the Max Brod bequest to Marbach." Extolling the German archives' "cutting-edge capabilities for professional storage and archiving" and

specialists in conservation, restoration, deacidification, and digitiza-
tion, Raulff wished to add Kafka's manuscripts to the estates of more
than 1,400 writers the Marbach archive already held in storage facilities
kept at a constant 18°C–19°C (about 66°F) and a relative humidity of 50
percent–55 percent. These include the Helen and Kurt Wolff Archive,
which contains the estates of over two hundred authors and scholars
who were persecuted by the Nazi regime and subsequently went into
exile.* Raulff added that Marbach already houses one of the world's
largest collections of Kafka manuscripts—second only to Oxford.†

"The Israelis seem to have become crazed," remarked Kafka scholar
Klaus Wagenbach (whose own papers are archived in Marbach) when
the suit to stop Esther Hoffe's will was announced. Yet during the hearings before Judge Kopelman Pardo, Marbach gradually took a less con-
frontational approach, and stressed that the imminent battle over Kafka
need not be a zero-sum game. Marcel Lepper, research director of Mar-

---

* These include the estates, in whole or in part, of Hannah Arendt, Else Lasker-Schüler,
Heinrich Mann, Joseph Roth, Nelly Sachs, and Stefan Zweig. Today the estate of Ste-
fan Zweig is scattered all over the world, including the National Library in Jerusalem,
British Library in London, Reed Library of the State University of New York, and the
Marbach archive. Marbach also holds the papers of Martin Heidegger (an acquisition
Hannah Arendt and Heidegger's son Hermann made possible in 1969), Erich Auer-
bach, Hans-Georg Gadamer, Karl Jaspers, and Marcel Reich-Ranicki, among others;
the archives of publishers (including Samuel Fischer and Ernst Rowohlt) and publishing
houses (including Suhrkamp and Piper); as well as the private libraries of Gottfried Benn,
Paul Celan, Siegfried Kracauer, Martin Heidegger, Hermann Hesse, and W. G. Sebald.
† In April 2011, the Bodleian Library in Oxford and the Marbach archives jointly purchased over a hundred letters and postcards written by Kafka to his favorite sister Ottla.
Marbach's own holdings include Kafka's original manuscripts of *The Trial*, "The Village
Schoolmaster," "The Stoker," and "The Rejection"; the nearly complete original typewrit-
ten draft of Kafka's letter to his father (on permanent loan from Hamburg-based publishers Hoffmann und Campe Verlag, who bought it at auction in 1982); two-dozen letters to
Grete Bloch; and several letters to Max Brod, Felice Bauer, and Milena Jesenská, among
others. Marbach also holds more than 120 letters from Max Brod to various correspondents, including Kafka, Arthur Schnitzler, Felix Weltsch, Stefan Zweig, and to Marbach
itself (two letters dated 1961 and 1967); as well as a 240-page handwritten manuscript of
Brod's debut collection of stories, *Tod den Toten!* (1906).

bach, pointed out that "with funding from the German Federal Foreign Office, the Rosenzweig Minerva Research Center at the Hebrew University of Jerusalem and the German Literature Archive here set up a joint research project in 2012 that helps to preserve German-Jewish collections in Israeli archives. . . . Cooperative, decentralized projects are more appropriate to the particular German responsibility in the context of German-Israeli relations."

Eva saw things in a starker light. "Marbach doesn't dare to challenge the Israeli claims openly," she told the German weekly *Die Zeit* in 2009. "There is still a guilty conscience because of the war and the Holocaust." Speaking of Germany and Israel, she told me "the two cultures—European and Levantine—are simply incompatible."

The Marbach archive hired Sa'ar Plinner, one of Israel's top intellectual property lawyers, to represent its interests in the Hoffe case. Plinner submitted to the court a statement from the director of the manuscripts department at Marbach, Ulrich von Bülow, claiming that Brod had visited the archive in the 1960s and explicitly stated that he wanted his estate to go there. Plinner argued that the proceedings were nothing but a pretext for Israeli state seizure of private property. What began in intimacy, between Kafka and himself, had become the ever-widening property of Brod, and then the Hoffe family, and now possibly the state itself.

At a later stage of the trial, Plinner pointed toward the first intimacy of the case: the friendship between Kafka and Brod. He asked the court to distinguish between the manuscripts Kafka had given Brod as gifts, and the manuscripts Brod had taken from Kafka's desk after Kafka's death. The latter, Plinner suggested, properly belong neither to the Hoffe family nor to the National Library, but if anyone to Kafka's sole living heir, Michael Steiner in London.

Some have disputed Brod's rights even to the gifts he received directly from Kafka. Kafka biographer Reiner Stach, for instance, writes that although Brod claimed that Kafka had given him various unfinished manuscripts as an outright gift, in fact Kafka had only handed them to Brod as a kind of "permanent loan," and Kafka later explicitly asked Brod to burn these, too. Because of his merits in laboring on behalf of Kafka's legacy, few challenged Brod's claim. Michael Steiner wrote to me:

> The interest of the Kafka Estate in this whole affair was the possibility that the manuscripts which were the subject of the litigation may have included some which had never been given to Max Brod by Franz Kafka and which therefore belonged to the Estate. It took many years for us to get hold of the inventory and even then, since it was not prepared by a scholar, there remained and remain ambiguities as to whether certain manuscripts were indeed ever gifted to Brod. All the judges over the years were at pains to stress that they were not dealing with that question, but solely with who was the rightful owner of manuscripts which did belong to Brod under his will or might have been gifted by him in his lifetime.

———

The debates before Judge Kopelman Pardo echoed outside the courtroom as well. In January 2010, Reiner Stach took a stand in the Berlin daily *Tagesspiegel*:

> Marbach would certainly be the proper place for the Brod estate, because it has the scholars and the expertise to deal with Kafka, Brod, and German-Jewish literary history. That the Hoffe daughters are now seriously negotiating with Marbach has aroused some resentments or covetousnesses in the Israeli National Archive [*sic*]. But they lack the people with knowledge of the language and milieu of those German texts from the cultural space between Vienna, Prague and Berlin. As a young man, Brod was in contact with Heinrich Mann, Rilke, Schnitzler, Karl Kraus, Wedekind,

and composers like Janáček, and discussed these correspondences with Kafka. But this was decades before he came to Palestine. To speak here of Israeli cultural assets seems to me absurd. In Israel, there is neither a complete edition of Kafka's works, nor a single street named after him. And if you wish to look for Brod in Hebrew, you have to go to a second-hand bookshop.

It is true that Mordechai Nadav set up the National Library's archival department only after 1966, when it received the literary estates of Martin Buber and Israeli Nobel laureate S. Y. Agnon. Only in 2007 did the library establish separate manuscript and estate departments. But some Israelis bristled at the suggestion that Israel lacked the expertise and resources needed to act as custodians of Brod's manuscripts. "As a native of Prague who at the Hebrew University is researching, along with my colleagues in Israel and abroad, its Jewish culture and history in all periods—in its languages, Hebrew, German, and Czech—I strongly protest these hypocritical and outrageous claims that challenge our legitimacy to carry out these studies and to take proper scientific care of primary sources in general, and the estates of Kafka and Brod in particular," Professor Otto Dov Kulka told the Israeli newspaper *Haaretz*. "They say the papers will be safer in Germany. The Germans will take very good care of them," Kulka told the *New York Times* in 2010. "Well, the Germans don't have a very good history of taking care of Kafka's things. They didn't take good care of his sisters [who perished in the Holocaust]."

In February 2010, Kulka joined two-dozen leading Israeli scholars in issuing an open letter in Hebrew and in (slightly imperfect and old-fashioned) German. "We the undersigned . . . are appalled by the way Israeli academia is portrayed in the German press, as if we have neither interest in nor the historical or linguistic aptitude to research the Brod archive. Brod is part and parcel of the history of the state of Israel, a writer and philosopher who authored numerous articles on Zionism, and who after his flight from Prague and the Nazis settled in Israel (then Palestine) and lived here for over thirty years until his death."

Nurit Pagi, who wrote her dissertation on Brod at the University of Haifa, was the driving force behind the open letter. "One reason Brod's wide-ranging works have not received the recognition they deserve is because his archive—which is 20,000 pages in size—has been inaccessible to scholars since his death in 1968, despite his request that it be given to the National Library," Pagi told *Haaretz*. "Now there is a one-time opportunity to correct the injustice done to him for many years and to allow Israeli researchers and others to shed new light on his work and his heritage," she added.

Pagi told me that her mother and Eva Hoffe had studied together at the Ben Shemen Youth Village, an agricultural boarding school founded in 1927. Pagi first chanced across Brod's novels in the 1960s at a public library in Haifa and in time became fascinated by how Brod's turn to Zionism moved him toward a realist style and vocabulary in his writing. She also took Brod as an instance of a wider truth: "Zionism was written in German," she told me. She was referring to the Zionist movement's deep roots in German-speaking culture, beginning with the writings of Viennese journalist Theodor Herzl, the early Zionist Congresses in Basel, and Zionist newspapers like Robert Weltsch's *Jüdische Rundschau*.

Several years ago, Pagi learned that the son of one of Israel's foremost poets said he was concerned about leaving his mother's literary archive in Israel, because, he said, "we have no future here." "The struggle to keep the Brod archive in Israel," Pagi wrote in 2011, "could demonstrate the contrary . . . It could demonstrate that we believe in our existence and our future here; that we believe that the Zionist project is far from realized, and that the legacy of Central European Jewry plays an important role in its realization. In fact, the struggle to keep Brod's archive in Israel is one of the most important of the struggles over our continued existence here."

Andreas Kilcher, a prominent Zürich-based scholar of Kafka and German-Jewish literature, cited Pagi's remarks on "the struggle" as an example of the Israeli "bellicose rhetoric" around the trial, and as a "gesture of culture-war" ("*kulturkämpferischen Gestus*").

The semantics of scholars on both sides—"resentments," "outrageous claims," "culture-war"—revealed the rivalry between Germans and Israelis over a shared literary heritage.

———

At the next hearing in the Tel Aviv Family Court, shortly after Cohen's cross-examination, it was Eva's turn to plead her case. After the "ambush" at the first hearing, she and her sister Ruth had first turned to Arnan Gabrieli, one of the leading intellectual property litigators in Israel. Gabrieli had represented their mother, Esther, and had negotiated the controversial sale of the archives of the Jerusalem poet Yehuda Amichai to Yale University. According to Eva, Ruth badgered Gabrieli to such a degree—including repeated calls to his home—that Gabrieli declined to take the case. Eva instead hired the lawyers Uri Zfat and Yeshayahu Etgar. (As a twenty-four-year-old law student at Bar-Ilan University, Zfat had clerked for Judge Shilo in 1975.)

From the outset, the two lawyers portrayed the National Library's position as an attempt, in effect, to nationalize private property. They argued that Judge Shilo's 1974 ruling against the state's attempt to appropriate the Kafka manuscripts should stand, and reminded Judge Kopelman Pardo that in contrast to the present proceedings, Shilo had the advantage of hearing Esther Hoffe's testimony directly. "The library's claims have already been raised as part of a judicial process . . . and were decided in a manner that leaves no room for raising them again."

Uri Zfat noted that Kafka's papers ought not be deemed part of Brod's estate at all. The fact that Brod made no separate mention in his will of the Kafka papers, Zfat said, demonstrates that he was well aware that they were no longer part of his estate; he had already given them as gifts to Esther Hoffe. Finally, Zfat said, during the years the National Library conducted negotiations with Esther Hoffe for the Kafka trove, it never acted as if it regarded itself as the rightful heir.

Shmulik Cassouto, court-appointed lawyer for the Esther Hoffe estate, and author of the book *Signature in Promissory Notes* (1997), added that the state's attempt to seize the manuscripts amounted to "open paternalism," and as such "does not befit a democratic state, as Israel likes to present itself." "It is not for us to determine whether Brod left his estate to the most 'suitable' person," Cassouto said. "Nor is it our place to cast doubt on the inner desires of his heart. Perhaps the state is right to claim that Brod would have done better had he not been so soulfully connected to Mrs. Hoffe, or that he would have done better to leave his 'treasure' to a more fitting heir—and there is no more fitting heir than the state of Israel itself. But Brod *was* connected to Mrs. Hoffe. He saw in her his only remaining family, and wished to give to her all that he had. This will must be respected."

Since Brod gave Esther the Kafka manuscripts as a gift during his lifetime, Cassouto claimed, both de facto and de jure, those manuscripts are not part of Brod's estate, and thus not subject to the interpretation of his will. As for Brod's own estate, Cassouto said, his will clearly left to Esther Hoffe the right to determine where it should go, and under which conditions. Furthermore, if it wished to conduct itself honorably, he said, the National Library would negotiate with Eva Hoffe for the acquisition of the manuscripts rather than to attempt to strong-arm her. The notion that the National Library should get the manuscripts without compensating Eva Hoffe he dismissed as "absurd."

Beyond the legal intricacies, however, the hearings in the Tel Aviv Family Court were suffused with broader considerations of where the legacies of Kafka and Brod properly belong. "Like many other Jews who contributed to Western civilization," Meir Heller said of Kafka, "we think he, his legacy . . . [and] his manuscripts should be placed here in the Jewish state." Ehud Sol (of Israel's prestigious law firm, Herzog, Fox and Neeman), court-appointed executor of the Brod estate, likewise argued that in deciding between Marbach and the National Library, the court must factor in Kafka's and Brod's attitudes "toward the Jewish world and the Land of Israel," as well as Brod's views on Germany after the Shoah. The significance of the Jewish people and its political aspirations to both Kafka and Brod would prove central to the trial—and to the judges' verdicts.

4

Flirting with the Promised Land

Ballroom of the Hotel Central, Prague
January 20, 1909

If I haven't emigrated to Palestine, I would at any rate have
traced the way there on the map.

— Franz Kafka to Max Brod, March 1918

The theologian Martin Buber, apostle of a new spiritually dynamic
Judaism, was speaking in Prague's Hotel Central. He had been
invited by the Bar Kochba Association, the Zionist group led by Hugo
Bergmann, Kafka's classmate from first to twelfth grade, together with
Felix Weltsch and Hans Kohn. Buber, the author of popular antholo-
gies of traditional eighteenth-century Hasidic tales, was giving his first
of three lectures (in January 1909, and April and December 1910) on the
regeneration of Judaism.[*] It wasn't his first encounter with the Prague
Zionists—Buber had visited in 1903, to celebrate Bar Kochba's tenth
anniversary—but it would be his most momentous.

---

[*] Buber's lectures would be published as *Drei Reden über das Judentum*, Rütten & Loening, 1911.

Max Brod, twenty-five, seated in the packed hotel ballroom, had enjoyed the warm-up act: in an alluring voice, sixteen-year-old actress Lia Rosen gave a recitation of poems by Hugo Hofmannsthal (to whom Rainer Maria Rilke had introduced her in Vienna in November 1907). She also sang Richard Beer-Hofmann's "Lullaby for Miriam" (*Schlaflied für Mirjam*), with the lines:

> Buried with me will be that which I won.
> None to be heir to us, we heirs to none.[*]

When Buber took the stage, his eyes seemed to Brod to blaze with a fierce intelligence. Brod thrilled to the sage's rhetoric of Jewish self-determination, the fevered eloquence of spiritual renewal. What does it mean to call ourselves Jews? Buber asked. And what demands does Jewishness make on our inner lives?

Brod later said he went into the lectures as a "guest and opponent" and came out a Zionist. Before then, he says he felt not a trace of Jewish self-hatred, but neither did he feel a particular Jewish pride. The encounter with Buber recalibrated Brod's relationship to Jewish life, and in turn to Kafka and Kafka's writing. Here began what Brod called his "struggle with—and for—Judaism." Buber's lectures spurred Brod to articulate something he and many other German-speaking Jews had only vaguely sensed: their attempt to identify with the "*deutscher Geist*" (the German spirit) had failed. On the heels of that failure, Brod became preoccupied with what Robert Weltsch would call *die persoenliche Judenfrage* ("the personal Jewish question"). Brod "moved from an almost exclusive and deliberate preoccupation with

---

[*] Lia Rosen would later play at the Vienna Burgtheater, Reinhardt Ensemble Berlin, and in New York's Yiddish theater, and would star in the movie *Der Shylock von Krakau* (1913). She emigrated to Palestine in 1928, died in Tel Aviv in September 1972, and was buried not far from Max Brod in Trumpeldor cemetery. Much of her estate (photographs, screenplays, and letters) is now kept at the National Library in Jerusalem (Arc. Ms. Var. 465).

aesthetic aspects to complete identification with the Jewish people," Weltsch reported.

The question arose from a sense of strangeness. "The German Jew in Czech Prague was, so to speak, an incarnation of strangeness and will-to-be-strange," writes Pavel Eisner. "He was the people's enemy without a people of his own." Some Prague Jews escaped the strangeness of their condition by escaping to places where they hoped their liminality might dissolve: to Vienna (Franz Werfel), Berlin (Willy Haas), or America (like the parents of Louis D. Brandeis). Others embraced radical socialism (Egon Erwin Kisch, who declared "my homeland is the working class") or baptism. Some of Prague's Jews took up Zionism more as trendy fashion (*Mode-Zionismus*) than as serious commitment. Gershom Scholem derisively called them *Hatschi-zionisten*, endowed as they were with all the intensity of a sneeze. Others, like Max Brod, would take up Zionism with the utmost seriousness.

Prague's notoriously tiny Zionist circles centered on the Bar Kochba Association, named for the leader of the last revolt of Jews against Rome.* If the ceiling of a certain café would collapse at a certain time, a common joke had it, the entire Zionist movement in Prague would be wiped out at a single stroke. Numerically small as it was, however, the movement managed to create an intoxicating blend of Zionism and socialism so successfully that, after 1918, Zionists would command two mandates in the city council of Prague. The leaders of the Zionist movement in Prague, Brod writes,

> were young men of a singular purity of character and most inten-
> sive intellectuality, a group of shining exemplariness the kind of

---

* Shimon Bar Kochba led the Jewish uprising against Rome between 132 and 135 CE until his death in battle at Beitar, in the Judean hills. He was also the hero of a popular 1897 play by the Czech poet and playwright Jaroslav Vrchlický (1853–1912), which draws implicit parallels between the Jews and the Czechs as two beleaguered minorities. In 1910, the Bar Kochba Association counted fifty-two active members.

which I never met again in my subsequent life. The student organization Bar Kochba was its center of crystallization.... All of us
were united in the conviction that our work had to be realized
through personal sacrifices and deeds, not through front-page
articles or inflammatory speeches but through quiet efforts in the
midst of the people. Our first goal was the renewal and elevation
of the ethics and morals of the humiliated, maligned Jewish community which, after all, had in many ways corroded in the diaspora.... The Jewish state we wanted to prepare "over there," in
Palestine, was to be founded on justice and selfless love between
individuals and included, as a matter of course, offering friendship
and help to our next-door neighbors, the Arabs.

During the decade 1900–1909, Brod had remained indifferent to the
Zionist zeal Bar Kochba embodied. He said that in 1905, he had never
even heard the name Theodor Herzl, the founding father of political
Zionism. (Brod remembered the first time he saw a portrait of Herzl
on the wall of Hugo Bergmann's living room in the Podbaba district of
Prague. "Who's that?" Brod asked.)

But beginning in 1909, he began to seek after the meaning of
Jewish identity, and the moral commitments it entailed. After the
Austrian-Hungarian Empire dissolved and Czechoslovakia was created, Brod would be elected honorary member (*alter herr*) of Bar
Kochba, would serve as vice-chairman of the Jewish National Council. He would also become one of the leading spokesmen of Czech
Jews in the newly founded republic, instrumental in negotiating significant autonomy concessions that President Tomáš Masaryk granted
Czechoslovakian Jewry. During his Zionist activity, Brod said, a line
from Kafka's story "Josephine the Singer, or the Mouse Folk" inspired
his selflessness:

Our folk, ever calm, without showing the slightest sign of distur-
bance, practically in the guise of the master—a mass that is at one

with itself and essentially an entity that despite all appearances to the contrary is one that can only give gifts to others but is never able to receive any.

In that story, Kafka's narrator reports that Josephine, the mouse singer, "is a small episode in the eternal history of our people." The mouse people, the narrator adds, "has always, somehow or other, saved itself, though not without sacrifices which fill historical researchers with horror."

Brod looked to cultural Zionism not only with an eye to reassessing his attachment to the Jewish people but also with a view to criticizing the tendency of new nation-states to erode the collective identities of minorities. "For me," he wrote in the Zionist weekly *Selbstwehr*, "there can be no doubt that the 'Jewish nationalist' may not be a 'nationalist' in the sense of the word commonly in use today. It is the mission of the Jewish-national movement, of Zionism, to give the word 'nation' a new meaning." The regeneration of Judaism—and the resurrection of the Hebrew language—could come about only if it were rooted in the Land of Israel. "Above all," Brod wrote to the Prague-born writer Auguste Hauschner (1850–1924), "Jewish nationalism must not create just another chauvinistic nation. Its sole purpose is to bring back to health the reconciliatory, all-inclusive humane genius of the Jew which today has degenerated."

As the Habsburg dynasty disintegrated, the upwelling nationalism gave Brod's mission new urgency. "The Jew who takes the national problem seriously," Brod wrote, "finds himself today in the midst of the following paradox: he must fight nationalism with the aim of establishing universal human fellowship . . . and he must simultaneously stand with the young Jewish national movement."

During World War I, Brod taught classes on world literature—what today we might call a "great books" course—to young Jewish women, refugees from Eastern Europe fleeing the war. In the first issue of *Der Jude*, he called the experience his "only solace in this spiritless time." "An enchanting freshness and naiveté emanates from the girls," he writes. They are "spiritual through and through." In an essay the following month, Brod contrasts his students with the more superficial "Western Jewesses." "The Galician girls as a whole are so much fresher, more spiritually substantial, and healthier than our girls."

Brod justified the increasingly central place Judaism occupied in his life with a six-hundred-page treatise called *Paganism, Christianity, Judaism* (1921, published in English in 1971). In this *opus, magnum* or not, he distinguishes three attitudes to worldliness: an affirmation of this world (paganism); a denial of this sinful world in favor of the "world to come" (the Christianity of "My kingdom is not of this world"); and an affirmation that this imperfect world can be redeemed (Judaism). This last attitude Brod calls the *Diesseitswunder*, or this-worldly miracle. Robert Weltsch said that for Brod, "paganism is the religion of the *Diesseits*, of human life in this world which ignores what is beyond sense experience. Christianity is the religion of the *Jenseits*, the world beyond. Judaism . . . is the religion which takes into account both worlds and believes in the coincidence of opposites, Grace and Freedom."

Attracted to sensuality and spirituality both, Brod chose Judaism. And that choice entailed the choice of Zionism. "Zionism provides Jewish religiosity with a body, which it had lost," Brod writes in the closing pages of *Paganism, Christianity, Judaism*. By providing him refuge from the neo-Paganism threatening to engulf Europe with what he calls "the bestialization of politics," Zionism would also save his life.

———

On August 13, 1912, Kafka arrived an hour late at Max Brod's apartment on Prague's Skořepka Street. He wanted to discuss the final order of the pieces in what would be Kafka's first published collection, *Meditation*. The moment he stepped into the apartment, Kafka noticed a twenty-four-year-old woman, a distant relation of Brod's, sitting at the table. "Bare throat," he records in his diary. "A blouse thrown on. Looked very domestic in her dress although, as it turned out, she by no means was. (I alienate myself from her a little by inspecting her so closely . . .) Almost broken nose. Blonde, somewhat straight, unattractive hair, strong chin. As I was taking my seat I looked at her closely for the first time, by the time I was seated I already had an unshakeable opinion."

In the course of their first conversation, the young woman reported that she worked in the Berlin offices of Carl Lindström AG, marketing a new dictation device. She also remarked that she had studied Hebrew and mentioned her Zionist leanings; "and this suited me very well," Kafka says. He took the liberty of suggesting a trip to Palestine together the following summer. She agreed, and they shook hands on it. In his jacket pocket that evening, Kafka carried the August 1912 issue of the journal *Palästina*, featuring a German translation of an essay by the cultural Zionist Ahad Ha'am about his recent visit to Palestine. Kafka jotted down her Berlin address on the title page before escorting her back to her hotel, Zum Blauen Stern (the very place where in 1866 Bismarck had signed the peace treaty between the Kingdom of Prussia and the Austrian Empire).

Felice Bauer was the woman Kafka would never marry. Over the next five years, and through hundreds of tumultuous letters (Kafka sometimes transcribed passages from his letters to Felice into letters to Brod, and quotes letters from Brod in his letters to her), he courts her affection, which he then finds overwhelming and retreats from. He loves her and flees from her. Separated by the six-hour train ride between Prague and Berlin, they would be twice engaged and twice separated.

Kafka's ambivalence toward Zionism can be read as a subtext of his ambivalence toward Felice—and other women he would love at a distance—as though Zionism and marriage were two aspects of one preoccupation, twin ways of saying "we" for a man who suffered a debilitating case of "we-weakness" (*Wir-Schwäche*). As though intuiting this subtext, when Kafka and Felice first became engaged, Brod gave them a present: Richard Lichtheim's book *The Zionist Agenda* (*Das Programm des Zionismus*, 1911).* But Kafka's ambivalence only deepened with time. Writing to Felice's close friend, Grete Bloch, in 1914, Kafka confessed: "I admire Zionism and am nauseated by it."

Kafka never set foot in Palestine, but in the first line of the first letter he wrote to Felice, five weeks after meeting her at Brod's apartment, Kafka uses the fantasy of Palestine as the opening gambit of flirtation:

> In the likelihood that you no longer have even the remotest recollection of me, I am introducing myself once more: my name is Franz Kafka, and I am the person who greeted you for the first time that evening at Director Brod's in Prague, the one who subsequently handed you across the table, one by one, photographs of a Thalia trip, and who finally, with the very hand now striking the keys, held your hand, the one which confirmed a promise to accompany him next year to Palestine.

This promise freed something in Kafka. On the eve of Yom Kippur, two nights after writing her this letter, he poured forth his breakthrough story "The Judgment" in a single ecstatic sitting from ten o'clock at night to six o'clock in the morning. He dedicated the story to Felice.

Judith Butler, professor at the University of California, Berkeley, remarks that for Kafka "Palestine is a figural elsewhere where lovers go, an open future, the name of an unknown destination." Throughout their correspondence, Felice becomes identified in Kafka's mind with that elsewhere. In February 1913, Kafka wrote to Felice about running into a young Zionist acquaintance who invited him to come to an

---

* Richard Lichtheim (1885–1963) edited the Zionist organ *Die Welt* from 1911 to 1913, and served as president of the German Zionist Federation from 1907 to 1920. He also served as a Zionist emissary in Constantinople (1913–1917) and Geneva (1939–1946), and wrote a series of volumes on the history of the Zionist movement in Germany.

important Zionist meeting. "My indifference regarding his person and any Zionism was boundless and unspeakable at that moment," Kafka writes. He accompanied the young man to the gathering, but only "up to the door of the café." He did not allow himself "to be escorted inside." It was as though in his relationship both to Felice and to the Jewish national ambition—and to his own writing—Kafka vacillated on the threshold of consummation.

The most vivid expression of this comes in Kafka's late unfinished story, "The Burrow" ("Der Bau," a title supplied by Brod), written in the winter of 1923. The story depicts a solitary badger-like creature which has devoted its life to building an elaborate underground fortress, with which it identifies itself: "the vulnerability of the burrow has made me vulnerable; any wound to it hurts me as if I myself were hit." The creature does not inhabit this well-defended refuge, but remains vigilantly outside, on the threshold:

> At times, I was seized by the childish desire never to go back to the burrow at all but rather to settle in here near the entrance and find my happiness in realizing all the time how the burrow would keep me secure if I were inside it.*

After breaking off his engagement with Felice for the second time, Kafka linked the image of being "near the entrance" to Zionism to subsequent lovers, too. In 1919, Kafka met and in short order became engaged to Julie Wohryzek, unassuming daughter of an impoverished cobbler and synagogue caretaker. She was a woman who "possesses an inexhaustible and unstoppable store of the brashest Yiddish expressions," Kafka told Brod. (Neither her pedigree nor her Yiddish appealed to Kafka's father, who considered her déclassé.) Julie, whose first fiancé,

---

* In July 1922, a year before writing "The Burrow," Kafka wrote to Brod: "Dearest Max, I have been dashing about or sitting as petrified as a desperate animal in his burrow. Enemies everywhere."

a young Zionist, had been killed in the trenches of the First World War, had attended Brod's lectures on Zionism. Almost immediately upon meeting Julie, Kafka asked Brod to send her a copy of his 1917 essay "The Three Phases of Zionism."

———

Thanks to Brod, even before meeting Felice, Kafka had already touched, in a tangential way, on Zionist circles. In 1910, he began going with Brod to meetings and lectures of the Bar Kochba group. Unlike Theodor Herzl, members of Bar Kochba were more concerned with reviving Jewish culture than with the politics of realizing the Jewish state. They understood Zionism not as an end unto itself but as a means of spiritual renewal. In August 1916, Kafka alluded to this in a postcard to Felice: "Zionism, accessible to most Jews of today, at least in its outer fringes, is but an entrance to something far more important."

Kafka's dialogue on the subject began years earlier with his friend Hugo Bergmann, who joined Bar Kochba at age sixteen in 1899 and was elected to chair the association at age eighteen. In 1902, the nineteen-year-old Kafka expressed bewilderment at his friend's commitment to Zionism. Bergmann replied:

> Of course, your letter does not lack the obligatory derision of my Zionism. . . . Again and again I have to wonder why you, who . . . were my classmate for so long, do not understand my Zionism. If I saw a madman before me and he had an *idée fixe*, I would not laugh at him, because his idea is a piece of life for him. You think Zionism is also an *idée fixe* of mine. . . . I did not have the strength to stand alone, like you.

Bergmann would leave Prague for Palestine in 1920, where he would serve as the first director of Israel's National Library. Under his leader-ship, Max Brod said, it became "the largest, most content-rich, and most modern library in the Middle East." Bergmann was later appointed rec-tor of the Hebrew University in Jerusalem. Kafka followed his career there with great interest. In 1923, Bergmann briefly returned to Prague to deliver a lecture at the Zionist club Keren Ha-Yesod. Kafka told him afterward, "You gave this talk only for me."

We can assume that Bergmann told Kafka something of the library's origins. In 1872, a certain Rabbi Joshua Heshel Lewin of Volozhin issued a call in *Hachavazelet*, the first Hebrew weekly pub-lished in Jerusalem, "to establish a library which shall become a focal point in which the books of our people shall be collected—not one shall be lacking." With the help of British financier and philanthro-pist Sir Moses Montefiore, funds were raised and a board recruited, including Eliezer Ben-Yehuda, father of modern Hebrew. In 1905, the library came under the auspices of the Zionist Congress in Basel. But the time was not yet ripe. A national library requires, by definition, a nation concentrated in one country, speaking one language.

It was at Bar Kochba, in January 1912, that Kafka attended a talk on Yiddish folk songs by Nathan Birnbaum, the forty-seven-year-old Viennese writer who twenty years earlier had coined the term *Zion-ism*. "Kafka hung on every word of Birnbaum's lecture," Reiner Stach writes. Kafka also went to Bar Kochba to hear talks given by the Zionist (and future author of the children's book *Bambi*) Felix Salten, and by Kurt Blumenfeld, secretary-general of the World Zionist Organization. He listened to leading cultural Zionist Davis Trietsch, a founder of the Jüdische Verlag and an editor of the journal *Palästina*, talk about the Jewish colonies in Palestine.

In September 1913, along with some ten thousand other participants (including his future publisher Salman Schocken and future first prime minister of Israel David Ben-Gurion), Kafka attended the eleventh World Zionist Congress in Vienna. (His main purpose for coming to

Vienna was work-related: the second International Congress for Rescue Services and Accident Prevention.) There he heard speeches by Nahum Sokolow, Menachem Ussishkin, and Arthur Ruppin, among other leading Zionist voices. Delegates were granted a premiere screening of a 78-minute silent documentary film, produced by Noah Sokolovsky, that offered panoramic views of the new city Tel Aviv, the landmarks of Jerusalem, and Jewish agricultural settlements in Judea, Carmel, and the Galilee.

The boisterous gathering left Kafka cold. "I sat in the Zionist congress," he remarked to Brod, "as if it were an event totally alien to me, felt myself cramped and distracted by much that went on." "It is hard to imagine anything more useless than such a congress," he told Brod. In his diaries, Kafka mocked *Palästinafahrer*, or those who journeyed to Palestine, who "constantly mouthed about emulating the Maccabees."

———

Caught in Prague's cultural cross-currents, Kafka was no less wary than Brod and his Zionist friends of the ambient anti-Semitism. Like them, he was all too aware that Jews were seen by Czechs as Germans, and by Germans as Jews. "What had they done," Theodor Herzl wrote in 1897, "the small Jews of Prague, the honest middle-class merchants, the most peace-loving of all peace-loving citizens? . . . Some of them tried to be Czech—they were assaulted by the Germans; others, who tried to be German, were attacked by the Czechs—and by the Germans as well."

Like Brod, Kafka read hateful anti-Jewish articles in the Czech paper *Venkov*, and was no stranger to casual Jew-baiting. One evening Kafka attended a salon hosted by his boss's wife. Another guest remarked, "So you've invited a Jew as well."

The two Prague writers had opposite temperaments and fates but shared the charged experience of belonging to a Jewish minority within a German-speaking minority within a Czech minority within a hetero-geneous Austro-Hungarian Empire being pulled apart by the centrifu-gal force of rival nationalisms. Both experienced at first hand the rising *völkisch* anti-Semitism that accompanied the Empire's disintegration.

In December 1897, Kafka, age fourteen, witnessed a three-day riot in Prague. During the "December storm," as it came to be called, maraud-ers vandalized synagogues, plundered Jewish shops, and attacked Jewish homes, including Brod's. "In my home the windows also shattered at night," Brod recalled. "Trembling, we scurried out of the nursery, which faced the street, to our parents' bedroom. I can still picture my father lifting my little sister out of bed—and in the morning there was actually a big paving stone in the bed."

Two years later, Kafka followed the case of Leopold Hilsner, a young Jew from a Bohemian town charged in 1899 with the ritual murder of a Czech Catholic girl. He read an eyewitness account of a 1906 pogrom by his friend Abraham Gruenberg. He read reports in Prague's Zionist weekly *Selbstwehr* about the Beilis blood libel in Kiev, and according to Brod wrote a short story about the notorious affair (burned at Kaf-ka's request by his last lover, Dora Diamant). He was moved by Arnold Zweig's 1914 play *Ritual Murder in Hungary (Ritualmord in Ungarn)*, which dramatized a blood libel known as the Tisza affair. "At one point I had to stop reading, sit down on the sofa, and weep," Kafka told Felice. "It's years since I wept."

Closer to home, in 1922, Kafka watched students of the German Uni-versity in Prague run riot rather than receive their diplomas from a Jew-ish rector. In the same year, Kafka was moved to answer an anti-Semitic screed, Hans Blüher's *Secessio Judaica*, which denounced "Jewish mim-icry" and recommended the secession of the Jews from the Germans. Kafka saw all this frenzied hatred without illusions. Thus, for example, when Germany's Jewish foreign minister Walther Rathenau was assas-sinated in 1922, Kafka remarked that it was "incomprehensible that they should have let him live as long as that."

Acutely sensitive to simmering anti-Semitism, Kafka kept up an unceasing dialogue with Bergmann and Brod about the question of the precarious status of the Jews in Europe. In 1920, he read Brod's study, *Socialism in Zionism*. Unlike his two friends, however, Kafka did not turn to Zionist ideology to answer that question. "I've been spending every afternoon outside on the streets, wallowing in anti-Semitism," the thirty-seven-year-old Kafka wrote during a pogrom in Prague in April 1920. "The other day I heard the Jews called *prašivé plemeno* [mangy brood]. Isn't it natural to leave a place where one is so hated? (Zionism or ethnic feeling is not even needed here.) The heroism of staying on nevertheless is the heroism of cockroaches that cannot be exterminated even from the bathroom."

————

In a September 1916 postcard to his fiancée Felice, Kafka remarks on "the dark complexity of Judaism, which contains so many impenetrable mysteries." To begin to fathom those mysteries, and to share in the grammar in which they were expressed, Kafka launched into a serious study of Hebrew, in 1917. In this he was following the counsel of Hugo Bergmann. "If you want to know the Jewish people," Bergmann stressed, "if you want to participate in discussions of issues that determine its fate, then first learn to understand its language!"

Kafka was aided in his Hebrew studies by a popular textbook by Moses Rath and conversational lessons with his friends Friedrich Thieberger and Georg (Jiří) Mordechai Langer.* Langer, a homosexual who had met Kafka through their mutual friend Max Brod in 1915,

* Thieberger, a rabbi's son, contributed to the Zionist journals *Der Jude* and *Selbstwehr*, and participated in the Bar Kochba Association. He would escape Prague to Jerusalem in 1939. Both Thieberger and Langer would leave their personal archives to the National Library of Israel.

had at age nineteen left his middle-class family to become a follower of a Hassidic rebbe. He was the author of *The Eroticism of Kabbalah* (*Die Erotik der Kabbala*, 1923), which Brod edited (and enthusiastically reviewed). He also wrote an elegy in Hebrew for Kafka in 1929. In 1941, two years before his untimely death, Langer, by then living not far from Brod in Tel Aviv, would recall his student's joy in speaking Hebrew:

> Yes. Kafka spoke Hebrew. In his later years, we always spoke Hebrew together. He, who always insisted that he was not a Zionist, learned our language at an advanced age and with great diligence. And unlike the Prague Zionists, he spoke Hebrew fluently, which gave him a special satisfaction, and I don't think that I'm exaggerating when I say he was secretly proud of it. . . . Once when we were traveling together by streetcar and speaking about the airplanes that were circling the skies of Prague at that moment, some Czech people who were riding in the streetcar with us . . . asked us what language we were speaking. . . . When we told them, they were surprised that it was possible to converse in Hebrew, even about airplanes. . . . How Kafka's face lit up then from happiness and pride!

At the same time, Langer added that Kafka "wasn't a Zionist, but he was deeply envious of those who fulfilled the great precept of Zionism themselves, which simply means those who immigrated to *Eretz Yisrael* [the Land of Israel]. He wasn't a Zionist, but everything that happened in our land greatly moved him."

In 1918, Kafka proposed to Max Brod that they begin to correspond in Hebrew. Brod too had been fitfully trying to master the language. "Being a good Zionist," Brod writes in his memoir, "I started to study Hebrew over and over again. Year after year. Always from the beginning. But I always got stuck, only made it to the Hifil" (Hebrew's causative verb form). In a 1917 collection of his poems, *Das gelobte Land* (Promised Land) Brod includes one called "Hebrew Lesson" [*Hebräische Lektion*]. It opens with these lines:

> I was thirty years old
> Before I began to learn the language of my people.
> It seemed to me as if for thirty years I had been deaf.

Brod remarked that Kafka learned the language "with special zeal." "By studying Hebrew deeply," Brod recalled, "he left me far behind in this field too."

By the fall of 1922, despite his failing health, Kafka was studying Hebrew twice a week with a nineteen year-old student from Jerusalem. Puah Ben-Tovim—"the little Palestinian," as he called her—was boarding in Prague with Hugo Bergmann's mother. Puah's parents had come to Palestine with the wave of immigrants from Russia in the 1880s. For ten years she helped her father, a distinguished Hebraist, read to the students at Jerusalem's first school for the blind. After World War I, she was in the first graduating class of Jerusalem's Hebrew Gymnasium. While still in high school, she had volunteered to help Hugo Bergmann catalogue the German books in the National Library.

"Every so often he'd have a painful coughing spell that would make me want to break off the lesson," Puah recalled. "And then he'd look at me, unable to speak, but imploring me with those huge dark eyes of his to stay for one more word, and another, and yet another. It almost seemed as if he thought of those lessons as a kind of miracle cure."

With Puah's help, Kafka filled vocabulary notebooks with Hebrew words next to their German equivalents in looping, childlike handwriting: Fascist movement, tuberculosis, holiness, victory, genius. He also copied out Hebrew phrases, like "May God smash you!" (According to Raphael Weiser, former director of the National Library's manuscript and archival department, the eighteen-page notebook I consulted at the National Library was presented to the library by the Schocken family.) "There is no question that he was attracted to me," Puah recalled, "but it was more to an ideal than to the actual girl that I was, and to the image of a Jerusalem far away. He was constantly picking my brain about Jerusalem, and wanted to come with me when I went back." "When I first met him," Puah said of Kafka, "he already knew he was dying, and he desperately wanted to live. He still dreamed of Palestine; and, since that's where I just came from, it gave me a sort of mystique in his eyes. . . . I soon came to realize that, emotionally, he was thrashing about like a drowning man, ready to cling to whoever came close enough for him to grab hold of."*

Yet Kafka, whose writing was born of the impossibility of belonging, pulled away from offers of collective belonging. "It was his yearning to belong, and to gain the self-confidence that accompanies belonging, that drew him to Zionism," says Vivian Liska, professor of German literature and director of the Institute of Jewish Studies at the University of Antwerp. "It was his fear of dissolution as a self in a group that kept him from adhering to it fully." Hans Dieter Zimmermann, a leading German interpreter of Kafka, is more clear-cut: "Not by any means was he a Zionist. . . . He is an 'unbridled' individualist, as he himself once wrote."

In 1922, Brod asked Kafka to consider taking over the editorship of *Der Jude*, the Zionist monthly edited by Martin Buber and bankrolled by Salman Schocken. Five years earlier, in 1917, Kafka had published a couple of stories—"A Report to an Academy" and "Jackals and Arabs"—in the journal. In June 1916, Brod had written to Buber that Kafka's deep longing for community, for escaping rootless solitude, made him the "most Jewish" writer of all.

Kafka declined the offer, but not, as might be expected, for reasons of precarious health. "How could I think of such a thing," Kafka replies,

---

* In May 1983, during the first of what would be five visits to Israel, French philosopher Jacques Derrida gave a talk at the Van Leer Institute in Jerusalem on Kafka's parable "Before the Law." Though she could walk only with great difficulty, Puah, aged eighty and widowed for thirty years, came and sat in the back row.

"with my boundless ignorance of things, my lack of connection with people, the absence of any firm Jewish ground under my feet? No, no."

Both the Promised Land and promised community remained unattainably distant. "What is Hebrew," Kafka had written to a fellow tuberculosis patient Robert Klopstock in 1923, "but news from far away?"

———

In the final year of his life, Kafka at last moved out of his parents' apartment and escaped their orbit. From September 1923 to March 1924, he lived "a half-rural life," as he wrote to Brod, in the outlying Steglitz district on the outskirts of Berlin. He had come here to live with Dora Diamant, a woman twenty-one years his junior who had broken with her family's strict Hassidic orthodoxy. "The rich treasure of Polish Jewish religious tradition that Dora was mistress of," wrote Brod, who visited their Berlin home several times, "was a constant source of delight to Franz." Dora and Kafka attended introductory classes on the Talmud at the Academy for the Study of Judaism on Artilleriestrasse (today the Leo Baeck House) until January 1924, when his health deteriorated. He called the academy "an oasis of peace in wild Berlin and in the wild regions of the inner self."

At the pace of a page a day, Dora also guided Kafka through the first three chapters of Y. H. Brenner's bleak last novel *Breakdown and Bereavement* (*Shekhol ve-Kishalon*) in the Hebrew original. The novel, which has been called "the most brutal self-flagellation in Hebrew literature," was a remarkable choice. Brenner, the tragic rationalist of Hebrew letters, stressed that "exile [*galut*] is everywhere." For Brenner, the Land of Israel is yet another diaspora. "I am not enjoying the book very much as a novel," Kafka told Brod.

Dora later said that she and Kafka "constantly played with the idea of leaving Berlin and immigrating to Palestine to begin a new life." The couple fancifully imagined opening a Jewish restaurant in Tel

Aviv; Dora would cook and Kafka would serve as the waiter, a position from which he could observe without being observed. (In Kafka's eighteen-page handwritten Hebrew vocabulary notebook, he lists the Hebrew word for waiter—*meltzar*.) But the dream of Zion would remain a dream unfulfilled. Kafka allowed himself to imagine moving to Palestine only when his illness was so far advanced as to make the move impossible.

In July 1923, Hugo Bergmann and his wife, Elsa (née Fanta), made one final plea to Kafka, inviting him to Jerusalem with them. "Once again the temptation beckons," he said, "and again the absolute impossibility answers." The Bergmanns left Prague with a photograph of Kafka instead; when they returned to Jerusalem, they placed it on the piano in their salon.

As his tuberculosis waxed and his strength waned, Kafka reflected on the beginnings that went unfulfilled. "There was not the least bit of enduring resolve in the way I conducted my life," Kafka confides in his diary in 1922. He goes on to list a series of the broken radiuses of his life's circle: "anti-Zionism, Zionism, Hebrew. . . . attempts at marriage." As with Felice, Julie, Milena, and Dora, Kafka, with his dread of conjugality, loved at a distance. He confessed as much in a letter to Brod in 1921: "I can love only what I can place so high above me that I cannot reach it." Palestine—and the Hebrew language coming back to life there—proved unattainably distant. Marriage and the Promised Land: two forms of happiness deferred, yearned for but not possessed.

In Eva Hoffe's view, perhaps this was for the best. In the oppressive humidity of a midsummer's afternoon in Tel Aviv, Eva and I walked along Dubnow Street. She was wearing a T-shirt brightly printed with an image of Marilyn Monroe and a loosely draped skirt. She carried three plastic bags of photos and documents that she wanted to show me, including her birth certificate and Czech passport. "Although I'm an Israeli and a Jew," she said, "I can't say I love this place."

I mentioned coming across an interview Brod gave to the Israeli paper *Maariv* in October 1960. He had told the interviewer: "If Kafka had merited to reach the land of Israel, he would have created works of genius in Hebrew!" I added that in her forthcoming novel, *Forest Dark*, the American Jewish writer Nicole Krauss imagined a counterlife for Kafka and unspools a kind of "what if." Krauss' narrator discovers that Kafka came to Palestine between the World Wars, settling there in obscurity under his Jewish name Amschel (also the name of his mother's maternal grandfather).

Though she had never met Kafka, Eva reacted with acerbic incredulity. "Kafka wouldn't last a day here," she said, kicking the hem of her threadbare skirt against her shins.

Science Fiction:
F.K. Tel Aviv 1957

"Science Fiction: F. K. in Tel Aviv 1957,"
pen-and-ink drawing by Jiří Slíva, 2013.

"Franz Kafka in the Waves,"
etching by Jiří Slíva, 2013.

5

First and Second Judgments

Tel Aviv Family Court, Ben-Gurion Avenue 38, Ramat Gan
October 2012

Kafka is to Jewish literature what Dante is to Catholicism or John Milton to Protestantism: the archetype of the Writer.
—Harold Bloom, 2014

A s the hearings in the Tel Aviv Family Court continued, so had the sales of Kafka's manuscripts from Israel. In 2009, much to the consternation of Israeli authorities, two documents in Kafka's hand were auctioned off in Switzerland. Both had at one point been in Esther Hoffe's possession. One of the documents is an eight-page letter from Kafka to Brod (dated September 1922, and sold for 125,000 Swiss francs): "I know allusions of the terror of loneliness," Kafka writes to Brod. "Not so much the loneliness of being alone, as that among people." (Klaus Wagenbach called the letter "one of Kafka's most beautiful ever.") During the decade Esther had been selling off her Kafka manuscripts (1978–88), the National Library had never raised an objection. Now, it tried in vain to block the sale.

Even as the trial progressed, it remained unclear which manuscripts

Eva Hoffe kept at her home on Spinoza Street, and which in her bank vaults. Hoffe signed an affidavit in which she declared that she no longer had anything in her apartment that was written in Kafka's hand. Eva herself contributed to the concern about their fate when she claimed burglars had broken into her Tel Aviv apartment during the trial. To this day, it's not clear what was stolen from her apartment, if anything.

There had been one attempt to catalogue the estate. In the 1980s, Esther Hoffe commissioned Bernhard Echte, a Swiss philologist and then-director of the Robert Walser Archive in Zürich, to draw up an inventory of the manuscripts in her possession. His inventory, running to more than 140 pages, lists some twenty thousand pages of material. A closely guarded secret to this day, the Echte inventory was not made available to the court.

In 2010, Judge Kopelman Pardo of the Tel Aviv Family Court ordered the opening of the Hoffe family's deposit boxes—four in a Zürich bank, and six others in Tel Aviv (Bank Leumi on Yehuda Halevi Street). Eva was permitted to be present neither in Zürich nor Tel Aviv. In Tel Aviv, she tried, in a rush of rage, to enter the room. "They're mine, they're mine!" she shouted. "A wild animal performance," she remarked to me when she recalled that day.

The Hoffe vaults in Zürich, at UBS on the Bahnhofstrasse, were opened July 19, 2010. Yemima Rosenthal of the State Archives had asked Professor Itta Shedletzky to lead a court-appointed team to review the material in the Swiss vaults and help inventory their contents. She would be paid by the Justice Ministry. Shedletzky, a respected expert on German literature at Hebrew University, is the editor of Gershom Scholem's letters and coeditor of the critical edition of Else Lasker-Schüler's *Works and Letters*. She remembers as a teenager reading Brod's novel on Cicero (*Armer Cicero*, 1955), serialized in the *Neue Zürcher Zeitung*. For Shedletzky, born in Zürich in 1943, it was a curious homecoming. She found herself in the city of her childhood, on the very street where she used to go window-shopping with her mother.

Here, too, Eva showed up uninvited and tried to force her way into the vault room. She suspected the lawyers were hunting for a "hidden" will of Brod (later than his 1961 will), and feared one of the lawyers might pocket a manuscript. The Swiss bank manager threatened to summon the police if she did not leave the premises voluntarily. She adamantly refused. "I was trembling inside, but didn't show them my fear," she told me. Shedletzky took her aside and succeeded in calming her. "Ehud Sol looked at me as though I'd tamed a lion," Shedletzky told me.

Ehud Sol, executor of Brod's estate, recalled the moment. "In Switzerland, they took us to huge vault rooms, where the branch manager and staff were waiting for us, aware they were witnesses to an historic event. When we opened the vaults—and this is conduct unbecoming a lawyer—we had tears in our eyes," he told the Israeli newspaper *Haaretz*. Given Sol's reputation as a ruthless litigator, his admission that he had shed tears was a striking testament to the significance of the occasion. (Shedletzky, however, calls this story "nonsense.")

Four boxes yielded manuscripts Brod had deposited during the 1950s. The first glimpses proved tantalizing: In deposit box S6588, Brod had left a note, dated 1947, on a brown envelope, declaring that the enclosed three notebooks of Kafka's Paris diaries belonged to Esther Hoffe.

In deposit box S6577 they found, among other items, a brown file folder on which Brod had written in black ink: "Kafka's *Letter to his Father*, original (property of Mrs. Esther Hoffe.)" Underneath, in blue ink: "My property [*mein Eigentum*]. Ilse Esther Hoffe, 1952."

Deposit box S6222 held two folders. On the first, Brod had written: "Kafka's letters to me which have been published, originals, my property, belonging to Esther Hoffe." On the second, Brod had written: "Kafka—my letters to Franz—belongs to Esther Hoffe—April 2, 1952, Tel Aviv, Dr. Max Brod."

Brod's notes on the envelopes and files were photographed, and Ilan Harati of Israel's State Archives checked the state of preservation of their contents. The discoveries seemed to confirm that Brod had given Esther Hoffe possession of the Kafka manuscripts during his lifetime.

They also confirmed Brod's obsession with collecting everything, especially anything with Kafka's handwriting on it (including Kafka's sketches and doodles).

Shedletzky, tasked with jotting down an inventory of the material in the deposit boxes, felt unduly rushed by the Israeli lawyers in the vault room. But she had time enough to take note of correspondence Esther Hoffe conducted with the German editors of the critical edition of Kafka's works, letters that proved that despite claims to the contrary, Hoffe allowed "systematic and regular" access to the Kafka papers in her possession. Incredibly, Shedletzky was never asked to submit her findings to the court.

Her inventory remained incomplete in another way. Eva Hoffe told me she had been fined 15,000 shekels (roughly $4,200 today) for refusing a court order to submit her home to a search so that the manuscripts there could be inventoried. Such a search reminded her of "Gestapo tactics," she said.

The incomplete inventory of the Tel Aviv and Zürich vaults, running to 170 pages, listed some twenty thousand letters (likely including some seventy letters from Dora, Kafka's last lover, to Brod), Brod's unpublished diaries,* two-dozen unknown drawings by Kafka, and original manuscripts of Kafka's short stories (including "Wedding Preparations in the Country"). In late February 2011, the inventory was submitted to Judge Kopelman Pardo.

In the meantime, Eva Hoffe said she had to rely on handouts in order to survive. Although she, like her mother, received reparations from the German government, she said she had spent most of her savings to pay for her mother's rehabilitation at Ichilov Hospital after Esther suffered a stroke. And her legal expenses were mounting. Claiming financial hard-

---

* Reiner Stach, the only scholar to have consulted the diaries, dismisses their literary significance: "Brod produced little more than a succession of jottings, written in the kind of postcard language that gave no indication of a will to form or literary authorship." Kafka's diaries, by contrast, in which the writer limbered up, served as a "vestibule of literature," Stach says.

ship, she had her lawyer Uri Zfat petition the court to release at least the monetary portion of her mother's estate (including reparations Esther had received from Germany and that according to Eva had accumulated to some 4 million shekels, or more than $1 million). In August 2011, Judge Judith Stoffman of the Tel Aviv District Court granted the motion, and allowed Eva and her elder sister Ruth Wiesler to inherit 1 million shekels (roughly a quarter of a million dollars) each.

For Ruth, a retired seamstress and aromatherapist, it was too little and too late. She had been so distraught over the trial that she couldn't bring herself to attend the hearings or even to read the court protocols. She died of cancer at age eighty in 2012, leaving her sister Eva to carry on the battle alone. "I hold the National Library responsible for the death of my client," Ruth's lawyer Harel Ashwall told the *Sunday Times*. "They have behaved in a very aggressive and inappropriate manner. I think what they have done is to try and exhaust Ruth and Eva until they gave up." Ruth had two daughters, Anat and Yael. Anat likewise blamed the tribulations of the trial for her mother's demise. "A woman who was healthy all her life suddenly gets cancer and dies—she was absolutely annihilated from it," she told *Haaretz*.

————

In October 2012, half a year after Ruth's death and five years after Esther Hoffe's death, Judge Talia Kopelman Pardo of the Tel Aviv Family Court issued a fifty-nine-page judgment. She opened on a lyrical note. "It is not every day, and certainly not as a matter of course, that a judge plumbs the depths of history, revealed before her fragment by fragment, shard by shard, more enigmatic than intelligible. A simple request filed by the plaintiffs, the daughters of the late Mrs. Esther Hoffe, to execute her will has opened a portal onto the lives, desires, frustrations—indeed the souls—of two of the twentieth century's great spirits."

Justifying the reopening of a case brought against Esther Hoffe and decided by Judge Shilo forty years earlier, the judge took the unusual step of citing a passage of fiction—Kafka's *The Trial*:

> In an actual acquittal, the files relating to the case are completely discarded, they disappear totally from the proceedings, not only the charge, but the trial and even the acquittal, everything is destroyed. An apparent acquittal is handled differently. There is no further change in the files except the adding to them the certification of innocence, the acquittal, and the grounds of acquittal. Otherwise, they remain in circulation; following the law court's normal routine they are passed on to the higher courts, come back to the lower ones, swinging back and forth with larger or smaller oscillations, longer or shorter interruptions. These paths are unpredictable. Externally it may sometimes appear that everything has been long forgotten, the file has been lost, and the acquittal is absolute. No initiate would ever believe that. No file is ever lost, and the court never forgets.

The 1974 decision in favor of Esther Hoffe had not been forgotten, Judge Kopelman Pardo wrote, but now the unpredictable oscillations had swung in a different direction. Kopelman Pardo rejected Eva Hoffe's probate of her mother's will. She did not rule on whether Brod owned Kafka's manuscripts, but she did accept the Israeli state's argument that Brod had bequeathed his estate—Kafka papers included—to Esther Hoffe not as a gift but in trust. If certain conditions are not met, a gift may be legally invalid despite the donor's or testator's intention.

Although Brod intended to give the manuscripts to Esther Hoffe as a gift, they remained in his de facto control; he alone decided their fate. Even after signing notes in which he promised possession of the papers to Esther, Brod behaved as though the Kafka papers remained his. In April 1952, for example, Brod wrote to Marianna Steiner in London, listing which of Kafka's manuscripts belonged to him and which to Kafka's surviving family heirs. He makes no mention of having given anything to Hoffe. In August 1956, Brod signed a document specifying under what conditions he would allow the German scholar Klaus Wagenbach to consult those papers: only in Brod's apartment, only for research and not for publication, and so on. Brod, and not Esther, granted the permission and set the terms. Finally, in an interview he gave the Israeli newspaper *Maariv* in October 1961, Brod said: "I'm still deliberating what to do [with the Kafka manuscripts]." The interviewer asked if he could see them. "No! I keep them in a bank vault." He says *I*, not *Esther and I*. (Judge Kopelman Pardo did not address the testimony Esther Hoffe gave in the 1973–74 case, according to which Kafka's manuscripts of "Wedding Preparations in the Country" and "Descriptions of a Struggle" "were in my safe since 1947, and when he [Brod] wanted it for work, I brought it to him." In a hearing on January 11, 1974, Hoffe likewise testified to Judge Yitzhak Shilo about Kafka's manuscript of *The Trial*: "I received it, I think, in 1952, and put it in my safe. He [Brod] gave it to me. I took it out of his house. Only when he worked on it did I bring it to him.") In any case, Esther never dared to sell one of Kafka's manuscripts while Brod was still living. (Eva Hoffe claimed that her mother chose not to sell the manuscripts in Brod's lifetime for the simple reason that he was consulting them for his work in editing and publishing Kafka's writings.)

Under clause 873 of the seventh volume of Mecelle law, the Sharia-based civil code of the Ottoman Empire that Israel adopted until it passed its own gift laws in 1968, the judge ruled that Brod's gift to Hoffe had not been completed or consummated.* (Eva Hoffe took the

---

* According to clause 846 of the Mecellé law, if a recipient of a gift says to the donor "I have received the gift," the gift is considered valid. The current Israeli Gift Law, which came into effect on October 1, 1968, as part of an ongoing effort to update Ottoman laws, stipulates that even if a gift had not been fully delivered or consummated, it becomes property of the recipient upon the death of the donor. Section 6 of the Gift Law, which allows gifts to be given in writing, was not included in the original bill sent to the Knesset (the Israeli parliament). It was added during the second reading of the bill to make it more consistent with civil principles of traditional Jewish law ("Mishpat Ivri").

suggestion that the gift that had defined her mother's life was uncon-summated as an especially sharp affront.) The Kafka manuscripts had never left Brod's literary estate, Kopelman Pardo ruled. The judge inter-preted Brod's will as subject to the principle of "successive heirs." In other words, since Esther Hoffe had made no other arrangement in her lifetime, Brod's literary estate must be placed in the custody of a public library or archive as stipulated in Brod's will. Esther had the right to decide where the literary estate would go, but having not exercised that right she did not have the right to pass that decision to her daughters.

This was to be the last case over which Kopelman Pardo presided. After twelve years on the bench, having with Kafka's help reached the summit of her judicial career, she returned to private practice and started a boutique firm specializing in the area of inheritance and fam-ily laws. Eva told me she suspects that the judge retired not because of age, but because if she were no longer a judge she would be shielded from complaints that she had mishandled this case. But such suspicion seemed to derive from Eva's own unhappiness with the result, rather than any professional missteps on Kopelman Pardo's part.

Aviad Stollman, who managed the Kafka file at the National Library, welcomed the verdict: "In view of the role of the library to collect, preserve and make accessible the cultural treasures of the State of Israel and the Jewish people, we see this as a great success." Mark Gelber, a leading Kafka scholar at Ben-Gurion University, called it a "very courageous decision."

Brod's literary estate, Eva said throughout the trial, carries far more than commercial value. Protesting that the manuscripts and papers "are like limbs of my body," Eva refused Shmulik Cassouto's offer to mediate a compromise. "She preferred risking an all-or-nothing approach," Cas-souto said. Eva gave me a different version: After Kopelman Pardo's ver-dict, she proposed to sell the manuscripts to the Marbach archive and relay the profits to the National Library. The National Library declined, she said. "And they accuse *me* of profit-seeking!" A later mediation, led by Gabriella Shalev (a jurist and former Israeli ambassador to the United Nations), also failed to reach a compromise.

In November 2012, less than a month after the Family Court ruling, Eva entered an appeal at the Tel Aviv District Court. "Not even Kafka himself could have written such a Kafkaesque tale," she said. She hoped to keep her phantom limbs.

———

As the trial progressed from the Family Court to the District Court, moral pleading increasingly intruded into the legal proceedings. Attorney Meir Heller, representing the National Library of Israel, addressed a panel of three appellate judges of the Tel Aviv District Court—Isaiah Schneller, Hagai Brenner, and Kobi Vardi. Heller stressed Israel's precedence over Germany as the proper place for the Brod and Kafka estates. In emotionally charged language, Heller noted that Kafka's world was destroyed by the Nazis.

Each of Kafka's three sisters—"who loved and honored him as a sort of higher being," as the writer's niece Gerti Hermann recalled—fell victim to the Third Reich. Elli (the eldest, who reminded Kafka most of himself) and Valli (the middle sister) were deported to the Łódź ghetto in late 1941, and sent to the gas chambers of Chełmno in September 1942. Ottla, the youngest and most vivacious of the Kafka sisters, was deported from the Terezin ghetto 30 miles south of Prague to Auschwitz, Poland, where she was murdered in October 1943. Heller added that Max Brod's only brother Otto, who also knew Kafka well, was deported from Terezin to Auschwitz in late October 1944, where he perished together with his wife and daughter.

Heller might have added other victims of German crimes: Kafka's lover Milena Jesenská, a Czech dissident married to a Jew in Vienna, murdered in 1944 in the Ravensbrück concentration camp; Kafka's second fiancée, Julie Wohryzek, killed in Auschwitz in 1944; Kafka's favorite uncle, Siegfried, who killed himself on the eve of his deportation to Terezin in 1942; and Kafka's friend Yitzhak Löwy, the Yiddish actor, who perished in Treblinka. At least five of Kafka's high school class-mates were murdered in concentration camps.

Kafka himself did not live to see human beings exterminated like vermin. But Heller suggested that had Kafka not died in 1924, had he reached his late fifties, he too would have been murdered by the Germans as a Jew. Is there not, Heller concluded, something obscene in the argument that the papers "belong" in Germany, the country of the genocidal perpetrators, the country that gave unprecedented mechanized form to man's inhumanity to man? Kafka may have written in German, but not long after his death German became the language of those who organized the mass murder of Jews, the degraded language of the camps.

Shmulik Cassouto, court-appointed executor of Esther Hoffe's estate, said the Shoah "hung like a cloud over the courtroom."

———

On June 29, 2015, after two-and-a-half years of hearings, the three judges of the Tel Aviv District Court rendered their verdict. Justices Brenner, Vardi, and Schneller said they were not bound by Judge Shilo's 1974 ruling in favor of Esther Hoffe. Since the National Library had not been a party to that case, the outcome of those proceedings could not set a precedent for the present case.

The judges portrayed the appellant, Eva Hoffe, as "moved less by the fulfillment of Brod's true wish than by the desire to profit from the assets of the estate." They also condemned Esther Hoffe's past sales of the manuscripts to the Marbach archive (discussed further in Chapter 14):

Brod likely could not have imagined that those writings that he saw fit, for reasons that became clear, to give as a gift to his secretary Hoffe would be put up for public auction piecemeal and sold by Hoffe and her daughters to the highest bidder. As Brod himself boasted in a newspaper interview: "The whole world chases Kafka. I myself do not care: I will not take a penny for my work on his oeuvre. It is a debt I owe a distinguished friend!" Is it conceivable that Brod, were he asked, would give his blessing to this kind of auction?

Had the Kafka material been part of Brod's usual estate, they would go to his sole heir, Esther Hoffe (under paragraph 7 of his will, which designates her the heir of all his property). The judges ruled that because the Kafka material was part of Brod's *literary* estate, however, Esther's right to them was conditioned by paragraph 11 of Brod's will, which instructed her to arrange for the deposit of his estate "with the library of the Hebrew University of Jerusalem [since renamed the National Library of Israel], the Municipal Library in Tel Aviv, or another public archive in Israel or abroad."

The District Court judges further ruled that Brod could be considered the owner of those of Kafka's manuscripts that Kafka had given him in his lifetime, but not of the manuscripts that he had taken from Kafka's desk after Kafka's death. In the absence of other claimants, however, the latter group would be deposited together with Brod's literary estate. At the same time, the court made no demand that an effort be made to locate Kafka's heirs, nor did it list which of Kafka's manuscripts belong in the former category and which in the latter. (Four of Kafka's nieces survived the Holocaust: two daughters of his sister Ottla, Věra Saudková [1921–2015] and Helena Kostrouchová Davidová [1923–2005], both of whom lived in Prague; Gerti Hermann [1912–1972], a daughter of Elli who fled to Canada; and Marianna Steiner [1913–2000], a daughter of Valli who lived in London.[*])

The District Court judges also agreed with the lower court that Hoffe had not been entitled to sell off parts of Brod's literary estate, or

---

[*] According to Hélène Zylberberg (1904–92), who met Kafka's sisters in late 1936, Ottla "never accepted the fact that Kafka's works had been published as the result of some-

to give them as gifts, since Brod had wanted her to transfer his estate intact and in its entirety to a library or archive. Hoffe and her successors were entitled only to any royalties that Brod's literary legacy would earn.

Judge Brenner wrote the District Court's opinion:

> The judges unanimously upheld the lower court's decision: Esther Hoffe had no right to sell Kafka's manuscripts, to give them away, or to bequeath them to her heirs. I believe and hope this court of appeal, on whose gates someone knocked, even if it did not bring redemption in upholding the lower court's ruling, did offer a chance to open a door that will enable the public and history to judge Kafka's works and to see them, after Kafka's death, in all their great ethical and artistic worth—and not, as Kafka sometimes saw them in his lifetime, as "failed works" there was no point preserving. . . . It seems Max Brod would have rejected out of hand the possibility of his literary estate being transferred to an archive located in Germany.

In his brief concurring opinion, Judge Kobi Vardi wrote:

> Just as Max Brod regarded his unobjectionable duty to publish the "wonderful treasures" of Kafka's works as a consideration that overcomes any other consideration against the publication of those works—and Kafka's instruction not to publish them—so it is our duty and our right to fulfill this aim, through the legal tools available to us.

Vardi added that the appellate court's decision was "a fitting and just result that best expresses the integration of law, literature, ethics and

---

one's indiscretion. Franz had left a will and his deepest and most sacred wish that all he had written be burned ought to have been obeyed. For this reason, she was angry with Max Brod." Zylberberg later translated Brod's biography of Kafka into French (Gallimard, 1945).

justice—and, in my view, the true will of Kafka. Though some may argue that we have erred, everyone will at least agree that this is a remarkable Kafkaesque story."

In its language, the fifty-six-page ruling ranged across several registers, from technical legalisms to sweeping nationalistic rhetoric. In the end, it affirmed that Kafka was an essentially Jewish writer and that his literary legacy, as a cultural asset of national significance, properly belongs in and to the Jewish state.*

————

As expected, the National Library welcomed the District Court decision. Stefan Litt, head of the library's German-language archives, said: "The big question now is: What will we find in the Hoffe family's Tel Aviv apartment, and what else may have been hidden elsewhere throughout the world?" He would have to wait. Shortly after the appellate court's decision, police in Germany seized handwritten manuscripts of Max Brod on the suspicion they had been smuggled out of Israel.

Eva Hoffe now saw no choice but to appeal to Israel's Supreme Court. She entered the second and final appeal with no great optimism. The high court had already hinted which way it might lean. In June 2015, as the three judges of the Tel Aviv District Court were deciding the Kafka case, Israel's Supreme Court was hearing a dispute concerning Europe's second largest prewar Jewish community: Vienna. After the

---

* This was not the first time that an Israeli appellate court invoked such a principle. In November 2015, the Jerusalem District Court halted the proposed sale of twelve hand-written pages of drafts of Israel's Declaration of Independence that had been slated to go on sale at Jerusalem's Kedem Auction House. The judges said they acted to "ensure Israel's inalienable assets remained in the public's hands and are not removed from the country without the government's consent." ("We find it strange that the state abandoned this inalienable asset for 67 years, didn't bother to demand it, although the media and studies reported its existence several times," the auction house replied. "The state only remembered the drafts when they were put on public auction.")

Second World War, members of the Vienna Jewish community (*Israel-itische Kultusgemeinde Wien*) saw little future in Austria for their extensive library. (Its director from 1935 to the *Anschluß* in 1938 was Moses Rath, whose textbook Kafka had used when he began to teach himself Hebrew.) In 1952 and 1953, Israel's National Library was permitted to pick out the choicest parts of the Vienna Jewish library and bring them to Jerusalem. This permanent loan amounted to 75 percent to 80 percent of that collection. The community's invaluable prewar archives, meanwhile, dating back to the eighteenth century, were also brought to Jerusalem, on permanent loan to the Central Archives for the History of the Jewish People. (The Central Archives, founded in 1939, formally merged with the National Library of Israel in January 2013.)

In May 2011, Ariel Muzicant, elected in 1998 to lead the 7,500-member Vienna Jewish community, filed a lawsuit in Jerusalem demanding the archives be returned. In October 2012, the Jerusalem District Court rejected the petition, accepting the argument of state archivist Yaacov Lozowick that Israel serves as the cultural center of the Jewish people.

In June 2015, the Supreme Court upheld that decision. Justice Elyakim Rubinstein (who a year later would hear Eva Hoffe's appeal) wrote: "What was done all over occupied Europe by the Nazis and their helpers during the dark days of the Holocaust is what caused the transfer of the material to the Jewish state, Israel, which arose from the ashes of the Holocaust—instead of it being tossed aside. In terms of history, hasn't the archive found its rightful home?"

Muzicant was appalled: "As much as we support the state of Israel as Jews," he told me in a telephone conversation, "taking our property is totally unacceptable." He compared Israel's behavior in the present case with Austria's reluctance, after the Second World War, to restore property looted from Jewish families. In both cases, culture produced by European Jewry belongs in its original context. Muzicant added that he asked the Federal Chancellor of Austria, Christian Kern, to raise the issue with Israeli Prime Minister Benjamin Netanyahu when they met in April 2017.

Israeli Supreme Court Justice Hanan Melcer, the son of Holocaust survivors from Poland, concurred with Rubinstein, however: some "cultural assets" may be of such significance that even their legal owners have no right to do as they please with them. "This is the place to emphasize that the value of a 'cultural asset' is, for the most part, so great that even the person with the possessory or ethical right to it cannot order its destruction," Melcer wrote. "To use an analogy, I will mention that, considering the fact that Kafka's writings have been recognized as 'cultural assets,' there was no justification for obeying Kafka's instructions to have his writings burned." Although the case of the Vienna archives had ostensibly nothing to do with the case of Brod's literary estate, the language of "cultural assets" would play a decisive role when the Supreme Court heard Eva Hoffe's appeal.

6

Last Son of the Diaspora:
Kafka's Jewish Afterlife

Pension Stüdl, Schelesen, Czechoslovakia
November 1919

> I ... have not caught the hem of the Jewish prayer shawl—now
> flying away from us—as the Zionists have.
> —Kafka, *The Blue Octavo Notebooks*, February 25, 1918

The judges in Tel Aviv were hardly the first to attempt a post-humous recruitment of Kafka to the Zionist cause. Nor were the judges the first to read Kafka as an essentially Jewish writer, to read his works as monuments of Jewish culture, in the line of the teachings of Moses, Hillel, and Maimonides.

Kafka's friend Felix Weltsch set the tone in 1924 in a full-page obituary in Prague's Zionist weekly *Selbstwehr*. "The soul that moved his writings was Jewish throughout." Two years later, Weltsch opened an essay on his friend with a stark claim:

Kafka was one of ours. He was a Praguer, he was a Jew, and he was a Zionist. His Zionism did not take on an explicit external form, but was expressed in his avid study of Hebrew and his firm intention to resettle in Palestine. Such was the case with all his convictions, which lay beyond the scope of external form and action. The essence of his work touches upon the deepest element of the Jewish *Weltanschauung* [worldview].

Unlike Brod's novels, suffused with Jews and Jewishness, in all of Kafka's fiction, there is no direct reference to Judaism. One searches in vain for Jews, or Jewish patterns of speech, in Kafka's placeless fiction. Unlike his contemporaries James Joyce and Marcel Proust, Kafka rigorously strips his characters of discernable ethnic identities, of awareness of their own origins and traditions, and more often than not of surnames. They are simply "the gatekeeper," "the hunger artist," "the father of the family," or "K."

This lack of delineation has encouraged a universalist reading, as though Kafka's art consisted in translating his own Jewish experience into universal language: the condition of the Jew as the plight of modern man *überhaupt*, "as such." "Kafka is important to us," W. H. Auden remarked in 1941, "because the predicament of his hero is the predicament of the contemporary man." Kafka's nameless heroes, Hannah Arendt wrote in 1944, "are not common men whom one could find and meet in the street, but the model of the 'common man' as an ideal of humanity." It is no coincidence that one of the biographies of Kafka is called *Representative Man*. Julian Preece, a British scholar of Kafka, argues: "Kafka was first and foremost an internationalist and a European ... the most cosmopolitan of all German-language writers."

But what if Kafka's path to universalism led through Jewish particularism? Many readers have strained to unearth Jewish forms and motifs in Kafka's works, to read his stories as allegories of the modern Jewish experience, and to portray his characters as quintessential Jews—both assimilated and cast out—surveying "the borderland between solitude and community," as Kafka puts it in his diaries.

The first and most influential of these readers was none other than Kafka's closest confidant, Max Brod. After his encounters with

Martin Buber at the Bar Kochba Association in 1909 and 1910 and his conversion to Zionism, Brod began to put Kafka's writing under a Jewish light. As early as 1916, Brod wrote: "Although the word 'Jew' never appears in his works, they belong to the most Jewish documents of our times."

Later, Brod would insist that *The Castle* in particular overflows with "the special feeling of a Jew who would like to take root in foreign surroundings, who tries with all the powers of his soul to get nearer to the strangers, to become one of them entirely—but who does not succeed in thus assimilating himself." (In his 1911 novel *Jüdinnen* [Jewesses], a love story set in the Bohemian spa town Teplice, Brod satirizes the figure of the assimilated Jew in the character of Alfred, a "lover of Wagner" who "belonged to those young Jews who are strongly attracted to all that is Aryan and despise everything Jewish.") Brod read *The Castle*'s protagonist as a superfluous man (a term popularized by Ivan Turgenev's 1850 novella *The Diary of a Superfluous Man*), equally estranged from God and from human community, continually in search of acceptance. ("I don't fit in with the peasants," says the wandering hero of *The Castle*, "nor, I imagine, with the Castle.") "This is the meaning of Kafka's religious socialism," Brod writes, "which constitutes a significant part of his humanistic Judaism, whose fundamental meaning is the demand for justice. The fragmented, assimilated Jew cannot follow this ideal with full force. Only he who has become internally whole again, who has found his homeland, his 'castle,' is capable of realizing this ideal." In this unfinished novel, Brod adds, Kafka "has said more about the situation of Jewry as a whole today than can be read in a hundred learned treatises."

Following Brod's cues, other readers interpreted the animals in Kafka's fables as symbols of Jewish exile, otherness, and self-alienation. The symbols—a bug ("The Metamorphosis"), ape ("A Report to an Academy"), dog ("Investigations of a Dog"), mole ("The Burrow"), jackals ("Jackals and Arabs," published a month before the Balfour Declaration was issued), and mice ("Josephine the Singer, or, the

Mouse People")—were said to be all the more potent because the word "Jew" is left unsaid.*

In September 1915, Kafka noted in his diary: "The pages of the Bible don't flutter in my presence." Yet the formidable German-born Israeli scholar Gershom Scholem, for one, read Kafka as a master of Jewish commentary, obsessed with the Law (and its inaccessibility) in a world of accusers and accused in which the Lawgiver has gone missing and (in the Kabbalastic parlance) has "hidden His face."

> For Kafka knew better than anyone else did how to express that boundary where nihilism and religion meet. That is why his writings, the secularized representation of the sensibility proper to Kabbalah (which he did not know), have, for many readers today, something of the radiance of canonical texts, or of some shattered perfection.

Convinced that Kafka belongs not so much in the German tradition as "in the continuum of Jewish literature," Scholem went so far as to accord Kafka's writings the status of Holy Writ, wrapped (as he said to the German-Jewish publisher Salman Schocken) "in the halo of the canonical." According to his colleague Alexander Altmann, Scholem "considered Franz Kafka to be the most authentic spokesman of our age. . . . He told his students in the 1930s that before embarking on a study of Kabbala they should first read Kafka." Scholem announced to

---

* For the present purposes, three examples will suffice: (1) The German critic Günther Anders writes that in "The Giant Mole," Kafka "analyzes the relation between the cultured Jew, the *Bildungsjude* whose affiliation to Judaism has become questionable, and the Orthodox Jew." (2) Benjamin Harshav called "Investigations of a Dog" "a cleverly veiled allegory of the Jewish condition" in which Kafka's canine character considers the diminishing power of language as it passes through generations; he laments the loss of the "true word." (3) Kafka represents "history's menace to the Jew," Clement Greenberg argues, "in the unknown enemies of the animal hero of 'The Burrow'; in the cats (presumably) that prey on Josephine's mice nation."

the Bavarian Academy of the Arts in 1974 that for him there were three canonical Jewish texts: the Hebrew Bible, the Zohar (the masterpiece of Kabbalah), and the works of Kafka. The latter, if nothing else, are as relentlessly and endlessly interpreted as the first two.

In a 1929 essay, German-Jewish thinker Margarete Susman (1872–1966) portrays Kafka's fiction as the last burst of Jewish theodicy before the disintegration of European Jewry, the last link in a literary tradition of quarreling with God [*Hader mit Gott*] that began with the biblical Book of Job. "God's silence and its consequences are the ultimate object of Kafka's art," she writes. That art, she says, like the Book of Job, expresses the Jewish encounter with divine hiddenness and the incomprehensible suffering. Like Kafka's protagonists, Job, who suffers a guilt not his own and "prefigures in his fate the sorrowful fate of the Jewish people in exile," found himself in a trial he could not comprehend.

Robert Alter, a leading scholar of Hebrew literature at Berkeley, has more recently drawn affinities between Kafka and the Jewish interpretive tradition:

> Had Kafka lived a century or two earlier, had he grown up in a pious milieu with his schooling entirely in the classic Jewish curriculum of sacred texts, his qualities of mind would have made him an excellent Talmudist, a first-rate exegete, and a brilliant weaver of kabbalistic homilies. . . . [He was] one of the keenest readers of the Bible since the masters of the Midrash.

"Is modern literature Scripture?" Saul Bellow once asked. "Is criticism Talmud, theology?" For some of Kafka's readers, yes. For them, as for the Israeli judges, Kafka's alleged appropriation of Jewish texts and themes becomes the cipher to his entire imaginative world.

Kafka himself would doubtless be more circumspect of such readings. "Many people prowl around Mt. Sinai," he wrote. If Kafka's own works have now come to resemble a Holy Scripture, perhaps they are zealously guarded by those who can no longer decipher their mysteries but who remain in awe of their power.

What in fact did Kafka have in common with the Jews, whether defined as a nation, a race, a religion, or an ethnicity? Were his own ties to them so tenuous and idiosyncratic as to make it impossible to consider his achievement as a Jewish achievement? By what measure can we assess the National Library's claim to take Kafka as a touchstone of "Jewish culture"?

———

In November 1919, Kafka, then thirty-six years old, took a two-week break from his job at the Worker's Accident Insurance Institute to travel to Schelesen, a Bohemian resort town 20 miles north of Prague. One of only two Jews among the firm's 260 employees, he set premiums, conducted inspections of work sites, answered countless complaints, and wrote essays on accident prevention. (The Institute's neo-baroque building on Na Poříčí Street today houses the Hotel Century Old Town Prague.) Though he earned a reputation for diligence and acumen, Kafka chafed against the bureaucratic drudgery. "In the office," he told Rudolf Steiner, "I fulfill my duties satisfactorily, at least outwardly, but not my inner duties, and every unfulfilled inner duty becomes a misfortune that never budges."

Kafka's destination for this vacation was a boardinghouse that catered to guests with lung ailments. Max Brod joined him there for several days. ("It was so wonderful to be together with you," Brod wrote on returning to Prague.) When Brod returned to Prague, Kafka, cloistered in his room, poured forth a merciless letter of more than a hundred handwritten pages, the longest he ever wrote. He wrote parts of it in tears. It was addressed to his father.

Ever since they were granted the Tolerance Charter by Emperor

Josef II—the "Mozart Emperor"—Prague's acculturated Jews had considered themselves part of the German population. Issued in 1781–82, the
Tolerance Charter had required Jews to take German names, shave their
beards, and enroll their children in state-sponsored German-language
schools. But Jews were granted full civic equality only in 1849. Kafka's father, Hermann (Hebrew name Henoch), burly son of a kosher
butcher, typified the first generation of Bohemian Jews after they were
emancipated. He enjoyed the right to live in the cities and enter the
trades. He had served as a platoon leader in the Austro-Hungarian army
for three years (1872–75). He was a man accustomed to giving orders, a
self-made and self-satisfied man who had come from the provinces to
the capital, Prague, to rise in the world. He had a shop for what was
then called "fancy goods" (*Galanteriewaren*)—parasols, canes, gloves,
muffs, buttons, felt slippers, lace underwear, stockings, ribbons, buck-
les, and other adornments. In the eyes of his son, he was a domineer-
ing, unappeasable man. Hermann thought his impractical only son had
things too easy. He both belittled his son and expected gratitude from
him. Franz associated the paternal Kafka line with "strength, health,
appetite, loudness of voice, eloquence, smugness, worldly supremacy,
stamina, presence of mind, knowledge of human nature, a kind of lord-
liness." At the same time, he describes himself in the letter as a fearful
child who "lived under laws that had been invented only for me and
which I could never comply with, I did not know why."

Kafka told Brod that when he presented his newly published collection of stories, *A Country Doctor*, to his father, Hermann had said, "Put
it on my nightstand," never to mention it again. Franz's filial pain had
long grated on Brod. (Hermann Kafka once called Brod a "*meschug-
genen Ritoch*"—a crazy hothead.)

In how many talks did I not try and make clear to my friend—
whose deepest wound, I knew, without yet having seen the diary,
was just this—how he overestimated his father, and how stupid

it is to despise oneself. It was all useless; the torrent of arguments that Franz produced (when he didn't prefer, as he frequently did, to keep quiet) could really shatter and repel me for a moment.

Kafka's parents, like Brod's, were "four-day Jews": they attended synagogue on the high holidays and on the birthday of Kaiser Franz Josef I (August 18). In the letter to his father (more like a settling of scores), Kafka describes a crisis of Jewish continuity. He writes that going through the motions during their infrequent and perfunctory visits to synagogue had left him indifferent. Those visits were "merely a social event," which the father took as a chance to greet "the sons of the millionaire Fuchs."

> And so I yawned and dozed through the many hours (I don't think I was ever again so bored, except later at dancing lessons) and did my best to enjoy the few little bits of variety there were, as for instance when the Ark of the Covenant was opened, which always reminded me of the shooting galleries where a cupboard door would open in the same way whenever one hit a bull's-eye; except that there something interesting always came out and here it was always just the same old dolls without heads. . . . I was not fundamentally disturbed in my boredom, unless it was by the bar mitzvah, but that demanded no more than some ridiculous memorizing.[*]

This experience was hardly uncommon. Brod, too, derided his Jewish education as "mere routine, boredom, something utterly exhausted and spent." On one occasion, Kafka had discussed with Brod the relation of

---

[*] On the invitation to Kafka's bar mitzvah, celebrated in 1896 at Prague's Zigeunersynagoge, his parents had called it a "confirmation." Fifteen years later, on the eve of Yom Kippur, 1911, Kafka went to synagogue with his father and noticed the family of the owner of the Salon Suha brothel in the pews nearby. Kafka had visited the brothel two days earlier.

Jewish sons to their acculturated, bourgeois fathers. "In this case," he wrote to Brod, "I prefer another approach over psychoanalysis, namely the realization that this father complex that some draw on for intellectual sustenance applies not to the innocent father, but to the father's Jewishness. Most of those who started to write in German wanted to get away from Judaism, often with their fathers' ambiguous agreement (this ambiguity was what was really embarrassing); they wanted it, but with their hind legs they were still glued to their fathers' Judaism and with their front legs they were unable to find new ground."

Now, writing to his father as a prosecutor "in this terrible trial that has been pending between us," Kafka turns accusatory on just this point.

You still brought along, from your small ghetto-like village, a tiny bit of Judaism. It was not much and some of it got lost in the army and when you came to the city. Still those impressions and memories of your youth sufficed for a bare minimum of a Jewish life, especially for you who are of a robust endowment and did not need much by way of spiritual sustenance and were left cold by religious need if it did not merge with social status.

"It was conceivable," Kafka continues, "that we might have found each other in Judaism." But the flimsy vestiges of Judaism passed on to him, Kafka writes, were "an insufficient scrap . . . a mere nothing, a joke—not even a joke . . . It all dribbled away while you were passing it on."[*] In the letter, Kafka three times uses the word *Nichts* (nothing) to describe the nullity of his father's religion-by-rote. "In the face of Judaism, Kafka is an exile," Swiss literary critic Jean Starobinski writes, "albeit one who ceaselessly asks for news of the land he has left."

---

[*] In sensing the thinness of the inherited tradition, Kafka was typical of his generation. Kafka's friend Robert Weltsch, writing in 1917, two years before Kafka wrote the letter to his father, claimed that "Jewish Prague lives on within us, although the Jewish community is no longer 'alive,' has dissolved, and fallen into lethargy."

Kafka's fiction is full of latecomers for whom the old verities have lost meaning. Traditions are on the point of losing their authority—or their decipherability—as they dissolve into incoherence. The hoped-for revelation never comes. So it was in reality. His father's tradition—like the son's letter—was a message deadened before it arrived.

Franz, still living with his parents, felt unable to deliver this exorcism-by-writing, this damning oedipal indictment (almost the mirror image of Flaubert's affectionate tribute to his father, in the posthumous *Souvenirs, notes, pensees intimes*). According to Brod, Franz asked his mother, Julie Löwy, to pass the letter on to Hermann. She prudently returned it to her son undelivered, never to mention it again. Kafka stashed the letter into a drawer in his desk, where it remained until Brod discovered it after Kafka's death.

For Kafka, the Jews were a people loyal to the law of transmission, but the Jewish message, in its paternal form, had been rendered indecipherable—and incommunicable. He could not recognize himself in its accumulated traditions. And yet his autonomy begins with that failure. Here, the interruption of Jewish patrimony shares something with the emerging sense in Kafka's writing that modern life is accompanied by the gradual loss of traditional structures of authority, the failure to transmit the father's word. For Kafka, modernity calls into question the very idea of succession—and our place in its order.

Kafka described himself as "without forebears, without marriage, without descendants." He once talked with Felice about the obstacles to raising their children in the Jewish faith. "I would have to tell the children . . . that, as a result of my origins, my education, disposition, environment, I have nothing tangible in common with their faith. . . . You might still be able to give the children at least a sorrowful answer to their question; I could not even do that."

Nor did Kafka spare himself the same question. "What have I in common with the Jews?" he asked himself in a diary entry of 1914. "I have hardly anything in common with myself."

———

Martin Buber's 1909–10 lectures in Prague left Kafka unimpressed. "It would take more than Buber to get me out of my room," he writes to Felice Bauer. "I have heard him before, I find him dreary." But beginning in May 1910, he (like Brod) discovered an unlikely source of vitality: the performances of a Yiddish theater troupe in the Café Savoy on Ziegen Square in Prague's former ghetto district. In contrast to the more "academic" style of the Bar Kochba group, "this company illuminated for me the true concept of Jewish folklore," Brod wrote, "terrifying and repulsive yet at the same time magically attractive."

At age twenty-eight, eight years before writing the indictment of his father's moribund Judaism, Kafka became enchanted by a third-rate Yiddish theater troupe of eight actors from Lvov (Lemberg) that performed in Café Savoy. At Brod's invitation, he attended twenty performances over the next two years—melodramas, tearjerkers, operettas, and comedies. Among the fourteen plays he saw were Jacob Gordin's play about the late first-century heretic Elisha ben Abuya, Avrom Goldfaden's historical dramas *Shulamith* and *Bar Kochba*, Zygmund Faynman's play *The Vice-King*, and what a review in the weekly *Selbstwehr* called "not entirely tasteful cabaret."

The café was tawdry, its doorman a part-time pimp. Yet the burlesque performances "made my cheeks tremble," Kafka said. The actors who roamed the green-curtained narrow stage seemed at times self-sufficient and self-absorbed, drawn into their own magic circle as if unaware of their spectators, as if the curtain had never parted.

Kafka would fill over a hundred pages in his diary—some of the most enchanting pages, in fact—with incandescent accounts of these Yiddish actors and the plays they staged. They presented something more than the spectacle of a *pathos*. He was impressed by their authenticity and "vigor" (*Urwüchsigkeit*), and by the ironic idiom itself—in which high and low, biblical and vernacular rattled against each other. Here Kafka caught a first glimpse of an unself-conscious, living Eastern European

Jewish culture; a culture free of the contrived qualities of his father's Judaism.

This is not something the Yiddish actors intended to convey. They did not wish to use the stage to instruct or impart a message to their spectators. They were not pedagogues. And yet something in the theater's logic of transmission clicked for Kafka.

"The history of cultural encounters," writes Kafka scholar Ritchie Robertson, "can probably show few transformations so abrupt as the reversal in the attitudes of successive generations of Western Jews to their Eastern counterparts." The narrator of Saul Bellow's story "Cousins" (1975) refers to "the nearness of ghettos to the sphere of Revelation, an easy move for the mind from rotting streets and rancid dishes, a direct ascent into transcendence. This of course was the situation of Eastern Jews. The Western ones were prancing and preening like learned Germans."

Two of the troupe's actors embodied that East-West contrast for Kafka. The first object of his infatuation was a thirty-year-old actress-singer named Millie Tshissik. "Yesterday her body was more beautiful than her face . . . she reminded me vaguely of hybrid beings like mermaids, sirens, centaurs." Her exaggerated theatrical gestures transfixed him: "the hand pressed at the depth of the shabby bodice, short jerks of the shoulders and hips when expressing scorn. . . . Her way of walking is somewhat ceremonious since she has the habit of slowly lifting, extending, and moving her long arms. Especially when she was singing the Jewish national anthem, moving her hips with her arms. . . ." When they met backstage, Kafka could not look Millie in the eye, he notes in his diary, "because that would have shown that I love her." After one performance, Kafka presented her with flowers. "I had hoped that the bouquet would somewhat appease my love for her. It didn't. Only literature or coitus can satisfy it."

A second member of the troupe caught Kafka's eye: a Warsaw-born actor living from hand-to-mouth named Yitzhak Löwy. One night, instead of acting, Löwy gave a reading: a short story by I. L. Peretz, humorous sketches by Sholem Aleichem, and a Yiddish rendition of H. N. Bialik's scathing poem about the Kishinev pogroms of 1903, "In the City of Slaughter" (*In Shkhite Shtot*). "After the reading," Kafka wrote, "while still on my way home, I felt all my abilities concentrated." Years later, in his story, "A Friend of Kafka," the Yiddish writer Isaac Bashevis Singer described a meeting with an actor based on Löwy. "[Kafka] came backstage," the aging actor tells the narrator, "and the moment I saw him I knew that I was in the presence of genius. I could smell it the way a cat smells a mouse."*

Hermann Kafka, like a self-made man embarrassed by poor relatives, held his son's new Eastern European Jewish friends in low esteem. He considered Löwy a vagabond, a disreputable *Ostjude* (Eastern European Jew). When Kafka invited Löwy home, Hermann "gave himself sarcastic shakes, cut grimaces, and started talking about how just about anybody was being let into the house."

In the undelivered letter, Kafka reproaches his father for holding the Yiddish actor in such contempt. "Without knowing him you compared him, in some dreadful way that I have now forgotten, to vermin." (Here Kafka uses the same word, *Ungeziefer*, that he used to describe his character Gregor Samsa in the opening line of "The Metamorphosis," the novella he wrote in late 1912 and published, with Brod's help, in October 1915: "As Gregor Samsa awoke one morning from uneasy dreams, he found himself transformed in his bed into a monstrous vermin." Löwy would be deported to Treblinka in 1942.)† "Through my agency," Kafka adds, "Judaism became revolting to you, Jewish writings unreadable,

---

* Löwy was also a great admirer of Max Brod, "the first to encourage me to appear in public with excerpts, songs, and scenes from Yiddish literature," he said in 1934.
† In describing Gregor Samsa as a vermin, several translators of "The Metamorphosis" into English (including David Wyllie, Joachim Neugroschel, and Stanley Corngold) retain the literal meaning of the German word *Ungeziefer*. Corngold notes that in Middle High German, *Ungeziefer* referred to an "unclean animal not suited for sacrifice." According to Sigrid Weigel, "it is a word without clear imagery; it is collective and can denote any verminlike pests, not necessarily a roach or beetle as it is often translated."

they 'disgusted' you." If the father had earlier made Judaism impossible for the son, now the son was making Judaism impossible for the father.

The Yiddish theater taught the son that the father's will concerning Judaism need not be the first and last word; it opened to Kafka another way of thinking Jewishness, an alternative to the paternal patrimony.

On the heels of his encounter with Yiddish theater, as the reverberations of his father's voice grew fainter, Kafka began to give himself the nourishment denied him by his father. He subscribed to the Zionist periodicals *Die Jüdische Rundschau* (Jewish Review) and *Selbstwehr* (Self-Defense). He read the Bible in Martin Luther's translation, acquainted himself with Talmudic literature through Jakob Fromer's *Organism of Judaism* (*Der Organismus des Judentums*, 1909), and "eagerly and happily" devoured Heinrich Graetz's *History of the Jews* (1888–89). "I had to stop here and there in order by resting to allow my Jewishness to collect itself," he says. He also read about Yiddish in French. He absorbed Meyer Isser Pinès's history of Yiddish literature (*Histoire de la littérature judéo-allemande*, 1911); after finishing it in January 1912, Kafka records in his diary that he read "five-hundred pages with such thoroughness, haste, and joy as I have never yet shown in the case of similar books." He copied into his diary several passages from the book, including this phrase in Yiddish: "*Wos mir seinen, seinen mir / Ober jueden seinen mir*"—What we are, we are/ But Jews we are.

Kafka knew from his father how condescending a view the assimilated Jewish bourgeoisie took of Yiddish; they shunned it as a half-German half-Hebrew "hermaphrodite" jargon. In his *History of the Jews*, Graetz, for example, had called it a "mumbling gibberish" (*lallendes Kauderwelsch*).

The unsettling encounter with Yiddish altered Kafka's relationship with German, his inherited mother tongue (*Muttersprache*), and challenged him to reassess whether he belonged to German—or German to him. "Yesterday," he writes in his diary on October 24, 1911, "it occurred to me that I did not always love mother [*die Mutter*] as she deserved it and as I could, only because the German language prevented it. The Jewish mother is no *Mutter*." He had loved his mother in a mother tongue that, for all the precision with which he brandished it, rang false. In one letter to Brod, Kafka refers to "the German that we still have in our ears from our un-German mothers." In another, he refers to the Jewish use of the German language as "an overt or covert, or possibly self-tormenting usurpation of an alien property [*fremde Besitz*], which has not been acquired but stolen, (relatively) quickly picked up, and which remains someone else's possession even if not a single linguistic mistake can be pointed out." It was an inheritance he could not fully claim.

And so another, humbler linguistic inheritance offered itself. On behalf of his new "indispensable friend" Yitzhak Löwy, whom he had been trying to persuade to emigrate to Palestine, Kafka persuaded the Bar Kochba group to sponsor a benefit evening of Yiddish readings. It would take place in the banquet hall at Prague's Jewish Town Hall (Jüdisches Rathaus) opposite the Altneu Synagogue on Maisel Street. Kafka himself organized and would introduce the evening. He anticipated in his diary that his introduction "will come straight out of me as though out of a gun barrel."

On the night of Sunday, February 18, 1912, Kafka took the stage, mediating between the audience before him and Löwy waiting in the wings behind him. It was not to be a Yiddish performance as much as a performance in German about Yiddish. In his talk (which Max Brod would publish in 1953 under the title "Speech on the Yiddish Language"), Kafka counseled his German-speaking audience not to fear the Jewish past submerged beneath their emancipated facades:

> I would like [the effect of the verses of the Eastern Jewish poets] to be released, if it deserves it. Yet this cannot occur so long as many of you are so afraid of Yiddish that one can almost see it in your faces. . . . You understand far more Yiddish than you think. And once Yiddish has taken hold of you—and Yiddish is everything: word, Hassidic melody, and the very essence of this Eastern Jewish

actor [Löwy] himself—you will no longer recognize your former complacency. At that point, you will so powerfully feel the unity of Yiddish as to make you afraid—not of Yiddish any longer but of yourselves.

Afterwards, Kafka noted the "proud, unearthly feeling" that accompanied him as he spoke about the "Mameloshn" (mother tongue). For once, he surveyed what he had done and saw that it was good. Nowhere else, notes French essayist and translator Marthe Robert, was Kafka, usually so uneasy about his position as a Jew writing in German, "so confident of his talent, so proud of his ease of movement of action." It was to be the only public lecture Kafka would ever give. His father, Hermann, did not deign to come.

In the end, however, the verdict in the Israeli courts would turn not only on Kafka's relation to Jewishness, but also on the Jewish state's relation—equally ambivalent—to him.

7

The Last Ingathering:
Kafka in Israel

Offenbach Depot, American Zone of Occupation, Germany
July–August 1946

I am a memory come alive.

—Kafka's diary, October 15, 1921

Beyond its legal conundrums, the trial in Israel threw into stark relief the country's ambivalence toward Diaspora culture. Throughout the trial, Israel acted as though it can lay claim to any pre-state Jewish cultural artifact,* as though everything Jewish finds its culmination in

---

* Consider the case of Bruno Schulz, a Jewish-Polish writer and artist with no inclination toward Zionism (and the translator, with Józefina Szelińska, of Kafka's *The Trial* into Polish). In 1942, just before he was shot to death in the street by an SS officer, Schulz painted several fanciful frescoes in the children's room of a house in his village of Drohobycz (then in Poland, today in western Ukraine). The town's Jewish community of about fifteen thousand was reduced to four hundred by the end of the war. Schulz's murals were left to decay and presumed lost for good. In February 2001, a German documentary filmmaker named Benjamin Geissler traveled to Drohobycz with his father, Christian, and rediscovered the frescoes. Shortly thereafter, a Polish-Ukrainian commission led by Wojciech Chmurzyński began to restore them. In a clandestine operation in June 2001, however, an Israeli team removed the paintings from the walls and hauled them to Yad

the Jewish state, as though Jewish culture has been driven by a teleological thrust toward Jerusalem. During the trial, the National Library portrayed Kafka as a touchstone of modern Jewish cultural achievement, and portrayed Israel itself as the heir of the Diaspora's achievements. As David Blumberg, chairman of the board of the National Library, put it: "The library does not intend to give up on cultural assets belonging to the Jewish people."

Outside the main reading room at the National Library, an engraved inscription, dated 1899, reads: "In Jerusalem our holy city shall be built a great house, high and exalted, where all of the fruits of the spirit of Israel from the day it became a people shall be kept, and to this house will stream our rabbis, sages, and all the enlightened of our nation." If Israel is a country of return, the Zionist "ingathering of exiles" involved not just the physical return of Jews to the land, but the aspiration to serve as a haven for Jewish books—an aspiration that accompanied the National Library from its inception.

Five years after the founding of the Hebrew University in 1925, the Jewish National and University Library (JNUL), as it was then called, moved into its new building on Mount Scopus, a hilltop in east Jerusalem. Since 1933, two copies of every publication printed in the country must by law be deposited with the library. In 1948, the outbreak of Israel's War of Independence severed Mount Scopus from the rest of Jeru-

---

Vashem, which asserted "a moral right" to the works. Polish authorities, offended by the implication that Poles are not worthy stewards of Polish-Jewish heritage, charged the Israelis with harming both reconciliation efforts and the artworks themselves. (Most of Schulz's extant letters and drawings are kept in the Adam Mickiewicz Museum of Literature and the Museum of the Jewish Historical Institute, both in Warsaw.) In response, the Holocaust museum warned Poland of the wider consequences of demanding them back. "Yad Vashem is of the opinion that if Poland feels that they have an interest in assets that they see as their own, a discussion can be initiated regarding assets—cultural and other—which are part of the Jewish legacy in general and the Holocaust-era in particular, and are spread throughout Poland." See the dueling open letters published in *The New York Review of Books*: "Bruno Schulz's Frescoes" (November 29, 2001), and "Bruno Schulz's Wall Paintings" (May 23, 2002).

salem, and the library was forced to move its main holdings to the Terra Sancta building, a Franciscan property in West Jerusalem. Twelve years later, the library was transferred to the impressive building in which it is currently housed, on the Givat Ram campus of the Hebrew University. In 2007, the Knesset passed the National Library Law, which redefined the JNUL as the National Library of Israel.

Visitors there are today greeted by the stunning interplay of saturated blues and radiant reds of Mordecai Ardon's stained-glass windows, among the largest ever made. Ardon's masterpiece is dedicated to Isaiah's vision of peace: "For out of Zion shall go forth the Law and the word of the Lord from Jerusalem.... And they shall beat their swords into plowshares and their spears into pruning hooks; nation shall not lift up sword against nation, neither shall they learn war again." The central window transfigures Jerusalem's Old City wall into the Dead Sea Scroll of the Book of Isaiah, as though in Jerusalem words are more real than stone.

Until Isaiah's vision is realized, the library must serve as a safe haven for a culture that only narrowly survived extermination. Among the Jewish properties looted by the Einsatzstab Reichsleiter Rosenberg (Nazi Germany's state agency for looting, formed in July 1940) were vast libraries and archives. Some were intended for anti-Jewish museums dedicated to curating a culture destroyed. By war's end, millions of plundered Jewish books had been scattered across Europe. Some 400,000 books that had been plundered from French Jews were discovered in Tanzenberg Castle in Carinthia, Austria.* In Vienna, 330,000

---

* These came from France (157,000 volumes), the Soviet Union (64,000 volumes), the Netherlands (90,000 volumes), Belgium (1,124 crates), and other occupied countries. In 1947, Simon Wiesenthal visited Tanzenberg together with three rabbis. "Suddenly I heard a thump behind me. One of the rabbis lay on the floor sobbing. He had a prayer book in his hand and said: 'Look, that's a prayer book from my house. Here is a message from my sister: Whoever comes across this prayer book, please turn it over to my beloved brother Rabbi Hoschut Seitmann. The murderers are in our community. They are in the house next door. In a few minutes they'll be here. Please, don't forget us and don't forget our

confiscated books (including part of the renowned YIVO library in Vilna) were kept in a former bank building, and tens of thousands of volumes stolen from Austrian Jews ended up in a basement of the Hofburg Palace. The former central synagogue of Trieste, Italy, was turned into a warehouse for books looted from Jewish emigrants. In Berlin, hundreds of thousands more volumes were kept in the Reich Security Main Office (*Reichssicherheitshauptamt*).

In 1946, Robert Walsh, a journalist dispatched to Germany by the Israeli newspaper *Haaretz*, reported that a five-story reinforced-concrete building belonging to I. G. Farben in Offenbach, near Frankfurt, had become the world's largest repository of Jewish books. Workers there sorted some thirty thousand books a day. Their restitution created a host of political, administrative, and diplomatic difficulties, but it also drew on a long Jewish tradition of "redeeming" books, almost as though they were human captives.

In 1945, a group of German émigrés in Jerusalem (including Hugo Bergmann, Martin Buber, Gershom Scholem, and Judah Magnes) established a "Committee for the Salvage of Diaspora Treasures" at the National Library. The committee (called in Hebrew *Otzrot Ha-Golah*, or Treasures of the Diaspora), expressed the view that it was "a requirement of historic justice that the Hebrew University and the Jewish National and University Library in Jerusalem be made the repository of these remains of Jewish culture which have fortunately been saved for the world," and that the Hebrew University should be "regarded as the spokesman of the Jewish people in this regard." Judah Magnes, president of the Hebrew University, added: "We are to be the chief country for the absorption of the living human beings who have escaped from Nazi persecution.... By the same token we should be the trustee of these spiritual goods which destroyed German Jewry left behind."

The next year, the library dispatched Scholem, the eminent Kab-

---

murderers.'" See Evelyn Adunka, *Der Raub der Bücher: Plünderung in der NS-Zeit und Restitution nach 1945* (Czernin Verlag, 2002).

balah scholar and director of the National Library's Hebrew Division
(a position obtained with the help of Kafka's friend Hugo Bergmann),
to Europe to rescue heirless books and manuscripts. Scholem did everything in his power to repatriate these fragments of memory. He was
concerned that if the task were left to Allied authorities, the books
would end up not in Jerusalem, but in New York, where prominent
scholars Hannah Arendt, Salo W. Baron, Horace Kallen, and Max
Weinreich had set up the Commission on European Jewish Cultural
Reconstruction.

In Prague, Scholem pored through a catalogue of some thirty thousand volumes that had been brought there from Theresienstadt. Visiting
the Offenbach depot in July and August 1946, he placed what he had
managed to rescue into unlabeled crates, provided a fake name on the
invoice, and colluded with an American Jewish serviceman to smuggle the crates on a kind of Noah's ark from Offenbach to Paris, and
thence to Jerusalem. Although the Allies lodged a formal diplomatic
complaint, the Offenbach books remain to this day in Israel's National
Library. Their rescue and survival made all the more tangible that which
had been destroyed.

———

Even as Zionism involves ingathering of exiles and their culture, and
claims Jewish cultural products from the Diaspora as its own, the Jewish state also rests on a contrary impulse: a self-purgation of the ata-
visms of the Diaspora, on the notion that only in Israel—and only in
Hebrew—can one reenter history as a Jew. Zionists saw exile as fallen
and in need of redemption, as something to be overcome.

What then explains the National Library's insistence during eight
years of legal battles on "ingathering" a quintessential Diaspora writer
who died a quarter century before Israel came into being? The question deepens in light of the fact—which Marbach's lawyers did not hes-

itate to point out—that Kafka never became part of the Israeli canon, or of the project of national revival. There has never been a Kafka cult in Israel, as there was in Germany, France, the United States, and elsewhere.

During the trial, the Marbach archive subtly portrayed Israel as a latecomer to the Kafka industry. Israel can boast of neither a center of Kafka studies nor a significant school of Kafka interpretation. Nor does it grant a Kafka Prize (as in Prague, bestowed on Elias Canetti, Philip Roth, Ivan Klíma, Elfriede Jelinek, Haruki Murakami, and Amos Oz, among others). To this day, no Israeli city has named a street after Kafka—in contrast to Berlin, Munich, Frankfurt, Hannover, Nuremberg, Dortmund, Köln, Karlsruhe, Bielefeld, Bottrop, Müritz, and Vienna, among many others. (As of this writing, Otto Dov Kulka of the Hebrew University was petitioning the Jerusalem municipality to name the square in front of the new National Library, due to be completed in 2020, Kafka Square.)*

Comparatively few Israeli literary critics have written about Kafka, and when they did, they tended to stress the Jewishness of his work. (Under the dominant influence of Gershom Scholem, he was read there not as a writer of fiction, but as a theologian.) In April 1969, several months after Brod's death, the National Library in Jerusalem held a Kafka exhibition at the suggestion of the German embassy in Tel Aviv. Under the direction of German scholar Klaus Wagenbach, the exhibition had appeared in Berlin and Munich. The National Library's director, Issachar Joel, said at the time: "We thought it proper to enrich the exhibition by adding a number of items which would make the Jewish side of Kafka more pronounced than it was in the original." The first conference in Israel on Kafka, held on the centennial of his birth in 1983, was similarly initiated and funded not by Israelis but by the Aus-

---

* In the far reaches of northeast Tel Aviv, there is a narrow Max Brod Street, lined by unprepossessing modern apartment buildings. Esther Hoffe was a guest of honor at the street's dedication ceremony in 1999.

trian embassy in Tel Aviv. The first Kafka conference in Israel organized by Israelis (the Hebrew University, the Leo Baeck Institute in Jerusalem, and Ben-Gurion University) did not take place until 1991.

The Scottish translators Willa and Edwin Muir introduced Kafka to English-speaking readers in the late 1920s.* In Europe, translations of Kafka's work appeared similarly early.† In Israel, Kafka's novels were translated into Hebrew piecemeal and relatively late, mostly at the behest of Salman Schocken.‡ Brod's biography of Kafka, published in German in 1937, did not see light in Hebrew until 1955 (translated by Edna Kornfeld).

In Germany, Kafka's complete works were published before World War II. Between 1982 and 2004, an international team put together a German critical edition of Kafka's writings (published by S. Fischer Verlag with funding from the German government). The first French edition of Kafka's works (edited by Marthe Robert) came out in

---

* Harold Bloom calls the Muir translations, heavily influenced by Brod, "an almost perfect English equivalent." By 1946, a volume of Kafka criticism appeared in English (edited by Angel Flores and published by New Directions), featuring forty essays by writers including W. H. Auden, Albert Camus, and, needless to say, Max Brod.

† "The Metamorphosis" in 1928 and *The Trial* appeared in French in 1933 (both translated by Alexandre Vialette), for example, and "The Judgment" in 1930 (in the translation of Pierre Klossowski and Pierre Leyris). *The Trial* appeared in Italian in 1933 (in the translation of Alberto Spaini, and again, decades later, in the translation of Primo Levi), in Polish in 1936 (translated by Bruno Schulz), and in Japanese in 1940 (translated by Koichi Motono). The 1940s saw the first translations of Kafka's stories into Romanian (by Paul Celan) and Persian (by Sadeq Hedeyat).

‡ Schocken commissioned Yitzhak Schenhar (Schönberg) to translate *Amerika* (*Der Verschollene*) in 1945. This was followed in 1951 by *The Trial*, translated by Yeshurun Keshet (Jakob Kopelevitz). (Scholem thought the translation so shoddy that he urged Schocken not to publish it.) Not until 1967 did *The Castle* appear in the translation of Shimon Sandbank. Kafka's diaries, translated by Haim Isak, did not appear until 1978–79. As the Hebrew language changed, it became necessary to update Hebrew versions of the earlier translations. This task was given to Abraham Carmel (Kreppel), whose translations of Kafka were published during the 1990s. Finally, in the later 1990s, Ilana Hammerman launched a series of new Kafka translations at the Am Oved publishing house. In 2014, her son Jonathan Nierad retranslated Kafka's *Letters to Milena* (*Briefe an Milena*, published in German in 1952). (They were first translated into Hebrew by Edna Kornfeld in 1976.)

eight volumes between 1963 and 1965. The first Spanish edition of the complete works appeared in 1960 (translated by David Vogelmann and others). A seven-volume edition of Kafka's collected works in Serbo-Croatian came out in 1978. In Israel, by contrast, there is to this day no Hebrew edition of Kafka's complete works. (Nor, as of this writing, does the National Library in Jerusalem hold a copy of the German critical edition of Kafka's works.)

———

In one view, Kafka's cool reception in the Jewish state was determined by a resistance toward German language and literature, which had become associated with Nazi barbarity.

In 1942, Arnold Zweig (another celebrated writer all but ignored in Israel), invited to give a speech in German at Cinema Esther in Tel Aviv, was violently prevented by right-wing activists. Together with Wolfgang Yourgrau, Zweig was editing a short-lived local German-language weekly called *Orient*. Among the contributors to this small corner of the *Exilpresse*, or the German press in exile, was Max Brod. In February 1943, an arson attack destroyed the *Orient*'s printing-house, the Lichtheim Press, in Haifa.

On September 10, 1952, after highly charged negotiations, Israeli foreign minister Moshe Sharett signed an agreement with German Chancellor Konrad Adenauer on reparations between Israel and West Germany. The reparations enabled the newly born state to finance major infrastructure projects, such as the National Water Carrier. Although the Israeli economy was in dire straits and its citizens subject to strict austerity measures and rationing, many Israelis, led by future prime minister Menachem Begin, fiercely opposed accepting German "blood money."

Even those who accepted reparations refused to countenance normalization of cultural ties, and the Israeli government imposed severe restrictions on cultural, literary, and educational ties with Germany.

German-language films were banned by the Israeli "board for film and theater review" (a committee of censors abolished only in 1989, when Germany and Israel concluded a protocol on cultural relations). Israel's Minister of the Interior announced in a speech at the Knesset on July 16, 1958:

> It is the Board's opinion that any performance in the German language is offensive to the feelings of the Israeli public who cannot forget the fact that this is the language of the nation that, only recently, barbarically annihilated a third of the Jewish people.

In 1965, West German Chancellor Ludwig Erhard and Israeli Prime Minister Levi Eshkol established diplomatic relations and arranged for the exchange of ambassadors. Even then, pockets of resistance persisted. Some *kibbutzim* banned the use of the German language. When German author Günter Grass visited Israel in March 1967 and in November 1971, for example, his public appearances were disrupted by protests. According to Avi Primor, Israel's former ambassador to Berlin, "the Israeli protesters were not targeting Grass personally and their anger had nothing at all to do with his literature. It was the German effort to establish cultural relations with Israel to which they objected."

For some Israelis, it was still too soon. "My mother tongue, as stated, was German," the Israeli writer Aharon Appelfeld wrote in 1997, "the language of my mother's murderers. How do people once again speak the language drenched in Jews' blood?"

In 1964, Gershom Scholem of the Hebrew University was invited to contribute a piece on "German-Jewish dialogue" for a Festschrift in honor of the poet and essayist Margarete Susman's ninetieth birthday. His acerbic answer was telling:

> There is no question that Jews tried to enter into a dialogue with Germans, and from all possible perspectives and standpoints: now demanding, now pleading and imploring; now crawling on their

hands and knees, now defiant; now with all possible compelling tones of dignity, now with a godforsaken lack of self-respect. . . . No one responded to this cry. . . . The boundless ecstasy of Jewish enthusiasm never earned a reply in any tone that could count as a productive response to Jews as Jews—that is, a tone that would have addressed what the Jews had to give and not only what they had to give up. To whom, then, did the Jews speak in this famous German-Jewish dialogue? They spoke only to themselves.

Although numerous German-speaking scholars, like Scholem, taught at Hebrew University from its founding in 1925, there was no German literature department there until 1973. The university offered no German-language classes between 1934 and 1954. (The Institute for German History at Tel Aviv University [later called the Minerva Institute], the first of its kind in Israel, was inaugurated in October 1971 with support of the Volkswagen Foundation.) The university's first chair in German language and literature was founded in 1977, also with funding from the Volkswagen Foundation. Only in 2001 did the University of Haifa establish the Bucerius Institute for Research of Contemporary German History and Society, financed by the Hamburg-based Zeit Foundation. Even today, were it not for German funding, Israel's German departments, together with other humanities departments, would wither. The Martin Buber Fellowship in the Humanities, for example, founded in 2010 at the Hebrew University, is financed by the German Federal Ministry of Education and Research.

———

A second view holds that Kafka's afterlife in Israel fell afoul not so much of a resistance to Germanness in particular as much as of an aversion to pre-state *galut* (Diaspora) culture in general. In her novel *Forest Dark* (2017), Nicole Krauss has her narrator put it this way: "Zionism is predicated on an end—of the Diaspora, of the past, of the Jewish problem—whereas literature resides in the sphere of the endless, and those who write have no hope of an end."

The Hebrew writer M. Z. Feierberg had a central character in his classic novella *Whither* cry out for just such an end: "Blow out the candle of the Galut—a new candle must be lit!" In 1938, the first anthology of the new prose of Palestine was published in Jerusalem. The introductory essay, by Joseph Klausner, professor of modern Hebrew literature at the Hebrew University, captures something of the tone of the time: "Before us is a new Jew," Klausner writes, "a man-Jew."

> The typical Jewish cowardice has been terminated, the pallid color above the cheeks is gone, and the delicate palms of the hands are no longer. Excessive spirituality has passed from the world along with fear of dogs, of policemen, of the Gentile. The back has become straight and the bent-over body has grown erect.

Austrian-born historian Judd Teller, reporting from Israel in 1953, wrote:

> To the *sabra* [native-born Israeli], the life of Jews a half century ago or more is alien. He has been told that it was a humiliating existence, and finds horrible confirmation of its "sordidness" in the older Hebrew writing. He refuses to identify his own literature with that created under such shocking conditions.

Finally, perhaps Kafka exemplified to Israelis the political impotence and passivity—the pessimism that flows from a sense of one's powerlessness—that Zionists so vehemently rejected. In his book *Old Worlds, New Mirrors* (2009), Israel Prize–winning scholar Moshe Idel writes: "In the years during which Kafka's feeling of loneliness reached its peak in Prague and elsewhere, a new life was being shaped in the land of Israel." Had Kafka written in Hebrew and lived on a *kibbutz*, Idel suggests, he would not have been among those bleak German-Jewish writers "for whom desolation was nothing but a mood."

In a diary entry of October 1921, Kafka said he inhabited "this borderland between loneliness and community," a no-man's-land marked by self-banishment and a refusal of roots. Many of Kafka's fictions are tragedies of the defeated outcast, of characters condemned to be excluded or to exclude themselves.

Kafka's motifs—humiliation and powerlessness, anomie and alienation, debilitating guilt and self-condemnation—were the very preoccupations Israel's founding generations sought to overcome. A new ethos found expression in the words of Hebrew poet David Shimoni (1891–1956): "Don't mourn, don't cry / at a time like this. / Don't lower your head, / Work! Work!"

"Kafka was on the side of the mice or the moles," Israeli literary critic Dan Miron wrote in 2010, "and shared their instinctual flight to the hole or the burrow." He who recoiled from power, who feared its reach, did not speak to those seeking power. A hypochondriac declared unfit for military service during the First World War "on account of weakness," whose fictional characters (as in *The Castle*) "tremble at every knock at the door," did not resonate with comrades in arms risking their lives to defend the Jewish state.

In Kafka's writing, inadequate, enfeebled sons submit to the judgment of their fathers. His story "The Judgment," for instance, ends not with the killing of the father, à la Oedipus, but with the death of the son in meek submission to the verdict of the father. In the nascent state, self-reliant individualistic sons overthrew their ineffectual fathers, left behind exilic passivity and pessimism, and started afresh. As the Israeli writer Amos Oz puts it, they felt that the past belonged to them, but they did not belong to the past. Those busy making history could not be expected to be well disposed toward someone from the time and place in which other nations made history and the Jews were crushed under its wheels. Whether as a neurotic artist or an artist of the neurotic, the poet of non-arrival found scant audience among those who had at long last arrived and wished to make a clean start.

The vanguard that had freed itself from the ghettos and inherited the Promised Land, in other words, did not look for inspiration to the disaffiliated pariahs desperate to blend into a society that excluded them—the "disinherited minds," to use Erich Heller's term, of the Diaspora. "Again and again," writes the Prague-educated scholar Heller, "Kafka is tempted to side with the world against himself." For this very reason, pioneers straining to cultivate a sense of at-homeness saw in Kafka the quintessential rootless, timorous Jew—haunted and homeless.

Ironically enough, this attitude was prefigured in those talks Martin Buber had given in Prague in 1909–10, the very speeches which had so enthralled the young Max Brod. In his second talk, "The Meaning of Judaism" ("Der Sinn des Judentums"), Buber remarked that "this very intellectuality—out of touch with life, out of balance, inorganic, as it were—fed on the fact that, for millennia, we did not know a healthy, rooted life, determined by the rhythm of nature." In his third talk, "Judaism and Mankind" ("Das Judentum und die Menschheit"), Buber called Jewish exile the "era of barren intellectuality."

The German-Jewish critic Walter Benjamin, nine years younger than Kafka, once remarked that understanding Kafka begins with "the simple recognition that he was a failure." Concerned with the practical demands of agriculture, urban planning, and social welfare, the first generation of Israelis had no ear for either the masochistic strains in Kafka's imagination or his sensibility of failure. Kafka's stories somehow didn't befit the spirit of the Israeli Jew, to whom Joshua and King David seemed closer than Joseph K. or Gregor Samsa or the hunger artist.

Israel wanted to rest on an act of discontinuity. (Brod's novel, *The Kingdom of Love*, aptly captures this sentiment. Garta's/Kafka's brother insists that the Jews, "so sick with self-contempt, self-destruction, and self-corroding irony, must be given a new consciousness.") "Like most kids who came to this country [Israel] as Holocaust survivors," the Israeli writer Aharon Appelfeld said in an interview with Philip Roth, "I wanted to run away from my memories. What didn't we do to change, to be tall, blond, and strong, to be *goyim*, with all the outer trappings." The new country represented normalization; the Diaspora abnormality.

Needless to say, there are different orders of prescience or clairvoyant conviction. Twelve years before Hitler came to power, Ilya Ehrenburg writes in his novel *Julio Jurenito* (1921):

> Solemn Performances of the Destruction of the Tribe of Judah will take place shortly ... The program will include, apart from the traditional pogroms—a public favorite—a series of historical reconstructions in the spirit of the age, e.g. burning of Jews, burying some alive, sprinkling of fields with Jewish blood, as well as modern methods of "evacuation," "removal of suspicious elements," etc., etc.

But Kafka's premonitions were understood to be of a different and more essential kind. George Steiner, for instance, argues that *The Trial* "prefigures the furtive sadism, the hysteria which totalitarianism insinuates into private and sexual life, the faceless boredom of the killers." Taking another example, Steiner asks us to consider "Kafka's use of the word vermin in 'The Metamorphosis' of 1912 in precisely the sense and connotations that would be given to it by the Nazis a generation later.... From the literal nightmare of 'The Metamorphosis' came the knowledge that *Ungeziefer* (vermin) was to be the designation of millions of men."

For survivors like Appelfeld, Kafka's vaunted prescience did not work in his favor. After the Shoah, the horrors of Kafka's imagined penal colony and its torture machine sounded a quaintly obsolete tone in the ears of Israelis. Against the horrors, they pitted fact. Elie Wiesel asserted that "a novel about Auschwitz is not a novel—or else it is not about

Auschwitz." For many first-generation Israelis, the true horrors could be registered in documentary, not fictional mode. It was as though art was inimical to atrocity; as though fiction, with its liberties and licenses, had been annihilated by fact, pushed back by a surge of traumatic memory. No imagination, not even Kafka's, could hope to evoke what had been suffered. Many Israelis affirmed a new version of the Bible's sublime injunction against graven images: the Shoah needed no representation outside of itself, it was incommensurate with the parables and symbols of literary imagination.

True, Kafka's language, with its characteristic oscillations between humor and horror, echoed faintly if unmistakably through some of the higher peaks of Israeli allegorical fiction. Its strains can be heard in the nightmarish stories in S. Y. Agnon's *Book of Deeds* (*Sefer Ha-Maasim*, 1932), and in Aharon Appelfeld's novels of displacement and disorientation. Above all, they can be caught in A. B. Yehoshua's "Flood Tide" (1960), and in the early stories collected in *Death of the Old Man* (1963) and *Facing the Forests* (*Mul Ha-Yearot*, 1968), stories not anchored in a recognizable time or space. "I was shocked by my encounter with Kafka in the 1950s," Yehoshua told me, "by the electricity of metaphysics in each line, especially in the aphorisms. Kafka was my first and most important influence. Of my literary generation here, I was perhaps the closest to him. He helped to liberate me from the social realism of the Israeli writers of the generation of 1948." But neither as a reader of Kafka nor as a teacher of Kafka at the University of Haifa was Yehoshua tempted to reduce his work to a symbol of Jewish concerns. "I could absorb Kafka because I detached his writing from its Jewish and biographical context . . . I grouped him with Camus, Beckett, and Ionescu." At the Sephardic synagogue in Jerusalem's Rehavia neighborhood, Yehoshua came to know Hugo Bergmann. Precisely because Yehoshua knew that Bergmann had known Kafka, Yehoshua hesitated to ask about "Kafka the man." "It was as if I unconsciously wanted to distinguish Kafka's writing from the Jewish man himself," Yehoshua says.

Aharon Appelfeld (1932–2018), one of the most diasporic of Israel's writers, was the exception who proves the rule. Appelfeld began reading Kafka in the 1950s. "When I began to read Kafka," Appelfeld told Michael Gluzman of Tel Aviv University, "I saw at once that his German was the German that I knew down to my fingertips." "As a writer," Appelfeld said to Philip Roth,

> he was close to me from my first contact. He spoke to me in my mother tongue, German, not the German of the Germans but the German of the Habsburg Empire, of Vienna, Prague and Chernovtsy, with its special tone, which, by the way, the Jews worked hard to create.
>
> To my surprise, he spoke to me not only in my mother tongue, but also in another language which I knew intimately, the language of the absurd. I knew what he was talking about. It wasn't a secret language for me and I didn't need any explications. I had come from the camps and the forests, from a world that embodied the absurd, and nothing in that world was foreign to me. . . .
>
> Behind the mask of placelessness and homelessness in his work, stood a Jewish man, like me, from a half-assimilated family, whose Jewish values had lost their content, and whose inner space was barren and haunted.
>
> The marvelous thing is that the barrenness brought him not to self-denial or self-hatred but rather to a kind of tense curiosity about every Jewish phenomenon, especially the Jews of Eastern Europe, the Yiddish language, the Yiddish theatre, Hassidism, Zionism and even the idea of moving to Mandate Palestine. . . .
>
> The Fifties were years of search for me, and Kafka's works illuminated the narrow path which I tried to blaze for myself.

The task of digging a trench between the Diaspora and the Jewish state fell to the new country's eminent writers, many of whom spurned Kafka's influence and denied any affinities. S. Y. Agnon, for example—the greatest Hebrew novelist, and Israel's only Nobel laureate in literature—was four years younger than Kafka. Agnon consistently refused to recognize Kafka's paternity, despite obvious influences. (Gershom Scholem had suggested as early as 1928 that Agnon's work represented a revision of *The Trial*. Gershon Shaked, a colleague of Scholem's at Hebrew University and a founding father of Hebrew literary criticism, calls Kafka Agnon's "Diaspora counterpart.") Was this because Agnon saw Kafka as a diasporic writer? He didn't say. "My wife, long may she live, has frequently offered to read me a tale by Kafka, but she did not succeed. After she had read but one or two pages, I turned my ear from it. Kafka is not from the root of my soul," Agnon said in 1962, "and he who is not from the root of my soul I do not absorb, even if he is as great as the ten wise men who created the book of Psalms. . . . I know that Kafka is a great poet, but my soul is alien to him."

———

To return to our question: Why, despite all this, did Israel's National Library press so insistently for Kafka's manuscripts?

It cannot be explained as a by-product of a much-hyped generational shift in Israel. It is true that after decades of wariness, as the last of Israel's Holocaust survivors began passing away, time-tempered post-Shoah taboos have loosened their grip and a newfound fascination with German culture has taken hold. It is true that drawn by the city's affordable cosmopolitanism, Israeli expats in Berlin today run Hebrew-language kindergartens, a Hebrew literary magazine, Israeli restaurants in Prenzlauer Berg, and a Tel Aviv-style beach on the Spree. And it is true that German courses at the Goethe Institut in Tel Aviv continue to be oversubscribed. But none of this explains the National Library's belated insistence on owning Kafka.

In the end, perhaps no better answer can be found than Kafka's remark in a letter to Milena Jesenská:

> The insecure position of Jews, insecure within themselves, insecure among people, should explain better than anything else why they might think they own only what they hold in their hands or between their teeth, that furthermore only tangible possessions give them a right to live and that once they have lost something they will never again regain it, rather it will drift blissfully away from them forever.

Judith Butler of Berkeley suggests that another insecurity may be at play: Israel, a small and insecure country, wishes to recruit Kafka for its increasingly urgent fight against cultural delegitimation. "An asset," she says, "is something that enhances Israel's world reputation, which many would allow is in need of repair: the wager is that the world reputation of Kafka will become the world reputation of Israel."

In that case, the question is obvious: How can a literature of the helplessness of modern man, of his subjection to a world he neither governs nor understands, become an object of cultural prestige and national craving?

Shimon Sandbank, one of Kafka's leading translators into Hebrew, told me that he ascribes the National Library's lawsuit to "patriotism that has nothing to do with literature as such." And yet, Israel is hardly the only country anxious to secure the luster and prestige of writers.

Do Israelis kindle to Kafka's work largely because it is the work of a Jew? Do they thereby impoverish what is theirs by slighting its universal significance? Has the National Library blinkered itself to the possibility that greatest victory would be to let the Germans have Kafka, a permanent reminder that the greatest German modernist was a Jew? Our possessions do not always serve us in the way we imagine. "Everything I possess is directed against me," Kafka once confessed to Brod, "and what is directed against me is no longer in my possession."

Like many a Kafka story, this one remains unfinished and unfin-
ishable (Kafka's truth could be realized only in works given over to the
fragmentary). But the trial makes clear that Jerusalem once more saw
itself as the rightful heir and home to the cultural products of Diaspora;
in the eyes of its courts and its National Library, at least, Israel saw itself
as the ending of a story that began elsewhere.

General sorting room of the Offenbach Archival Depot,
Germany, 1946. (Yad Vashem)

8

Kafka's Last Wish, Brod's First Betrayal

Kafka family apartment, Oppelt House, Old Town Square 12, Prague
June 1924

Anyone who cannot cope with life while he is alive needs one
hand to ward off a little his despair over his fate . . . but with his
other hand he can jot down what he sees among the ruins, for
he sees different and more things than the others; after all, he is
dead in his own lifetime and the real survivor.

—Kafka's diary, October 19, 1921

If the fathers of the world [the patriarchs] had wished that their
resting place should be in the Above, they would have been able
to have it there: but it is when they died and the rock closed on
their tombs here below that they deserved to be called saints.

—Pinchas ben Hama, fourth century CE

On his deathbed, emaciated and robbed of strength, almost
unable to speak or swallow, his breaths short and percussive as
he coughed his life away, Kafka communicated with Dora Diamant and

his doctors by scribbling notes on slips of paper. "Usually these notes were mere hints," Max Brod said. "His friends guessed the rest."

As his energies ebbed, Kafka reviewed the proofs of his last and starkest short story collection, *A Hunger Artist*. Brod had urged the publisher to rush the volume into print. In the title story, Kafka's gaunt protagonist fasts himself to death in a circus cage, unnoticed and unappreciated.

> "Forgive me everything," whispered the hunger artist. Only the supervisor, who was pressing his ear up against the cage, understood him. "Certainly," said the supervisor, tapping his forehead with his finger in order to indicate to the staff the state the hunger artist was in, "we forgive you." "I always wanted you to admire my fasting," said the hunger artist. "But we do admire it," said the supervisor obligingly. "But you shouldn't admire it," said the hunger artist. "Well then, we don't admire it," said the supervisor, "but why shouldn't we admire it?" "Because I had to fast. I can't do anything else," said the hunger artist.

Kafka's lover and Czech translator Milena Jesenská had once written to Brod that Kafka's "asceticism is altogether unheroic—and by that very fact all the greater and more sublime."

Kafka had years earlier confided to Brod that he saw his lung hemorrhages as both punishment and liberation. "My attitude to tuberculosis today," he wrote Brod in 1917, "is like that of a child clinging to its mother's skirts." Describing Kafka's illness, Brod noted in his diary: "Kafka sees it as psychogenic, his salvation from marriage." "You are happy in your unhappiness," Brod said when Kafka disclosed the diagnosis. It was Brod who had consulted doctors behind Kafka's back, who had insisted that Kafka see laryngological specialists, and who had accompanied him to their waiting rooms. Speaking of himself in the third person, Kafka had admitted his fear of death to Max Brod. "He has a terrible fear of dying because he has not yet lived."

Kafka, convinced to the end of the insufficiency of his writing, was not granted the time to say all that he had in him. He died just short of his forty-first birthday in a private twelve-room sanatorium outside Vienna. He was buried a week later, at 4 o'clock in the afternoon of Wednesday, June 11, 1924, in a modest ceremony at Prague's New Jewish Cemetery.

Even in life, there seemed to have been something posthumous about him. In his journals, he dwelled often on death and on "casting off the self" (*Selbstabschüttelung*). The Prague-born author Franz Werfel wrote in November 1915: "Dear Kafka, you are so pure, new, independent, and perfect that one ought to treat you as if you were already dead and immortal." When she heard of his death, Milena Jesenská remarked that Kafka was "a man who beheld the world with such excessive lucidity that he could no longer bear it."

Kafka's writing had afforded him no fame, no literary prizes; public recognition had eluded him, as had any expectation that posterity would be more appreciative than his contemporaries. Unheralded, he hadn't completed a single novel. The little that had been published was passed over without wide acclaim. His second collection of stories, for instance, *A Country Doctor* (published by Kurt Wolff in 1920), was mentioned by only a single reviewer. To the chagrin of both his publishers and his impresario Brod, Kafka had not bothered to change this state of affairs. In November 1921, Kurt Wolff wrote to Kafka:

> None of the authors with whom we are connected comes to us with wishes or questions so seldom as you do, and with none of them do we have the feeling that the outward fate of their published books is a matter of such indifference as it is with you. . . . If over the course of time you could give us, in addition to collections of short prose pieces, a longer, extended story or a novel—since I know from you and from Max Brod how many manuscripts of this kind are nearly finished or even completed—we would be especially grateful.

Kafka never replied to the letter.

Brod described Kafka's untimely death as a "catastrophe." His twenty-two-year friendship with the man he called a *"Diesseitswunder"*—an earthly miracle—had been "the mainstay of my whole existence." At the graveside, he eulogized Kafka as a prophet in whom "the splendor of the *Shekhina* [divine presence] shone." When he returned from the funeral to the town center, Brod reports, the medieval clock on the southern wall of Old Town Hall—flanked by the figures of Vanity, Greed, Lust, and Death—had stopped at 4 p.m.: "its hands were still pointing to that hour."

After the funeral, Kafka's parents Hermann and Julie asked Brod over to their apartment on the top floor of the Oppelt House to go through their son's desk. According to biographer Reiner Stach, Hermann Kafka "signed a contract giving Brod the right to publish Franz's works posthumously." Beneath the clutter of pencils with broken points, collar buttons, and a paperweight from Karlsbad, Brod discovered a voluminous archive of Kafka's unpublished notebooks, unfinished drafts, and diaries.

As he spilled these papers out of the drawers, Brod also found two undated notes—one in pen and the other penciled—instructing him to burn Kafka's remaining papers. The first note reads:

Dearest Max,

My last request: Everything I leave behind me . . . in the way of notebooks, manuscripts, letters, my own and other people's, sketches and so on, is to be burned unread and to the last page, as well as all writings of mine or notes which either you may have or other people, from whom you are to beg them in my name. Letters which are not handed over to you should at least be faithfully burned by those who have them.

Yours, Franz Kafka

The second note, in pencil, which Brod believed preceded the first, reads:

Dear Max,

Perhaps this time I shan't recover after all. Pneumonia after a whole month's pulmonary fever is all too likely; and not even writing this down can avert it, although there is a certain power in that. For this eventuality therefore, here is my last will concerning everything I have written: Of all my writings the only books that can stand are these: "The Judgment," "The Stoker," "Metamorphosis," "Penal Colony," "Country Doctor," and the short story "Hunger Artist" . . . But everything else of mine which is extant . . . all these things without exception are to be burned, and I beg you to do this as soon as possible.

Franz

Brod could not summon much surprise at this instruction. He knew all too well that Kafka did not think highly of what he called his "scribbling." Kafka's diaries are steeped both in the preoccupation with what he calls *Schriftstellersein*, being-a-writer, and in self-slandering laments at how "dead" and "inert" he found what he terms his "feeble literary work." Take, for example, his diary entry of March 13, 1915:

Lack of appetite, fear of getting back late in the evening; but above all the thought that I wrote nothing yesterday, that I keep getting farther and farther from it, and am in danger of losing everything I have laboriously achieved these past six months. Provided proof of this by writing one and a half wretched pages of a new story that I have already decided to discard. . . .

Kafka regarded the ending of "The Metamorphosis," to take another example, as "imperfect almost to its very marrow." On the one hand, Kafka was aware of "the enormous world I have inside my head." On the other, he recognized that "the inner world can only be lived, not described." ("I am constantly trying to communicate something incommunicable," he wrote.) "Almost every word I wrote jars against the next," he noted in 1910. "My doubts stand in a circle around every word."

In 1917, when Brod had asked him to supply something for a reading in Frankfurt, Kafka replied: "The pieces I could send really mean nothing at all to me; I respect only the moments at which I wrote them." Later, Max's wife Elsa had also asked Kafka for something she could read in public. "Why resuscitate old labors?" he answers. "Only because I haven't burnt them yet? . . . What's the point of preserving such miscarried works, even if the miscarriage was artistic?"

In the last months of his life, Dora Diamant said, "he wanted to burn everything that he had written in order to free his soul from these 'ghosts.' I respected his wish, and when he lay ill, I burnt things of his before his eyes."

Kafka here tempts us to speculation: can his last instruction to Brod be understood as a characteristic gesture of a literary artist whose life was a judgment against itself? As a self-condemnation, with Kafka acting as both judge and the accused?

In the final scene of *The Trial*, Joseph K. is tempted "to seize the knife himself . . . and plunge it into his own body." In the end, he cannot bring himself to carry out his own execution. "He could not completely rise to the occasion, he could not relieve the officials of all their tasks; the responsibility for this last failure of his lay with him who had not left him the remnant of strength necessary for the deed." Like Joseph K., Kafka lacked the strength to carry out his own last sentence: the destruction of his writings both personal (letters and diaries) and literary (unfinished stories). It was as though even in self-renunciation Kafka was beset by indecision. He left the execution to Brod, the very man who since the beginnings of their friendship felt that Kafka's self-condemnation was several shades too harsh.*

---

* In Steven Soderbergh's 1991 movie *Kafka*, the stonemason and sculptor Bizzlebek, a stand-in for Brod, directs Kafka into a tunnel that begins beneath a gravestone. Half in

———

Brod was neither the first nor the last to confront such a dilemma. Tradition has it that the Roman poet Virgil was so dissatisfied with the *Aeneid* that on his deathbed in the year 19 BCE he ordered the manuscript to be burned. Needless to say, the executors of his estate did not comply. In October 1865, Samuel Clemens wrote to his brother Orion and his sister-in-law Mollie about his manuscripts: "You had better shove this in the stove—for if we strike a bargain I don't want any absurd 'literary remains' & 'unpublished letters of Mark Twain' published after I am planted." The English poet Philip Larkin instructed his secretary three days before he died in 1985 to burn all his diaries. They were incinerated in the boiler room at Hull University. When Vladimir Nabokov died in 1977, he left instructions for his heirs to burn the 138 handwritten index cards that made up the rough draft of his final, unfinished novel, *The Original of Laura*. Nabokov's wife, Vera, could not bear to destroy her husband's last work. Thirty years later, Dmitri Nabokov, their sole surviving heir, allowed its publication. Finally, before he died in 2016, the playwright Edward Albee, best known for "Who's Afraid of Virginia Woolf?," instructed in his will: "If at the time of my death I shall leave any incomplete manuscripts I hereby direct my executors to destroy such manuscripts."

Unlike those executors, Brod grappled with the difficulties inherent in discerning Kafka's "true will." Kafka had admitted in a letter to Brod: "concealment has been my life's vocation." (As Kafka wrote to his favorite sister Ottla in 1914: "I write not as I speak, I speak not as I think, I think not as I ought to think, and so it goes on into the deepest dark-

———

the grave, Kafka turns to Bizzlebek and asks for a favor. "If I don't see you later, go to my house and find my notebooks and destroy them. All my manuscripts, just burn them. Please." "What an extraordinary request," Bizzlebek replies. "It's my last and final one." "Then its authority is in doubt," Bizzlebek says. "A true friend would do it," Kafka insists. "Not necessarily," Bizzlebek says. "A wife would."

ness.") In justifying his disobedience, Brod claimed that Kafka put disproportionate pressure on his writing (which Kafka called "a form of prayer") and subjected his art to impossibly high criteria—"the highest religious standards," and "immoderate self-criticism," as Brod put it. He regarded Kafka's notes—notes, not legally binding testaments—as the products of "temporary depression."

> My decision to publish his posthumous work is made easier by the memory of all the embittered struggles preceding every single publication of Kafka's which I extorted from him by force and often by begging. And yet afterwards he was reconciled with these publications and relatively satisfied with them.

Brod understood that Kafka's reluctance to publish his work derived not from an intention to keep it secret but from a conviction of its incompleteness, of the fathomless gap between what had been realized and what had gone unrealized. In fact, the very first of Kafka's writings Brod published after Kafka's death were the two notes forbidding the publication of Kafka's works. In this, Brod wished to prove his true fidelity to Kafka: he published his work and at the same time Kafka's instructions not to do so.

In 1921, when Kafka had first mentioned his request to burn everything, Brod says he answered: "If you seriously think me capable of such a thing, let me tell you here and now that I shall not carry out your wishes." After Kafka's death, Brod claimed: "Franz should have appointed another executor if he had been absolutely and finally determined that his instructions should stand."

Why then did Kafka entrust Brod, of all people, with carrying out his last wish? Perhaps he wanted his unfinished work to see the light of day but without his imprimatur. Or perhaps for a simpler reason: Brod alone had access to the papers Kafka wished consigned to the flames. Other than the manuscripts he already had, Brod was the only one in a position to obtain them from Kafka's family and correspondents.

In the end, Brod preferred to act as a self-appointed literary executor rather than as literary executioner. He justified his betrayal of Kafka's stated instructions by appealing to a higher two-fold loyalty: to literary posterity, and to Kafka's true wishes.

———

Immediately after Kafka's death, Brod set out to write what he called "a living work of art" to resurrect his beloved friend. "Above all," he said of his next novel, "I wanted to bring him to life for myself in this new way. So long as I lived in this book, in working at it, he was not dead, he still lived with me."

In the novel, a roman à clef called *The Kingdom of Love* (*Zauberreich der Liebe*, 1928, English edition 1930),* Kafka appears in the thin disguise of Richard Garta, a tall, delicate man who wished to live "in complete austerity." Garta radiated both a "delicate sadness" and "a powerful, imperceptible, but irresistible force," Brod writes. "He did not speak to disciples, to the people, like Buddha, Jesus, or Moses. He remained shut within himself. But that was perhaps because he saw further into the great secret than they had done."

Garta, this "saint of our time," has died of consumption before the plot begins. Yet he is constantly present in the memories of his friend, thirty-four-year-old narrator Christof Nowy, a man who feels that to have a woman in his arms is "a kind of deliverance." As students, Garta and Nowy had developed "the most charming fellowship, untainted by the slightest touch of vanity or pretense." "They had no secrets from each other." Some in their circle murmured that Garta was the genius, and Nowy the mediocrity. "It was a verdict with

* The Czech-born writer Milan Kundera dismissed "this simpleminded novel, this garbage, this cartoon-novel concoction, which, aesthetically, stands at exactly the opposite pole from Kafka's art."

which Christof would have heartily agreed; but he did not understand why he should be compared or contrasted with the friend he so loved and admired." Garta, given to flashes of irony, offered Nowy a source of steadiness and consolation. Garta made him feel that "he could look calmly on the tumult of the world." "His whole behavior," Nowy says of Garta, "down to the smallest detail, even if you only watch the way he brushes his hair, is based on the belief that there is . . . a mode of life which is right, thorough, clean, and unshakably natural."

Nowy cannot reconcile himself to Garta's death. "His utter integrity," Nowy says, "marvelous as it was, led to nothing. I warned him, I struggled to save him. There is no doubt—he died of his devotion to perfection." Nowy "had taken charge of all Garta's literary remains, as, indeed, Garta had requested him to do, with the proviso that they should all be destroyed."

Nowy, like his author, defies the request, "in view of the inestimable value he attached to Garta's writings." Nowy says that Garta "made the ultimate demands on himself; as he had failed, his writings, that were but steps that exalted height, had no value for him. He, indeed, but he alone, had the right to despise them in this way." Nowy decides to keep Garta's papers in his safe, having concluded "that in our time the Saint could only show himself thus incompletely."

Unable to save his friend in life, Nowy endeavors to save Garta in death. To orchestrate the "fight for the spiritual legacy of his dead friend," he boards a steamer to Palestine to find Garta's younger brother, a pioneer living in a Communist settlement in the Jezreel Valley near Mount Gilboa, "a noble example of that integrity which Garta had so worshiped." ("Kafka's fundamental attitude," Brod writes elsewhere, "was that of the *chalutz*, the pioneer." In 1918, Kafka had sketched his vision of frugal life in a socialist kibbutz in a piece called "Workers without Possessions," envisioning a diet of bread, water, and dates. "Any existing possessions should be given to the state for the construction of hospitals [and] homes," Kafka wrote.[*])

In the novel's closing scene, the brother reveals that Garta had not only confessed the desire to settle in Palestine (a Zionist who never physically made it to Zion), but had left at his death a mass of manuscripts in Hebrew—"as much as in German."[†] Nowy resolves to return to Europe to edit his friend's posthumous papers.

Beset by a guilty conscience, Brod used his fiction to seek Kafka's blessing from beyond the grave.

---

[*] The French anarchist writer André Breton spoke about this text at a lecture in Paris in 1948.

[†] According to Dora Diamant, Kafka's last lover, "German is too modern a language, too much of the present day. Kafka's whole world longs for an older language. It was an ancient consciousness in him, ancient things and ancient fear." Quoted in J. P. Hodin, "Memories of Franz Kafka," *Horizon*, January 1948.

9

Kafka's Creator

Reich Ministry of Public Enlightenment and Propaganda
Wilhelmplatz, Berlin
July 22, 1935

The rise of Nazism put an end to the rich German-Jewish literary symbiosis that had so decisively shaped both cultures, and to the long and lively Jewish love affair with the German language. On July 22, 1935, the Reichsschrifttumskammer (Reich Chamber of Literature), newly headed by SS-Gruppenführer Hanns Johst (1890–1978), issued a report to the Gestapo: it had come to their attention that a Jewish publishing house in Berlin, Schocken Verlag, was distributing Kafka's collected works edited by Brod, although both authors appeared on a Nazi blacklist issued that April. The report of the Chamber—a body which literary critic George Steiner dubbed "the official whorehouse of 'Aryan culture'"—recommended confiscation of all books by the two Jewish authors.

For the previous eleven years, instead of obeying Kafka's last message, Brod had dedicated himself with singular passion to saving the manuscripts and rescuing Kafka from oblivion—transforming himself in the process into the greatest posthumous editor of the twentieth century. In effect, Brod claimed a monopoly; by means of literary beatification, he canonized Kafka (giving him a stature far beyond what Kafka enjoyed in his own lifetime), and made him into a saintly icon—an object of what Germans call *Dichterverehrung*, or poet-worship. "The category of sacredness (and not really that of literature)," Brod wrote in his 1937 biography of his friend, "is the only right category under which Kafka's life and work can be viewed."

Later readers of Kafka took issue with Brod on just this point. In his lecture on "The Metamorphosis," Vladimir Nabokov writes that "such poets as Rilke or such novelists as Thomas Mann are dwarfs and plaster saints in comparison to [Kafka]." But Nabokov rejects Brod's sanctification of the writer: "I want to dismiss completely Max Brod's opinion that the category of sainthood, not that of literature, is the only one that can be applied to the understanding of Kafka's writings. Kafka was first of all an artist, and although it may be maintained that every artist is a manner of saint (I feel that very clearly myself), I do not think that any religious implications can be read into Kafka's genius." In the footsteps of Nabokov, many have since accused Brod's posthumous editing either of serving as an accessory to a shallow grasp of Kafka's works or of suffering from misapprehension, as though something in Kafka's art remained alien to the man most selflessly devoted to it. (Novelist J. M. Coetzee, for instance, has said that Kafka was an artist "whom Brod revered yet utterly failed to understand").

To the degree that Kafka's reputation rests on texts he neither completed nor approved, the Kafka we know is a creation of Brod—in fact, his highest and most enduring creation. By betraying Kafka's last wish, Brod twice rescued his legacy—first from physical destruction, and then from obscurity. Kafka's posthumous fame—"the bitter reward of those who were ahead of their time," in Hannah Arendt's phrase—was Brod's doing. Without Judas, it has been said, there would be no crucifixion. And without Brod, there would be no Kafka. We cannot help but hear Kafka's voice through Brod; whether knowingly or not, we read Kafka Brodly.

Does creation involve possession? Some charge Brod with making Kafka in the image of his own Jewishness. Kafka biographer Reiner

Stach, for instance, speaks of "the gap between Kafka's ethics of truthfulness and Brod's identity politics," and of the sense that "Brod kept deceiving himself about the extent to which he 'knew' Kafka." Singling out Brod's efforts "to simplify Kafka's relationship to the Zionist movement," Ritchie Robertson (professor of German literature in Oxford and codirector of the Oxford Kafka Research Centre) writes that "in interpreting Kafka's works he [Brod] is too much inclined to ride his own hobby-horses." The New York intellectual Irving Howe remarked that Brod's biography of Kafka encompassed "too much Brod and not enough Kafka." According to Klaus Wagenbach, Germany's foremost authority on Kafka, "Brod increasingly made Kafka's writings serve his own aim of revitalizing modern Judaism in association with Zionism." William Phillips, coeditor of *Partisan Review*, likewise mocked Brod's slipshod attempt "to squeeze a Jewish over-soul out of Kafka."

At the time of Kafka's death in 1924, Brod was at the zenith of his literary powers. In 1925, Brod's novel about a sixteenth-century false messiah, *Reubeni: Prince of the Jews* (1925, published by Knopf in the United States in 1928, and in the Hebrew translation of Yitzhak Lamdan the same year), won the Czech State Prize, an honor he treasured.* His influential biography of Heinrich Heine was widely acclaimed. Stefan Zweig praised the pointillist portraits of his early fictions, and hailed him as "one of the most exquisite miniature painters in the German language."

Yet were it not for his role as the custodian, editor, and publisher

---

* Friedrich Torberg called the novel "one of the outstanding Jewish novels of our time." The real-life David Ha-Reubeni, claiming to represent an Arabian principality whose citizens descended from the biblical tribes of Reuben and Gad, met with Pope Clement VII in the 1520s. A decade later he was charged with heresy by the Inquisition and burned at the stake in Spain. Although Reubeni's origins are unknown, Brod imagines him as growing up in a Prague Jewish community facing expulsion. Brod has his "prince of the Jews" muse about power: "Perhaps those nations are so powerful and beloved of God . . . because they serve God—with their evil instincts also." When the fictional Reubeni is condemned to the flames, Brod's narrator echoes Kafka's *The Trial*: "The accused were told neither the nature of their indictment nor the names of their denouncers."

of Kafka's writings—the curator of Kafka's posthumous fame—Brod would have long since faded from public memory. With the exception of his 1937 biography of Kafka (published in English a decade later), Brod's own books have on the whole fallen into oblivion. To date, no biography of him has appeared in English, nor has his autobiography appeared in English. In Israel, the small number of his books translated into Hebrew have long since gone out of print. "Even among serious readers," the German-born writer Heinz Kuehn said, "only his role as Kafka's alter ego had kept his name alive."

Kafka's death only quickened Brod's determination to promote and publish his friend's writing and bring it into the public eye. Georg (Jiří) Langer, writing in 1941, remembered the savior's devotion some fifteen years earlier:

> It goes without saying that he [Brod] was a trustworthy caretaker of these writings, he prized them and guarded them like the apple of his eye. And behold, one evening a well-known writer visited him, and Brod wanted to show him Kafka's manuscripts, which he didn't allow just anyone to see, with the exception of this man, because even looking at them could harm them. He was already in the process of removing the manuscripts from their folders to show to the guest. But just at that moment, the lights in the entire house and all the neighboring houses went out due to some mishap with the electricity, and the honorable guest returned home disappointed; he hadn't seen a single letter.

Readers wouldn't have to wait long. In the three years after Kafka's death, as Brod became a leading culture critic for the *Prager Abendblatt* and the *Prager Tagblatt*, he organized the papers he had salvaged from Kafka's desk, cobbled together his late friend's three unfinished novels, and published them in rapid succession. "Today," Brod writes in his 1960 memoir, "every word of Kafka's is snatched up. But how hard it was for me in the beginning (i.e. after Kafka's death) to find a publisher for all his works." In 1925, he coaxed an avant-garde Berlin publisher (Die Schmiede, founded four years earlier) to publish *The Trial*, which Brod prepared for publication from Kafka's unfinished manuscript. In 1926, he persuaded the Munich publisher Kurt Wolff to publish *The Castle*, also left unfinished by Kafka. Wolff later complained that he had sold very few of the 1,500 copies of *The Castle* he printed. But the following year, Brod had Wolff bring out Kafka's first novel. Kafka's working title for the novel he began writing in 1912 was *The Man Who Disappeared* (*Der Verschollene*); Brod, insisting that Kafka often referred to the book in conversation as his "American novel," renamed it *Amerika*. Brod expressed the hope that "precisely this novel . . . will reveal a new way of understanding Kafka."

Confident that he was equal to the task, Brod then edited and brought out two volumes of Kafka's posthumous stories: *Beim Bau der chinesischen Mauer* (translated by Willa and Edwin Muir as *The Great Wall of China*, 1933), and *Beschreibung eines Kampfes* (translated by Tania and James Stern as *Description of a Struggle*, 1958). Brod followed these with his selections from Kafka's diaries, letters, and aphorisms.

Can we say with any certainty where Kafka ends and Brod begins? Brod invented titles for what Kafka had left untitled, and sequences for what Kafka had left loose and unnumbered. (It was his idea, for example, to end *The Trial* with Joseph K.'s execution.) Never beset by the notion that Kafka's texts were somehow unalterable or unrevisable, Brod aggregated and expurgated, in ways both subtle and significant. He rearranged sentences, tidied up Kafka's loose punctuation and orthographic peculiarities, edited out what he called "linguistic errors" (*Sprachunrichtigkeiten*) and Prague colloquialisms, tinkered with paragraph breaks and notes to typesetters, and entered his own scribblings in red on the manuscripts. He bowdlerized sexual, prurient, or unflattering references from Kafka's diaries and censored out references to people still living. (In his biography, *Franz Kafka: The Poet of Shame and Guilt*, Prague-born historian Saul Friedländer examines the discrepancies between Brod's version of the diaries and the newer critical edition.) Sometimes, as with Kafka's story "Description of a Struggle," Brod merged two manuscript versions into one. In one of his octavo notebooks, Kafka crossed out an entire draft of a short story. Brod gave it the title "Prometheus" and published it. "Savior though he was," Cynthia Ozick comments, "Brod also manipulated whatever came into his hands."*

In his book *Testaments Betrayed* (1993), the Czech-born writer Milan Kundera insists that Brod betrayed Kafka not only by propagating the myth of the suffering modern-day saint, but also by indiscriminately publishing Kafka's unfinished works and diaries, his undelivered letter to his father, and his love letters. With this indiscretion, Kundera writes, Brod created "the model for disobedience to dead friends; a judicial precedent for those who would circumvent an author's last wish."

But had Brod obeyed the author's last wish and consigned his manuscripts to the flames, most of Kafka's writing would be lost. We—and Eva Hoffe—owe our Kafka to Brod's disobedience.

———

Max Brod had been disappointed that the publications of Kafka's three unfinished novels had not gained more notice. Beginning in

---

* In a 2010 letter to the *New York Times*, Zvi Henri Szubin, professor emeritus at the City College of New York, reported an instance of such manipulation:

> In 1957, when I accompanied my mother on her visit to Brod's basement office at the Habima Theater in Tel Aviv, Brod said that in the process of deciding which of Kafka's papers to save, he, "like a surgeon on the battlefield, did not have the luxury of being sentimental." My mother, who up to that day viewed Brod, her beloved teacher and mentor, as "the most ethical person in the world" was astounded and accused him of deliberately destroying Kafka's continuing correspondence with her best friend, Regina. Accordingly, I am convinced that Brod calculatedly safeguarded Kafka's reputation and legacy in the image of his own creation.

1931, he tried in vain to interest the Berlin publisher Gustav Kiepenheuer (1880–1949) in the rest of Kafka's literary estate. The Nazi rise to power in 1933 scuttled the project. Meanwhile, an imperious autodidact and department store magnate named Salman Schocken (1877–1959) launched a publishing house on Berlin's Jerusalemstrasse. (Brod had known Schocken at least since 1915, when Schocken cofounded the Zionist journal *Der Jude* with Martin Buber.) In 1934, Brod offered Schocken, whom he called "the patron of the Jewish book," world rights to Kafka's works.

The offer met at first with rejection by Lambert Schneider, Schocken Verlag's editor in chief. According to Arthur Samuelson, who would later serve as editorial director of Schocken Books in New York, Schneider only reluctantly changed his mind. "He was urged by one of his editors, Moritz Spitzer, to see in Kafka a quintessentially 'Jewish' voice that could give meaning to the new reality that had befallen German Jewry and would demonstrate the central role of Jews in German culture."

Spitzer, thirty-four, had years earlier met Kafka at a meeting in Prague's Lucerna Palace of the Zionist-pacifist movement Ha-Poel Ha-Tzair. The founder of that movement, A. D. Gordon (1856–1922), visited Prague in the spring of 1920. Spitzer introduced the distinguished Zionist leader to Kafka. Spitzer recalled that Kafka "almost physically contracted" when he met new people. Ever since reading Kafka's first two short stories, which had appeared in *Der Jude*, Spitzer had been eager to get his hands on anything Kafka published.

On February 22, 1934, Kafka's mother (widowed in 1931) signed a contract with Schocken Verlag, negotiated by Brod, in which she gave the publisher world rights to Kafka's writings. Thanks to Schocken, Kafka gained some readership in Germany before the Second World War. In an advertisement for a Kafka anthology (*Vor dem Gesetz*) published in the Schocken Bücherei series in 1934, Hermann Hesse called Kafka a "younger brother of Nietzsche."

But as the Nazi noose tightened, "Aryan" publishers in Germany were forbidden from publishing Jewish authors, and Jewish publishers forbidden from publishing non-Jewish authors.* With the exception of *Tycho Brahe*, all of Brod's books were blacklisted in Germany in 1933. Kafka's works, by contrast, were not well enough known to be banned by the regime; but they were deemed "Jewish" enough to be off limits to "Aryan" publishers.

This changed with the Gestapo's instructions in July 1935. The change was likely prompted by a rave review published that month of the first of four volumes of the Schocken edition of Kafka's works. Writing in the exile journal *Die Sammlung*, twenty-eight-year-old writer Klaus Mann (son of Thomas Mann) wrote: "The collected works of Kafka, offered by the Schocken Verlag in Berlin, are the most noble and most significant publications that have come out of Germany . . . the epoch's purest and most singular works of literature." Mann added that the publisher was among the last bastion of culture in Germany.

In the fall of 1936, to get around German restrictions, Spitzer, with the help of a trusted lawyer named Josef Schlesinger, transferred the rights to Kafka's works to a publisher in Prague, Heinrich Mercy Verlag (using Julius Kittl Nachfolger, Keller & Co. as its distributor). Under the agreement, Schocken would cover any losses, and the rights would revert to Schocken upon request. Mercy Verlag brought out volumes 5 and 6 of Kafka's complete works. This arrangement lasted until the German occupation of Prague and the forced liquidation of Schocken Verlag in 1939. (Spitzer fled to Jerusalem in March of that year.)

In 1935, Salman Schocken managed to smuggle his library from Berlin to Jerusalem. The collection included several hundred Hebrew manuscripts; more than 4,500 pages of the German poet Heinrich Heine's manuscripts and letters; almost all manuscripts of Novalis' philosophi-

---

* In 1935, Schocken Verlag could still publish (as part of its Bücherei series) a book by the nineteenth-century Austrian writer Adalbert Stifter (in his biography of Kafka, Brod counts Stifter as among Kafka's favorite writers). Because Stifter was not a Jew, however, the book had soon thereafter to be withdrawn.

cal writings; autographs and manuscripts by Schopenhauer, Beethoven, and Schubert; and more than sixty thousand rare books (first editions of works by Goethe, Hölderlin, Lessing, Kleist, Schiller, Hofmannsthal, Rilke, and others). Five years later, in 1940, Schocken wanted to bring the printings of Kafka's works, and other stock, from the Czech warehouse to Palestine. Since Britain classified Czechoslovakia as an enemy state, British Mandatory Palestine refused to permit the shipment. Schocken didn't know that the entire stock, including the Kafka print run, was likely destroyed when the Gestapo seized the Julius Kittl company in the summer of 1939. Schocken had lost the stock but retained the rights.*

In a 1937 letter to Salman Schocken, sending greetings for the publisher's sixtieth birthday, Gershom Scholem hailed the decision to publish Kafka's works. Kafka had inscribed for us, Scholem wrote, "a secular statement of the Kabbalistic world-feeling in a modern spirit."

The transmission of that statement to Kafka's readers, however, had its flaws. In June 1937, Moritz Spitzer complained to Scholem that Brod's editing of Kafka was "sloppy, of course," and that "just between us, a real Kafka edition will have to wait until the day Brod is no longer sitting on the manuscripts."

---

* Just after the end of the Second World War, and with his usual confident élan, Salman Schocken established Schocken Books in New York. Joining bibliophilia to business acumen, he intended to create a library of uniformly produced essential books on Judaism. After a rocky start—Hannah Arendt called him "Bismarck personified," and Gershom Scholem wrote that Schocken was "a broken and miserable human being who has managed to antagonize everyone in America"—Schocken put Kafka at the center of his newly founded press. One of his first initiatives, in fact, was the English edition of Kafka's *Diaries*, based on Max Brod's typescript, which had not yet appeared in the original German. In 1946, Schocken Books reissued the existing Muir translations of Kafka's novels, helping to inaugurate a postwar Kafka craze in the United States. In 1951, Salman Schocken would in turn sell the German rights to Kafka's work to Gottfried Fischer, owner of the esteemed S. Fischer Verlag, which the Nazis had shut down during the war. "Kafka put our newly reestablished publishing house squarely into the public eye," Fischer said. More recently, S. Fischer Verlag has published Reiner Stach's definitive three-volume biography of Kafka: *Kafka: Die Jahre der Entscheidungen* (2002); *Kafka: Die Jahre der Erkenntnis* (2008); and *Kafka: Die frühen Jahre* (2014).

Salman Schocken, ca. 1950. (Lotte Jacobi)

The Last Train:
From Prague to Palestine

Ostrava, Czech-Polish border
March 15, 1939

He over whom Kafka's wheels have passed has lost forever both any peace with the world and any chance of consoling himself with the judgment that the way of the world is bad.
—Theodor W. Adorno, "Commitment," 1962

At 9 p.m. on Tuesday, March 14, 1939, fifteen years after Kafka's death, Max Brod, fifty-four, and his wife, Elsa, stood at platform 2 of Prague's Wilson Station. The station, known to the Czechs as Wilsonovo nádraží', was named after former U.S. President Woodrow Wilson, whose statue faced the station from a high pedestal across the street. Max and Elsa carried British immigration visas to Palestine in their coat pockets. It had been an eventful day. That morning, they had watched columns of Nazi youth marching four abreast down Prague's main avenues chanting *"Sieg Heil!"* That evening, Hitler had summoned the President of Czechoslovakia, Emil Hácha, to the Reich Chancellery in Berlin. The Brods boarded the train not knowing whether they would be permitted to cross the Czech-Polish frontier. They were seen off by three men who had helped arrange the last-minute escape of Czech Jews: Jacob Edelstein (head of the Palestine Office in Prague), Fritz Ullmann (a Zionist leader and representative of the Jewish Agency), and Robert J. Stopford (British Treasury liaison officer in Prague for financial and refugee questions).*

Max Brod's experience of the First World War twenty-five years before had awakened him not only to the tenuous position of Prague's Jews but also to the realization that politics cannot be wishfully ignored. Brod, then thirty years old, felt that the high-minded intellectuals and "men of spirit" (*Geistigen*) had held themselves and their beautiful thoughts dangerously aloof from political realities. "We were an over-indulged generation. . . ." Brod recalled in his memoir. "Debates about Richard Wagner's music, the foundations of Judaism and Christianity, impressionist painting, etc. seemed far more important. And now this peace had suddenly come to an end, overnight. Never has a generation been so brutally trampled by the facts." Until then, Brod said, the word "war" carried an atavistic medieval ring; it seemed to belong to an earlier age. "We writers had done too little," he writes of the decisive year 1914 in *Paganism, Christianity, Judaism*. "We had not been concerned enough about the forces of reality. . . . The demons had caught us unawares."

This time, he would not be caught unawares by a society coming apart at the seams. Five years before he boarded the last train out of Prague, he had authored a pamphlet called *Rassentheorie und Judentum* (Race Theory and Judaism, 1934), in which he assailed the new German racial theory. But the anti-Semitism and racist group-think only swelled. At the end of September 1938, immediately after the Munich Agreement allowed Nazi Germany to annex parts of Czechoslovakia, Brod resolved to leave. "He felt rejected by the culture that he loved—the German cul-

---

* The private papers and diaries of R. J. Stopford, kept at the Imperial War Museum, London (catalogue number 12652), shed light on his heroic work on behalf of refugees from Czechoslovakia.

ture," writes Gaëlle Vassogne, author of *Max Brod in Prague: Identity and Mediation*.

An exile, as the saying goes, is a refugee with a library. Standing on the platform, Brod was a refugee with a bulky, cracked-leather suitcase stuffed with loose bundles and leaves of Kafka's manuscripts: journals, travel diaries, rough drafts, fair copies, sketches, hundreds of letters, and thin black notebooks in which Kafka earnestly practiced his Hebrew. (Brod left his own manuscripts in a trunk to be shipped later.) Brod had carefully collected even the smallest scraps of Kafka's furtive fragments. According to the English playwright and poet Ben Jonson, Shakespeare "never blotted a line." Not so Kafka. The pages in the suitcase showed all the marks of Kafka's hand: passages crossed out with bold diagonal strokes, doodles, scatterings of shorthand, false starts, and reworkings.

———

Some have conferred on Kafka almost divinatory powers of prescience, if not of prophecy. Milena Jesenská said of Kafka: "He heard signals of impending peril where others, deaf to the truth, felt safe and secure." More than he pursued the truth, she believed, the truth pursued him. Kafka's name has become a byword for the dehumanizing effects of faceless bureaucracies that pervade public and private spheres alike. He is said to have distilled the irrational state power that renders individuals insignificant, transforms a man from subject to object, and makes terror a routine banality. "The crucial moment towards which everything in Kafka is directed," the German-Jewish social critic Theodor W. Adorno remarked, "is that in which men become aware that they are not themselves—that they themselves are things."

In this view, Kafka foresaw, or foreshadowed, the corrosion of individual freedom under totalitarianism, with its grotesquerie of arbitrary arrests, show trials, self-denunciations, inscrutable tribunals, tortures in the name of edification, and punishments that precede crimes—in other words, judicial violence.

Some of his earliest readers understood Kafka's writing, so full of dread, as envisioning the machinery of fascism. In his memoir *The Prague Circle*, Brod writes: "Where angst speaks from the letters and diaries of Franz, it is justified angst. It is the angst before the approaching horrors of Hitlerism which he foresaw in a kind of spiritual clairvoyance and even described before they happened." Did he have premonitions of what was to come? German playwright Bertolt Brecht answered in the emphatic affirmative:

Kafka described with wonderful imaginative power the future concentration camps, the future instability of the law, the future absolutism of the state *apparat*, the paralyzed, inadequately motivated, floundering lives of many individual people; everything appeared as in a nightmare and with the confusion and inadequacy of nightmare.

In June 1938, less than a year from Brod's flight from Prague, Walter Benjamin wrote to Gershom Scholem that Kafka's world was "the exact complement of his era which is preparing to do away with the inhabitants of this planet on a considerable scale. The experience which corresponds to that of Kafka, the private individual, will probably not become accessible to the masses until such time as they are being done away with."

The texts that in the eyes of some anticipated the totalitarian upheavals of the twentieth century now themselves became threatened by those same upheavals. Brod would not allow the Nazis to fulfill Kafka's will by sending them up in flames in one of their funeral pyres of Jewish books.

———

The Brods' train departed Wilson Station at 11 p.m., scraping through countryside just occupied by the Wehrmacht, and pulling into Ostrava on the Czech-Polish border at 4 a.m., March 15. When the train came to a halt, Brod looked out the window of his compartment and stared at a motionless German soldier guarding the platform. He looked "like the statute of a Roman legionnaire," Brod said. "Truth be told, he was rather beautiful." Brod noticed that his legionnaire was not alone; the tracks were lined with fully armed Wehrmacht soldiers. "It's hard to say why this sight caused me no fear," Max Brod recalled. "I think it was because I was so tired, so sleepless, and had thought I was still dreaming. And because the young soldier standing closest to me was such a beautiful specimen. This was always my weakness: beauty, in any form, always aroused my wonderment, and has more than once in my life brought me to the very edge of total disaster."

Felix Weltsch and his wife Irma shared the Brods' train compartment. Felix, who had known Max since grade school, watched his friend cast glances at the bulky suitcase. "I didn't take my eyes off it," Brod later said. Brod might have been thinking of the young Karl Rossman in Kafka's first novel *Amerika*, who during the voyage to the New World watched his suitcase "so carefully for the whole crossing that his watchfulness had almost cost him his sleep" only to lose it the moment he arrives at the New York harbor. Perhaps Brod already attached a talismanic importance to the contents of the suitcase, hoping that they would protect him from the unluckier fate of those he left behind.*

It was to be the last train to cross the Czech-Polish border before the Nazis closed it. Later in the day, when the train pulled into Krakow, Poland, Brod saw the disheartening newspaper headlines: Czechoslo-

---

* A dozen years later, Brod would write a book about his classmate Victor Mathias Freud, a Zionist, early member of the Bar Kochba group, and much-loved schoolteacher (*Beinahe ein Vorzugsschüler*, Almost an Exemplary Student, 1952). Denied a British immigration visa to Palestine, Freud was deported from Prague to Terezín in July 1943 and thence to Auschwitz in October 1944. He too believed he was protected by sacred texts. His last words before boarding the deportation train: "Nothing much can happen to me. I have the Bible and Goethe's poems in my pocket."

vakia was no more. The country so dear to his heart, where he came to know joy and grief, had passed into oblivion and left him in the lurch.

On the afternoon of March 17, the Brods arrived in the Romanian port of Constanța on the Black Sea together with 160 other refugee families from Czechoslovakia. The train took them straight to the docks, where they had booked cabin 228 on an old Romanian liner called the *Bessarabia*. The ship took them to Tel Aviv with stopovers in Istanbul, Athens, Crete, and Alexandria.

Brod had first set eyes on Palestine eleven years earlier. During a six-week visit in 1928, he had visited Kibbutz Beit Alfa and the adjacent Kibbutz Heftziba (both founded in 1922 by immigrants from Czechoslovakia, Germany, and Poland).* Some of his writing had been published in Palestine before the war. *Tycho Brahe* had appeared in Hebrew in 1935 (in the translation of the Polish-born poet Mordechai Temkin).

Brod did not in those years entertain thoughts of *aliya* (immigration to Palestine). "The Diaspora will remain anyhow," he wrote in 1920, "since Palestine can at best become the home for one-eighth of Jewry." In 1922, Brod published an article in which he remarked on his "heart-felt reservations against Palestine, that is, against the *exclusivity* of Palestine as the salvation for the Jew." (Brod, ever the redactor, deleted this passage when he republished the piece in 1966.) Brod had been determined, Mark Gelber writes, "to live his life indefinitely in the diaspora as a Jewish nationalist." (Decades later, in 1957, Brod remarked to his friend Fritz Bondy, a Prague-born translator who wrote under the pseudonym NO Scarpi: "The state of Israel cannot exist without the Jews in the Diaspora, neither can the Diaspora survive without the state of Israel.")

Even now, on the eve of the Second World War, Palestine was not Brod's first choice. Friends in Palestine, he writes in his memoir, "warned me against *aliya*. Men of intellectual professions, especially

---

* Czech president Tomáš Masaryk had visited Beit Alfa the previous April—the first visit of a head of state to British Mandatory Palestine.

those above a certain age, are not in particular demand here. What is required there are sturdy young men, pioneers, men of action, engineers, chicken-coopers, farmers, shepherds." In early 1939, Brod wrote in a tone of desperation to an old acquaintance, German novelist and Nobel laureate Thomas Mann. Sensing impending catastrophe, Brod declared he was determined to emigrate to America while there was still time. He mentioned an attack on him published in the *Völkische Beobachter*, the Nazi Party daily, which sought to discredit Brod on the basis of "some erotic passages from works of my youth, written decades ago."

Brod was familiar with the extraordinary roster of European Jewish émigrés who had the foresight to escape to the United States, despite the stiff quotas: Albert Einstein, Hannah Arendt, Leo Strauss, Herbert Marcuse, Theodor W. Adorno, and Max Horkheimer, not to mention the musicians, painters, and sculptors who together would make an incalculable contribution to postwar American culture. Brod now begged Mann to arrange an invitation to an American university. (Mann had secured himself an offer to teach at Princeton.) Brod listed what he could offer to an American university: courses in Czech politics, Zionism, and music—and a treasure of unique value. "I would bring with me the whole still-unpublished literary estate [*Nachlass*] of Franz Kafka," he wrote to Mann, "and would edit it there and set up a Kafka archive."

When he received Brod's plea, Thomas Mann was just putting the finishing touches on his novel *Lotte in Weimar*. There he has Goethe warn that the German people "submit to any mad scoundrel who appeals to their lowest instincts, who confirms them in their vices and teaches them to conceive nationalism as isolation and brutality." All too aware of the new Nazi brutality, Mann tried to bring Brod to the New York Public Library. In a letter dated February 27, 1939, Mann turned to H. M. Lydenberg, director of the library, and asked for help in bringing Brod to the U.S. as a "non-quota alien":

I have known and admired Dr. Brod for many years. He is now fifty-four. For the past twenty years and more, he has worked for his country, not simply as a writer, but as a civil servant and also as editor of the *Prager Tagblatt*. He is a gifted and cultured man, but now, because he is a Jew, he is no longer permitted to write what he thinks and believes, and is being ridiculed and vilified in the German press.

Mann also relayed to Lydenberg that Brod

> is willing to give his collection of the books and manuscripts of Franz Kafka to any institution of repute which would accept it and in return offer him a position to act as assistant or curator of the collection, and so make possible his entry into this country. . . . Perhaps you will agree with me that the possibility of acquiring the manuscripts and books of so well known a writer as Franz Kafka is an opportunity deserving of consideration quite apart from the human tragedy of the individual for whom the collection represents the one real chance of escape from an intolerable situation.

In his autobiography, Brod gives the story a somewhat different spin: "When the danger of Hitlerism rose later on and remaining in Prague meant torture and death, Thomas Mann took me under his wing without my having to ask. Through Mann's intervention, everything was so deftly handled that a professorship was waiting for me at an American university. I chose to follow the genius of my life and go to Palestine." In fact, although Mann did succeed in getting Brod an offer from Hebrew Union College in Cincinnati, the letter of appointment failed to reach him by the time he fled Prague. According to Gaëlle Vassogne of the Université Stendhal in Grenoble, France, even after he arrived in Tel Aviv, Brod still tried to find a position in an American university.

Brod's attempt to tempt America with the Kafka manuscripts came to naught. Clutching his suitcase, he and Elsa headed to Tel Aviv instead. On at last arriving in Palestine, Brod said he had "only one plan: to act for the memory of my friend Franz Kafka in this country that he missed."

What would Brod do with the relics of the sainted Kafka once he had brought them to the Promised Land?

On May 5, 1940, with Germany poised for the invasion of Belgium, France, Luxembourg, and the Netherlands, Brod wrote from Tel Aviv to the Rector of the Hebrew University in Jerusalem:

> The turbulent times we live in cause me to turn to you with an urgent request. Would it be possible for you to keep a suitcase of mine containing very important manuscripts? In this suitcase is the estate of Franz Kafka, my musical compositions and my unpublished diaries. You understand that this suitcase, most precious to me, in these times cannot be secure in a private place. I would like it to be secured with you, if it is possible for anything today to be secure.

The protracted negotiations between Brod and the Hebrew University were interrupted: on September 9, 1940, the Italian air force bombed residential areas of Tel Aviv, killing 137 people, including 53 children. Brod decided to deposit his treasures neither at an American university nor at Hebrew University but in a fireproof safe at the Schocken Library on Balfour Street in Jerusalem. In a document dated December 6, 1940, Salman Schocken affirmed that Kafka's manuscripts were deposited in a safe at the Schocken Library, and that only Brod would have a key to that safe.

It proved to be a false promise. It seems Schocken had the key duplicated and had the Kafka material hastily photographed without Brod's permission. In a letter dated February 22, 1951, Brod protested to Schocken that he had made a copy of the key to the safe. When Brod requested the manuscripts to be returned, Schocken dragged his feet.

"He hoped that if he wore Max down for long enough, Max would eventually throw up his hands," Eva Hoffe told me.

On April 26, 1951, Brod wrote to Kafka's niece Marianna Steiner to say that Schocken had broken his promise and had a spare key to the safe. Steiner (née Pollak) had fled to London with her husband and son in April 1939. On April 2, 1952, Brod again wrote to Marianna Steiner to say that he had opened the safe in the presence of one of Schocken's clerks "and found everything in best order." According to Brod's inventory, the manuscripts included:

1. Kafka's manuscripts of his three unfinished novels: *The Trial*, *The Castle*, and *Amerika*
2. Kafka's drafts of several short stories, including "Description of a Struggle," "The Burrow," "The Hunger Artist," "A Little Woman," "Blumfeld," and "Josephine the Singer, or the Mouse Folk"
3. Kafka's diaries (thirteen quarto notebooks) and travel journals
4. Kafka's blue octavo notebooks (eight notebooks filled with Kafka's aphorisms and stories)
5. The original typescript of Kafka's letter to his father
6. Kafka's Hebrew exercises
7. Kafka's letters to Brod

Brod noted that Kafka's letter to his father, and the manuscripts of *The Trial* and "Description of a Struggle," "are my property." Kafka's letters to Brod "do not belong to the Kafka estate, but I myself deposited them there temporarily." "Everything else," Brod added, "belongs to the heirs of Kafka."

In August 2015, a month after the Tel Aviv District Court decision, Marianna's son Michael Steiner, for many years a partner in a leading London law firm, wrote to the Israeli lawyers in the Hoffe case in his capacity as executor and trustee of the will of his mother and as representative of the Kafka estate. Referring to Brod's claims in the 1952 letter, Steiner writes:

> My mother accepted these claims throughout her life and the Kafka Estate does not adopt any different position . . . At this point I should like to make it clear that the Kafka family has always been grateful to Max Brod for everything that he did for Kafka's literary reputation, for his selfless behavior after Kafka's death, and for the assistance he gave the family, in particular in its negotiations with Schocken, the publishers. . . . In 2010, I was approached by the National Library for information and it was mooted that the Kafka Estate might wish to be joined in the litigation that was in prospect. I was not able to understand how, after so many years, the construction of Brod's will determined by Judge Shilo could be relitigated. I supplied what information I could to Meir Heller [the National Library's lawyer], explained what the Estate's objectives had been in the past, and asked to see a copy of the court-ordered inventory to enable me to compare it with Brod's letter of April 1952. I also made it clear that the Estate regarded itself as the owner of all items which Brod had himself accepted did not belong to him, which might include manuscripts of Kafka not listed in the letter, but the existence of which had for some reason not been listed by Brod. The inventory has never been supplied to me. I think it now should be.

In the same letter, Michael Steiner adds that in 1956, "Schocken transferred the manuscripts to a safe in Switzerland without informing either my mother or Max Brod. It appears that before that happened Brod had already taken away the manuscripts of which he claimed ownership in the letter of April 1952, with some other items which he may have wanted for his editorial work." More than six decades later, the episode has hardly faded from Eva Hoffe's memory. The Schocken family is "monstrous," she told me.

In April 1961, manuscripts which Brod conceded belonged to the Kafka estate and which were in the Swiss bank vault were collected by the scholar Sir Malcolm Pasley on behalf of the Kafka estate and deposited with the Bodleian Library in Oxford. Pasley brought the manuscripts from Switzerland to Oxford in his small private car.[*]

---

[*] In August 1969, Marianna Steiner also deposited with the Bodleian the manuscript of "The Metamorphosis" (*Die Verwandlung*) and the next year a box containing Kafka's letters, which had been in the possession of her cousins in Prague. Another Kafka niece, Gerti Kaufman, the daughter of Kafka's sister Elli, bequeathed her share to the Bodleian Library in 1972. In 1989, Miriam Schocken, a grand-daughter of Salman Schocken, gave the Bodleian a further batch of Kafka's papers. The critical editions of Kafka's works, published by S. Fischer Verlag, are based on the manuscripts in Oxford. Marianna Steiner bequeathed her share of the manuscripts to the Bodleian Library on her death in 2000. Under the editorship of Roland Reuss and Peter Staengle, Stroemfeld Verlag published facsimiles of the Bodleian Kafka manuscripts.

Max Brod in Prague, February 1937.
(Czechoslovak News Agency)

11

The Last Tightrope Dancer:
Kafka in Germany

Theodor Ackermann antiquarian booksellers, Ludwigstrasse 7, Munich
November 1982

> In the organism of humanity, there are no two people which
> attract and repel each other more than the Germans and the
> Jews.
>
> —Moses Hess, 1862

> From early on they [the Jews] have forced upon Germany things
> that might have come to it slowly and in its own way, but which
> it was opposed to because they came from strangers.
>
> —Franz Kafka to Max Brod, 1920

In November 1982, almost a century after Kafka's birth, Werner Fritsch, managing director of the venerable Munich bookseller Theodor Ackermann (founded 1865), got the offer of a lifetime. A man he declines to identify told Fritsch that, unlike Kafka's family, the writer's personal library of some 279 books somehow survived the Nazi regime more or less intact. The collection promised to throw light on a previously obscure question: With whom did Kafka keep mental company? After showing the books to Professor Jürgen Born to verify their authenticity, Fritsch sold the library for an undisclosed sum to Born's Institute for the Study of Prague's German Literature at the University of Wuppertal.

The accent of Kafka's library lay heavily on German classics: the works of Goethe, Schiller, Schopenhauer (Kafka had nine volumes of his collected works), and Friedrich Hebbel, along with world classics in German translation: nine volumes of Shakespeare, and several novels of Dostoyevsky. The Jewish components of Kafka's library proved rather meager. Among other works, it included Theodor Herzl's diaries; some volumes of Jewish folklore collected by M. Y. Berdichevsky (described as "the first Hebrew writer living in Berlin to be revered in the world of German letters"); Richard Lichtheim's *The Zionist Agenda* (*Das Programm des Zionismus*, a gift from Brod); Moses Rath's Hebrew study book (1917); and an anthology published by the Bar Kochba Association. It also includes a 1921 edition of Brod's book, *Paganism, Christianity and Judaism*, with the dedication: "For my Franz, for your recovery, Max."

The composition of the library supports the Marbach archive's position throughout the trial in Israel over the Brod estate: German literature—not the Jewish tradition—indisputably constituted Kafka's cultural canon. If Judaism was for Kafka a foreign but acquired frame of reference, his natural home was in German literature. He revered the Lutheran writer of Alemannic folktales Johann Peter Hebel (Kafka called his "Unexpected Reunion" "the most wonderful story in the world"), Heinrich von Kleist (especially *Michael Kohlhaas* and *The Marquise of O*), and the Viennese dramatist Franz Grillparzer (especially his diaries and *The Poor Minstrel* [*Der arme Spielmann*]). Among his contemporaries in the world of German letters, Kafka admired Hugo von Hofmannsthal, Robert Walser, and Thomas Mann.

But above all he had esteemed the greatest classicist, Goethe. According to Marthe Robert, a member of the editorial board of the German critical edition of Kafka's complete works, the young Kafka "sought the Promised Land in Weimar, and Goethe was his Bible." In the summer of 1912, Kafka and Brod traveled to Weimar for six days to pay homage to the writer who had made his home there for more than half a century. "To hear Kafka talk about Goethe with awe was something quite out of the ordinary," Brod remembers. "It was like hearing a little child talk about an ancestor who lived in happier, purer days and was in direct contact with the Divine."

At the same time, Kafka was not above mocking the German national sanctification of Goethe. His friend Oskar Pollak's pilgrimage in 1902 to the Goethe National Museum elicited a letter from Kafka in which the word "national" is described as "the most delicate, miraculously delicate irony." To Pollak's mention of visiting Goethe's study, the writer's holy of holies, Kafka replies: "We cannot ever have the all-holiest of someone else, only our own." There is nothing to possess of the great Goethe, Kafka says, except "the footsteps of his lonesome walks through the countryside."

Kafka attended a German university, studied German jurisprudence, and steeped himself in German literature. More to the point, the austere music of Kafka's art was inseparable from—and made possible by—the German language. In the movement and momentum of his perfectly weighted sentences, Kafka forged that necessity into a stainless and unstilted prose of spare precision, economy, and translucency, a merciless German that pares away superfluity and slack. (Even the barmaids and peasants in his fiction speak a flawless German, uninflected with dialect.) His beautifully calibrated language, Hannah Arendt remarked, was "the purest German prose of the century." That language "is fire," Brod said, "but it leaves no soot behind."

Is Kafka possible only in German? Time and again, the Marbach archive's lawyers intimated that Kafka is German because his language is German and his art could not be expressed in anything but the German language. They were neither the first nor the most eloquent advocates of this view. "His language was German," Cynthia Ozick writes, "and that, possibly, is the point. That Kafka breathed and thought and aspired and suffered in German—in Prague, a German-hating city—may be the ultimate exegesis of everything he wrote." "When he crucially, even triumphantly, announced, 'I am made of literature and nothing else,'" Ozick adds, "it could only mean that it was German idiom and essence, German root and rootedness, that had formed and possessed him."

Whether he possessed *it* is altogether another matter. In a letter to Brod, Kafka depicts the prose of Jews writing in German as "a literature impossible in all respects, a gypsy literature which had stolen the German child out of its cradle and in great haste put it through some kind of training, for someone has to dance on the tightrope." Kafka's mastery of German is inseparable from his fear of falling from that impossible tightrope.

———

Why did the German Literature Archive persevere through eight years of legal wrangling for the chance to acquire Kafka's literary remains? Did it involve the ways Kafka figured into Germany's overcoming of its repressed past?

Kafka recognized "the pride which a nation gains from a literature of its own." A national literary archive, whether in Marbach or Jerusalem or anywhere else, is neither a neutral repository nor an arbitrary accumulation; it is a shrine to national memory and to the continuity of that memory. Like a church consecrated by its relics, or a temple by its Holy Ark, the archive as reliquary participates in the effort of a nation to distinguish itself from other nations. The archive is a tabernacle that derives its legitimacy by what it preserves. If we whisper in libraries and archives as we whisper in churches, this is why.

If the archive is where the writer is translated into a saint, it is also where the private coalesces into the public, where inanimate literary remains are invested with collective symbolic significance. (And like any other material thing, a literary relic may be possessed by one person or group to the exclusion of another.) No matter how self-effacing, its curators serve not merely as guardians and conservators, but as privileged interpreters who include and exclude, give the stamp of authenticity, and authorize veneration. They decide *what* material to archive, *how* to order it, and *who* may access it. The word "archive" itself points in this direction: it derives from the Greek *arkhe*, literally "beginning, origin, first place." Control of the archive is a form of power.

This is especially true of Germany, where until 1871, when Bismarck's Prussia consolidated the various smaller states, there was no people that could claim the title "Deutsche." There were only Saxons, Bavarians, Swabians, Prussians, East-Franks, and so forth. According to a well-known quip, there is no German identity other than the search for an identity. Despite political divisions, the German people, it is often said, found itself in its literature. In this nation of *Dichter und Denker* (poets and thinkers)—a nation preoccupied with the unanswerable question of what it means to be German—affirming national identity vitally involved turning toward German literature. (To be sure, as Heinrich Mann remarked in 1910, Germans are perfectly capable of revering their writers as keepers of the national conscience without necessarily absorbing their ideas.)

Language and literature acted not just as a vehicle of communication but as a crucible of national cohesion in which a "German" identity was forged and membership in the imagined community called Germany was determined. German literature long preceded the unified German state (just as Jewish literature long predated the Jewish state). In Germany (as later in Israel), the founding documents are not those that announce the birth of the state (e.g., the Constitution and Declaration of Independence in the United States), but texts that long precede the birth of the state.* The masters of German prose and poetry—Luther, Goethe, Schiller, Kleist, Heine—predate the establishment of modern Germany in 1870.

---

* See, for example, Benjamin Netanyahu's remarks addressed to then Prime Minister Yitzhak Rabin on October 5, 1995: "You said the Bible is not our land registry. I say: The Bible *is* our registry, our mandate, our proof of ownership. . . . This is the very foundation of Zionist existence."

In January 1889, German philosopher Wilhelm Dilthey issued a far-reaching call for the state to establish and support German literary archives in order "to foster our national awareness." The time was ripe. Later that year, Schiller's estate was incorporated into the Goethe Archive that had been founded four years earlier. Ever since, to a degree unthinkable elsewhere, literature has played—and continues to play—a consolidating role in helping Germans come to terms with their *Volksgeist*.

Precisely for this reason, the National Socialists both commandeered German-language literature and called it into question. The fall of the Third Reich, in turn, ushered in more than just a political crisis; it demanded a reassessment of the interactions of *Geist* and *Macht*, of literature and power-politics. After the war, in the shadows of the ruins, some German writers sensed that German literature had lost its way and had to be reset. (The German language, the poet Paul Celan said after surviving the war, "had to pass through its own answerlessness.") After what became known in West Germany as the *Stunde Null*, or "zero hour," they felt the need to begin anew. In a conversation in Berlin, the literary scholars Sigrid Weigel and her husband Klaus Briegleb told me that the loose-knit circle of German writers known as Gruppe 47, prominent leftist apostles of the so-called *Nachkriegsliteratur* (postwar literature), called for a radical new beginning, a *Traditionsbruch* (rupture with tradition). They refused to continue to write as if nothing had happened, as if the horrors had been exaggerated by anti-German propagandists; instead, they looked to literature to help them face the traumas their country inflicted.

Between 1947 and 1967, the most prominent writers of the Federal Republic—Heinrich Böll, Günter Grass, Martin Walser—fixated on a past that would not pass away. Grass declared that the struggle to overcome the repressed past (*Vergangenheitsbewältigung*) was the ultimate aim not only of his own writing but of German literature as such.

It was into this milieu that the Marbach literature archive came into being in 1955 on the outskirts of Marbach (population fifteen thousand), the birthplace of the German poet Friedrich Schiller. (On June 21, 1934, for the poet's 175th birthday, some fifteen thousand Hitler Youth, looking to Schiller as a standard-bearer of National Socialism and the "eternal German spirit," marched through Marbach.) The archive is nestled in a grove of plane trees on a hillock overlooking the Neckar River. Behind the archive, a block of thirty apartments, called the Collegium House, offers accommodation to researchers. The archive itself stands adjacent to the domed Schiller Museum—opened in 1903 and expanded into its present dimensions in 1934—which houses the poet's relics: his death mask, vest, gloves, and socks. Across the lawn, the Museum of Modern Literature (Literaturmuseum der Moderne, known as LiMo), beckons visitors into environmentally controlled exhibition galleries, illuminated by subdued artificial light, where material from the archives' collections is displayed. The permanent exhibition—organized by year rather than by writer or theme—includes Kafka's high school matriculation certificate (1901); the original manuscripts of *The Trial* (1914–15) and his unfinished story, "The Village Schoolmaster" (1915); a letter to Max Brod (1917); three letters (1920) and a postcard (1923) to Milena Jesenská; and even one of his spoons. Here the old veneration of writers like Schiller and Goethe was translated into the present, grafted onto modernist writers like Kafka.

And it is here that Kafka's past came to impinge on Germany's present.

———

In June 2017, I sat down with the director of the Marbach archive, Ulrich Raulff. Before his appointment, Raulff served as editor of the culture pages of the *Frankfurter Allgemeine Zeitung* and as managing editor of the *Süddeutsche Zeitung*. He also coedited a volume on "Heidegger and Literature," and published an award-winning book on Stefan George, the German poet to whom some National Socialists looked as an important influence. When Raulff came to Marbach in November 2004, he brought with him ambitions to raise the archive's public profile. (He is set to be replaced as director in January 2019 by Sandra Richter, currently head of the department of modern German literature at the University of Stuttgart.)

Raulff began our conversation with a smile that was also a glower, "So," he said, "is there anything I can do against you?"

From the outset of the legal proceedings in Israel, he said, he had wished to maintain "clear neutrality," and instructed his attorney, Sa'ar Plinner, to act as an observer merely. Raulff presented himself as a man thrust against his will into the spotlight; as though despite his best intentions, he had been unwittingly drawn into controversy.

By 2010, the policy of neutrality had run aground; Raulff became worried about the bad press the archive was getting, first in Israel and then internationally. He claimed the controversy took him by surprise. "Perhaps Israeli sensibilities had changed," he said, "and there was a new heightened awareness in Israel of the country's cultural heritage."

That year, Raulff came to Israel to meet with both Eva Hoffe and representatives of the National Library. To placate the Israelis, he proposed co-ownership of the Brod estate along the lines of the partnership the archive in Marbach would set up with the Bodleian Library in Oxford with regard to the hundred letters and postcards Kafka sent to his favorite sister Ottla between September 1909 and January 1924. (The two institutions had jointly bought the letters for an undisclosed fee in April 2011.) There were already several joint cataloguing projects between the Marbach archive and the National Library in Jerusalem, too.* But Raulff's malleability was not reciprocated, and the attempted compromise failed.

---

* These joint projects, supported by the German Federal Foreign Office (Auswärtiges Amt), include the papers of leading Orientalist S. D. Goitein, a pioneering researcher of the "Cairo Geniza"; Josef Horovitz, founder and first head of the School of Oriental Studies; Curt Wormann, director of the Jewish National and University Library; Netti Boleslav, a German-language writer in British Mandate Palestine and Israel; and Jewish-German orientalist Martin Plessner, a professor in the Department of Islamic Culture at the Hebrew University. Each of these collections is housed at the National Library in Jerusalem.

Not long after, Raulff told me, the trial had brought him another unpleasant surprise. He had been on the verge of getting a generous grant for the archive from the Alfried Krupp von Bohlen und Halbach Foundation, one of the largest philanthropies in Germany. Between 2001 and 2008, a 169,000-euro grant from the Krupp Foundation had made it possible for the Marbach archive to photograph and digitize its entire collection of Kafka manuscripts. Against the backdrop of the Kafka trial, however, the new funding had run aground because of the foundation's complicated past. During the Second World War, its founder, the industrialist and arms manufacturer Alfried Krupp, had used concentration-camp prisoners supplied by the SS to work under brutal conditions in his factories. In 1948, he had been convicted of crimes against humanity by a U.S. military court in Nuremberg. Without warning, Raulff said, the Krupp Foundation had suddenly pulled the new grant, citing the need to shield its name and reputation from even indirect suggestions that it supported seizing cultural heritage from Israel.

By 2012, Raulff said, he regretted getting involved in the first place, and instructed Plinner to drop the case. He valued long-term partnership and good working relations with the National Library of Israel over short-term gain, and preferred "the logic of research" over "the logic of acquisition." His interests, if any, rose above national boundaries. Why then did Plinner address the Supreme Court in 2016 in the name of the Marbach archive, I asked. Had Plinner consulted him, Raulff said, "I would have told him not to appear in the Supreme Court."

I sensed a deep ambivalence: on the one hand, as one of the central bankers of the literary republic, adept in assessing the value of literary capital and prestige and in understanding how the "culture industry" congeals literature into commodity, Raulff wanted to seize a once-in-a-lifetime chance for the archive. (Goethe once spoke of a "world market of intellectual goods.") Both the German and Israeli will to appropriate, whether lofty or low, attempted to convert Kafka's works into usable goods.

On the other, he could not risk the appearance of "seizing" cultural heritage from the Jewish state. "Had Eva won and turned to us," Raulff said, "it would have been a catastrophe for us." I asked what he would have done had Eva offered to sell Brod's estate to Marbach. "I would have had sleepless nights," Raulff replied.

Throughout the conversation, he seemed persuaded that only the Israelis had interests, that the Marbach archive acted in this case as an unobjectionably disinterested, neutral, even passive observer; he spoke as if Germany represented the true home of the human spirit. This reflects a position of strength, of a majority culture: only those who have fulfilled their interests can speak in a "disinterested" way, and only those who have accumulated literary capital can allow themselves the luxury of persuading themselves of the pure timeless universality of literature. (A German only has an explicit interest, a colleague quipped, when an Israeli compels him to put it on paper.) It is possible to want something and at the same time not to admit to oneself that one wants it. But the fact is that it would have been highly unusual, to say the least, for Plinner to appear, file briefs, and argue in the Supreme Court without Raulff's knowledge and authorization.

———

Did the German state itself wish to appear to be free of interests? If politics, especially cultural politics, is a form of aesthetics, to appear disinterested is a matter of good taste. The postwar German uneasiness with avowed interests may correspond to an ambivalence toward the uses and abuses of sovereign power and the state's latent violence. Postwar Germany is famously reluctant to admit to being a state, like other states, that pursues its national interests, as if an unsheathed expression of national interest today might portend the staccato of marching jackboots tomorrow.

The German party to the legal dispute in Israel wished to appear as honest brokers acting not in the name of Germany but of literature per se, as though it represented European universalism against Israeli particularism, or the eternal light in which other cultures are refracted. In a 2011 documentary film about the trial called "Kafka's Last Story" (directed by Sagi Bornstein), Ulrich Raulff addressed the question of Kafka's belonging: "He is nowhere at home—thus everywhere."

Needless to say, Marbach is not "everywhere." It is in a Germany that in its postwar reckoning, in its "coming to terms with the past" (or *Vergangenheitsbewältigung*), was anxious to overcome the old canard that Jews could not authentically master German, even if they wrote it flawlessly; that they were poachers, or at most tolerated guests, on the fertile lands of German prose; that the German idiom used by Jews was an appropriation of someone else's property. In this view, the Jewish writer, essentially uncreative, could only ape the language of Kant, Schiller, and Goethe. (Kafka's story "A Report to an Academy," published in Martin Buber's monthly *Der Jude*, features a speaking ape.*) In his notorious essay "Judaism in Music" ("Das Judentum in der Musik," 1850), the German composer Richard Wagner writes: "The Jew speaks the language of the nation in whose midst he dwells from generation to generation, but he speaks it always as an alien. . . . In this Speech, this Art, the Jew can only imitate and mimic." The German historian Eduard Meyer (1855–1930), in his 1896 book *The Emergence of Judaism* (*Die Entstehung des Judentums*) contrasts Aryan creativity to the Semites' deriv-

---

* At one point in "A Report to an Academy," Kafka has his ape look out at a man looking in at him: "He could not understand me, he wanted to solve the enigma of my being." Max Brod called this story (published in *Der Jude*, November 1917), "the most brilliant satire of assimilation which has ever been written." The translator Peter Wortsman calls the story "an allusion to the attempts of assimilated Jews to imitate Aryan ways, so as to pass in a hostile and often perilous society." We know that Kafka read a pamphlet by the Russian Zionist Max Mandelstamm, which remarked on the similarity between an assimilated Jew, with his "capacity for mimicry," and an ape.

ative nature. Jews were said to be set apart because they spoke another language (Hebrew, Yiddish) or spoke German with a "Jewish" accent. However much they mastered mimicry, the purities of German speech and spirit receded beyond their grasp.

Some Jewish writers internalized the myth of Jewish mimicry. In an essay called "Imitation and Assimilation" (1893), leading cultural Zionist Ahad Ha'am argued that "the Jews have not merely a tendency to imitation, but a genius for it. Whatever they imitate, they imitate well." In *The Star of Redemption* (1921), the German-Jewish philosopher Franz Rosenzweig writes that Jews, having no idiom of their own, have spoken languages borrowed from their hosts; Hebrew, their holy tongue, belonged to God alone.

If not mimics, the Jews were seen, and sometimes saw themselves, as mere custodians of German literature and language. In 1912, the Zionist literary scholar Moritz Goldstein published an essay called "The German-Jewish Parnassus" in the prestigious journal *Der Kunstwart*. It aroused a great deal of controversy. "We Jews are administering the spiritual property of a nation which denies our right and our ability to do so," he claimed. Decades later, Max Brod, too, spoke of Jews as stewards of the German language. In a letter to Martin Buber, he remarked:

> We Jews treat German quite differently from a real German such as Gerhart Hauptmann, Robert Walser, or even a mediocrity like Hermann Hesse. We merely hold the language in trust, hence in purely linguistic matters we are uncreative.

Perhaps there was a recognition that to bring Kafka—precisely as a Jewish guardian of German prose, and as a Jew who died before he could fall victim to the Nazis—back into the German fold would be to erase the moral stains of the past, to regain a forfeited standing, and to recover a German language not yet defiled by the nihilistic bellowing of

Hitler and Goebbels.* Herein hides another irony with which the story of Kafka's last trial is salted: the attempt to use the writer who raised self-condemnation into art as a means of self-exculpation.

West Germans pressed Kafka into service against the immediate National Socialist past. After the "zero hour," to prove that it had rid itself of Nazi thinking, the guilt-ridden majority literature embraced a cultural symbol of antitotalitarian minority thinking—a Jew from Prague. The Czech writer and Kafka scholar Alena Wágnerová suggests that the passionate embrace of Kafka in Germany has functioned as "an ingenious displacement mechanism" ("*ein raffinierter Verdrängungs-mechanismus*"). Commenting on "the fervent curiosity that broke out among Germans after 1950," the philosopher (and Hannah Arendt's first husband) Günther Anders (1902–1992) goes farther:

> Those who were guilty of and complicit in the excessive crimes of the Hitler regime, who knew very well what they had done and yet were not only not charged with or punished for anything, but rather, with few exceptions, continued to live in a self-satisfied and smug manner—they were presumably thankful to have been supplied with an *antipodal* figure. . . . *The idolization of Kafka dissolved the fact that millions of his kinsmen had been murdered*" (emphasis in the original).

What Anders calls "the Kafka epidemic [*Kafka-Seuche*]," he adds, "infected those Germans who were the half-hearted accomplices and who wished to prove, also to themselves, that they could accept the guilt

---

* In his short history of German literature, Heinz Schlaffer of the University of Stuttgart remarks on the disproportionate numbers of twentieth-century German writers who were Jews. "If one grasps 'German' not as an ethnic species but as a cultural mindset, then the emancipated Jews can be considered the more serious Germans. With their expulsion and extermination, German literature logically forfeited its standing and lost its character." See *Die kurze Geschichte der deutschen Literatur*, Hanser, 2002.

imposed on them by the victors at least in the form of literature, and thereby work through their remorse in the form of artistic admiration."

The notion that postwar Germans looked to Kafka for feel-good absolution, if valid, might also obliquely throw light on the place of German-Jewish studies at Marbach. At a talk he gave in 2004 in Tel Aviv, Mark Gelber of Ben-Gurion University said:

> Scholars who visit the archives sign their names in the guest book daily upon arrival, noting also their home city or country, the date, and the specific topic of research. Visitors, if they care, have some sense of the identity of the other colleagues and what they might be researching, thus facilitating conversations during coffee breaks and the like. During an extended research visit in Marbach in 2003–2004, I could not help but notice the egregiously dispropor-tionate number of scholars working in the area of German-Jewish literary studies. Although I did not keep an exact record, and even though it may seem at first ludicrous, it would probably be fair to say that about one-third to one-half of the visiting scholars during this period were working on some aspect of the poetry of Paul Celan or another topic related to German literature and the Shoah. Another quarter, perhaps, were working on topics related to a major figure or topic in German-Jewish literary or cultural history; for example, Kafka and Walter Benjamin seem to be very popular right now. . . . The study of German literature seemed to have been displaced by German-Jewish Studies at the very altar of one of its central temples.

During the trial in Israel, Germans regarded Israelis as latecomers to Kafka studies. But in another sense the Germans themselves were burdened by belatedness. From World War II until the 1980s, Kafka's Jewishness was virtually ignored in Germany. Günther Anders, writing in German in 1951, offers a representative example: "To claim Kafka as the continuator of the Jewish religion and Jewish theology is completely and absolutely off the mark."

The first German conference to address Kafka's Jewishness was convened by Karl Erich Grözinger and Hans Dieter Zimmermann in Frankfurt in 1986. The Stuttgart-born scholar Grözinger (b. 1942) argued, as he would subsequently put it in his book *Kafka and Kabbalah*, "whenever Kafka speaks of judgment, sin, atonement and justification, he is working from the direct context of a Jewish theology." Grözinger tells me that many leading German scholars, including Hartmut Binder, declined to come to the groundbreaking conference. Those who did attend were dismayed by what they heard. "They acknowledged that Kafka was a Jew, but didn't know how to interpret his Jewishness," Grözinger says, "and resisted the notion that the great German writer would be snatched from their hands." It was as though they feared Kafka would be Judaized or "Jewified."

German literary critics have worked assiduously to rehabilitate Kafka and claim him as their own. In his monumental studies published in 1958 (*Franz Kafka* and *Die Weltkritik von Franz Kafka*), Wilhelm Emrich argued that Kafka completed German classicism, and "poetically renewed the classical legacy of German humanism that he adored and honored throughout his life." Beginning in the 1960s, a popular edition of Kafka's stories (*Sämtliche Erzählungen*, edited by Paul Raabe) sold a million copies in Germany.

Today, the German weekly *Die Zeit* publishes a supplement on the history of German literature for high school students, divided into the standard periods: Middle Ages, Baroque (1600 to 1720), Enlightenment (1680 to 1789), *Sturm und Drang* (late 1760s to early 1780s), Weimar Classicism (1772 to 1805), Romanticism (1790s to 1880s), Biedermeier (1815 to 1848), and so forth. Only one writer merits his own category. In between *Moderne* and *Expressionismus*, Kafka perches permanently in the German canon.

Kafka is reported to have said that Jews and Germans "have a lot in common. They are ambitious, able, diligent, and thoroughly hated by others. Both are pariahs." And yet Kafka almost never mentions Germany in his letters or diaries, and when he does it is with indifference. Although he briefly lived in Berlin with Dora Diamant, and although all his publishers were in Germany, Kafka was neither German nor non-German. "I have never lived among German people," Kafka remarked to Milena Jesenská. (Of the correspondence with Milena, only Kafka's letters to her remain. She gave them to their mutual friend Willy Haas in 1939, shortly before the Gestapo arrested her and deported her to the Ravensbrück concentration camp. Shortly after Kafka's death, she had asked Brod to burn her letters to Kafka.) "Kafka wrote in German, of course," Philip Roth notes, "but he was not a German in any way. He was, to the core, a German-speaking citizen of Prague and a son of Prague Jews."*

* As I was researching this book, I was occasionally asked why the Czechs chose not to apply to join the legal proceedings in Israel and made no claims on the manuscripts Brod had rescued from Prague. Czech, after all, was the first language into which Kafka's works were translated: "The Stoker" (the first chapter of *Amerika*) in 1920; *The Trial* in 1923 (seven years before its French publication); and *The Castle* in 1935. The world's first dissertation written on Kafka ("The Feeling of Loneliness and Communion in Franz Kafka," by Mathilda Slodka) was written in Czech and submitted to Charles University in Prague in 1939.

After the Second World War, Communist authorities in Prague banned Kafka's books in his own city. "A regime that is built on deception," the Prague writer Ivan Klíma later said, "that asks people to pretend, that demands external agreement without caring about the inner conviction of those to whom it turns for consent, a regime afraid of anyone who asks about the sense of his actions, cannot allow anyone whose veracity attained such fascinating or even terrifying completeness to speak to the people."

As a result, Kafka was little known in his native country until 1963, the year Marxist intellectuals from across the Eastern bloc convened a heated two-day conference in the Liblice Castle near Prague to mark what would have been the author's eightieth birthday. (Max Brod had to decline an invitation to attend for reasons of ill health, but he did come from Israel the next year to open a Kafka exhibition in the Prague Museum of Czech Literature, and once more in 1966 to present his book, *The Prague Circle*.) The symposium aimed to rehabilitate Kafka's reputation in the Soviet bloc and bring the author out of the shadows to which he had been consigned. Austrian Communist Ernst Fischer told

In his life, as in his afterlife, Kafka would often be defined with a reductive simplicity that belied the complexities of his own self-definition. In the last months of his life, Kafka wrote from Berlin to his sister Elli:

———————

the participants: "Let us get Kafka's works back from their involuntary exile! Let us grant him a permanent visa!"

Some regarded the conference as a catalyst for the short-lived Prague Spring of 1968. Gustáv Husák, Czechoslovakia's leader from 1969 to 1989, is reported to have said that the Prague Spring "began with Kafka, and it ended with counterrevolution."

"In 1968," Milan Kundera writes, "the Russians occupied my country to crush the so-called counter-revolution. Their official statements declared that the first sign of the counter-revolution in Czechoslovakia had been the rehabilitation of Kafka! Their argument may seem absurd, but it is less stupid than telling: Kafka's work had long ago come to stand for the principal values that Czech intellectuals defended against totalitarian idiocy." The West German writer Heinrich Böll witnessed a remarkable scene as Soviet tanks rolled in to suppress the Prague Spring in August 1968. "A tank stood in front of Kafka's birthplace, its cannon aimed at the bust of the author," he wrote.

The months and years after gave ample examples of the fury the Liblice conference had aroused in the Communist regime. In September 1968, the official newspaper of the ruling party in the GDR indicted the conference as "an important milestone in the growth of the influence of revisionist and bourgeois ideology." In 1970, a booklet called *Beware Zionism* was published in Czechoslovakia. It included a long essay by Yevgeni Yevseev (a pen name of Svatopluk Dolejs), editor of the anti-Semitic Prague weekly *Arijsky Boj* (The Aryan Fight) between 1941–44, and later a member of the secret police. Intertwining anti-Zionist and anti-modernist polemics, Yevseev called Kafka's writing "decadent" and substandard," and the conference "a carefully premeditated political operation of a subversive character." Finally, in 1972, a Czech Communist literary critic named František J. Kolár wrote in a Czech magazine:

> If we are to discuss the influences of Zionism on the events in Czechoslovakia in 1968—and particularly what led up to them—we must make a detailed analysis of "Kafkaism" and of the "alienation" connected with it. Those who propagate this fashionable ideology, which was deviously introduced to this country from the West, have always emphasized the Jewish and Judaic origins of Kafkaism.

Today, Prague commercializes Kafka as kitsch, puts his image on graffiti, coffee mugs, refrigerator magnets, and T-shirts in souvenir shops, and affixes his name to tourist cafés in the Old Town. Two monuments—a 12-foot-high bronze Franz Kafka Monument by Jaroslav Róna and a 36-foot-high head of Kafka with chrome-plated moving parts—offer photo ops for visitors.

Recently I had an amorous escapade. I was sitting in the sun in the Botanical Garden ... when the children from a girls' school walked by. One of the girls was a lovely long-legged blonde, boyish, who gave me a coquettish smile, turning up the corners of her little mouth and calling out something to me. Naturally I smiled back at her in an overly friendly manner, and continued to do so when she and her girlfriends kept turning back in my direction. Until I began to realize what she had actually said to me: "Jew."

We might say that this Jew was precariously suspended between impossibilities. Jewish writers, Kafka once wrote to Max Brod, "live beset by three impossibilities: the impossibility of not writing, the impossibility of writing in German, and the impossibility of writing differently. And we could add a fourth impossibility: the impossibility of writing at all." Kafka neither purposed nor proposed to untangle that knot of impossibility.

12

Laurel & Hardy

King Solomon Hotel, Tel Aviv
March 1939

K. continuously had the feeling he was losing himself or had
strayed farther into foreign parts than anyone before him, into
a foreign world in which even the air was nothing like the air
at home, in which one might suffocate on the foreignness. . . .
—Kafka, *The Castle*

J ust after Max Brod arrived in Tel Aviv, several groups came to greet
him in his temporary lodgings in the King Solomon Hotel. The first
was a delegation of Hebrew writers. One of them, sixty-three-year-old
Russian-born poet Shaul Tchernichovsky, pulled him aside. "You've
heard enough speeches for now. But maybe you're in need of a little
money?" The truth is that Brod had to live from loans until his money
transfer arrived via London, and his two "lifts"—shipments of his
books, furniture, and beloved piano—arrived from Prague.

The second group was a delegation from the flagship Habima theater (founded in Moscow in 1917, established in Tel Aviv in 1931, and
officially recognized as Israel's national theater in 1958). Habima had

attracted Brod's attention years earlier, in February 1928, with its first-rate performances in Prague of *The Dybbuk* by S. Ansky. Its representatives now offered Brod a job.

Brod was fifty-five when he arrived in Tel Aviv. In his three-piece suits, worn with a certain dated dignity, the most prominent representative of the last generation of Prague's Jewish authors cut a solitary figure on the city's boulevards. Safe in Tel Aviv but grieving for a lost world, Brod pinned on his lapel a memento of his youth: a black-red-gold ribbon from the German Student's Union where he first met Kafka. Prague, though now flooded by blind nationalism, was still in his heart, in ways both loud and voiceless.

Brod's day-to-day reality had little in common with the lofty Zionism he had espoused in Prague. He complained about the sun-scourged city's "cruel humidity," and sensed that his Central European sensibilities were at odds with Tel Aviv's literary climate. In Prague he had found it easy to make a reputation. Here he found it hard to fall into the Hebrew stride, to find a way to join the Middle East with Mitteleuropa, and so did not become a vibrant presence in Tel Aviv's literary circles. Ever the resourceful networker, Brod did meet the brightest stars in the Hebrew firmament—S. Y. Agnon, Natan Alterman, Haim Hazaz. He befriended the poet Shin Shalom and the writer Aharon Megged (a literary editor at the *Davar* newspaper). He kept in touch with Martin Buber and light-heartedly suggested Buber be appointed Israel's foreign minister. Yet like writers who lived in Israel but wrote in German (including Werner Kraft, Ilana Shmueli, Ludwig Strauss, and Schalom Ben-Horin), he did not feel plugged into the main action; he could not reprise his old role as a public intellectual. The acoustics had changed.

In one of his poems, Robert Lowell writes: "You can't carry your talent with you like a suitcase." In Prague, Brod's talent had been accustomed to acclaim. In Tel Aviv, Brod's books met by and large with indifference. Some of his historical novels, like *The Redemption of Tycho Brahe*, had appeared in Hebrew even before he came to Palestine. But none of his philosophical or religious works, which Brod considered to be the core of his writing, were translated into Hebrew. In 1942, Brod complained of this to the Israeli critic and translator Dov Sadan:

> Concerning your question why I neither had my *Paganism, Christianity, Judaism* nor my *The Miracle on Earth; or the Jewish Idea and its Realization* published in Hebrew, I can tell you that I would like nothing better than a Hebrew edition of my books! But all the attempts I have made here with Hebrew publishers have failed. It truly is not my fault but theirs!

In a 1948 letter to Shin Shalom, Brod complains of neglect at the hands of Hebrew University: "I was invited by the universities in Zürich and Basel to lecture on Kafka (an invitation the likes of which the university in Jerusalem never entertained!)" Brod complained to Shin Shalom that however warmly he was greeted as a person, as an author he was treated coolly by the Hebrew literati: "Only when I do nothing, e.g. on my 60th birthday, do people find me delightful."

Hebrew literature—then still under the Romantic spell of Y. H. Brenner and M. Y. Berdichevsky—was itself out of step with European literature, which had long put Romanticism behind it. Much later, in the mid-1960s, Jerusalem mayor Teddy Kollek appointed Brod to the jury of the Jerusalem International Book Fair Prize (together with the Hebrew poet Avraham Shlonsky and the Jewish Alsatian poet Claude Vigée). But on the whole, the Israeli republic of letters showed scant interest in Jewish writers like Brod who did not write in Hebrew. "He was a foreigner here," Aharon Appelfeld said of Brod.

It didn't help that Brod struggled with the language.* He found it easier, he reports in his memoir, to talk about the arts in Hebrew than

---

* In 1941, Brod wrote in German to Fischel Lachower, Polish-born editor at the Israeli publishing house Mossad Bialik (founded in 1935), with whom Brod was arguing about the translation and publication of his books: "Excuse me for writing in German. The Hebrew orthography is still causing me problems."

to shop for vegetables in the old-new tongue. To the end of his life, he transliterated his Hebrew into Latin characters. In a handwritten note to a Mr. Cohen in the state archives, for instance, Brod writes: "Ledaavoni hagadol, hineni assuk joter midaj. Bilti-efshari li leharzot al Kafka" (To my great regret, I am too busy. It is impossible for me to lecture on Kafka). He did the same whether he was composing little poems for Esther Hoffe's daughters or preparing notes for his Hebrew lectures. Habima's star actress Hanna Rovina, known as the "First Lady of Hebrew Theatre," approached Brod after a joint appearance in Haifa, where they read works of Stefan Zweig: "Your essay was excellent, your Hebrew is beautiful. Just one thing is disturbing: one can see your eyes moving from left to right."

But Brod refused to be remaindered by the past. Neither in Prague nor now in Tel Aviv did the self-declared "Jewish poet of the German tongue" regard Hebrew as the only adequate language for Jewish literature.

Some writers, "strangers in a strange land," are crippled by emigration and exile. Others find their true measure in the gap between "over there" and "here." Dante's *The Divine Comedy*, Voltaire's *Candide*, Victor Hugo's *Les Misérables*, and Heinrich Heine's *Germany: A Winter's Tale* (*Deutschland. Ein Wintermärchen*) were each created in exile. "A loss of harmony with the surrounding space," the Polish poet Czesław Miłosz writes in an essay called "On Exile," "the inability to feel at home in the world, so oppressive to an expatriate, a refugee, an immigrant, paradoxically integrates him in contemporary society and makes him, if he is an artist, understood by all."

Brod's prolific productivity continued unhindered in the new country. He adapted his novel *Reubeni* for the stage, and directed its premiere at Habima on June 1, 1940. He wrote a tragedy in four acts in 1942 about the biblical King Saul (a version he reworked with the poet Shin Shalom was published in 1944). Together with the composer Marc Lavry and Shin Shalom (pseudonym of Shalom Joseph Shapira), he created a two-act libretto for the first Hebrew opera in history, *Dan the*

Guard, which debuted in 1945. He authored a historical novel about the desperate love of Judas for Jesus (*Der Meister* [The Master], published in German in 1951 and in Hebrew in 1956 under the title *Achot Ketanah*). He devoted himself to writing a two-volume philosophical work (*Diesseits und Jenseits* [Here and Beyond], 1947).* He also authored the first comprehensive study of music in Israel (*Die Musik Israels*, 1951).

He wrote a regular column (called *Pinkas Katan*, or Small Ledger) on arts and culture in the Hebrew trade-union newspaper *Davar*, where he reviewed Hebrew productions of Shakespeare, and occasionally remarked on his continuing devotion to Kafka's legacy. "I wanted to establish a Kafka archive," he writes in his November 14, 1941, column, "and in addition a Friends of Franz Kafka's Work that will disseminate his writings, deepen our understanding of them, and publish his still unpublished manuscripts. None of these plans have yet come to fruition, apparently because of the war."

———

Closer to his heart, Brod accepted the position of dramaturge at Habima. His modest starting salary: 15 Palestinian pounds a month. Much of his job involved reviewing submissions and writing rejection letters. In April 1945, for instance, he writes to the theater critic and playwright Gershon K. Gershuni: "I've read your play, *Banner of the Uprising* [*Nes Ha-Mered*] with great interest, but I regret that it is impossible to produce; these terrible events are too close to us, and we don't yet have the necessary distance in time from them. For this reason, the Theater has in principle decided not to stage plays about the Warsaw Ghetto for the time being." Brod also seems to have been flooded with

---

* The second edition of *Diesseits und Jenseits* bore an epigram from Kafka: "A man cannot live without a steady faith in something indestructible within him, though both the faith and the indestructible thing may remain permanently concealed from him."

unsolicited plays on biblical themes. "After rejecting five plays named 'Moses,' ten 'King Ahabs,' and a dozen 'Ezras,' I wished to hang on my door a sign that it is preferable to read the Bible in the original than getting excited over its staged versions."

Despite the resistance of the clique that ran the theater, Brod widened its horizons in the postwar years beyond folksy plays by Jewish writers like Aharon Ashman, Sholem Aleichem, and S. Ansky. Before Brod joined the theater, Habima had only two of Shakespeare's plays in its repertoire: *The Merchant of Venice* and *As You Like It*. Now Brod invited the director Julius Gellner from London to stage Shakespeare's *A Midsummer Night's Dream* (1949) and *King Lear* (1955). British director Peter Coe directed *Julius Caesar* (1961). Tyron Guthrie, another English director, mounted Sophocles' *Oedipus Rex* (1947). Austrian-Swiss director Leopold Lindtberg put on Brecht's *Mother Courage* (1951).

"He found quite a comfortable, though not very influential, role as intermediary between local and foreign writers and the theater," writes Freddie Rokem, a professor in Tel Aviv University's Department of Theatre Arts. "My decision to work at Habima was absolutely right," Brod records in his memoir. "Even in times of acute crises at the leading Hebrew theater, I never entertained any doubts about that decision. I always remained faithful with Habima and she with me."

Whether the theater reciprocated his loyalty is another question. In Eva Hoffe's view, Habima took advantage of Brod's international connections but never accorded him the recognition he deserved. He was never granted voting rights, for example, in the collective that decided which plays to stage, and his recommendations were sometimes overruled. "He was so disappointed in this country," Eva said. "He had tremendous expectations when he arrived here, and what a slap in the face he got." Another sign of neglect may be read in the fate of Brod's Habima archives. When plays were submitted to Habima, Brod wrote readers reports on note cards in which he registered his opinion (in German) on whether the theater should produce them. During renovations after Brod's death, Habima apparently threw out Brod's archive of nearly four hundred of these boxed notecards (what the Germans call *Zettelkasten*). Long believed lost, they were rediscovered in late 2016 by Professor Tom Lewy of Tel Aviv University. Lewy told me that Shimon Lev-Ari, a Romanian-born actor, historian of Hebrew theater, and the founder of the Israeli Center for the Documentation of the Performing Arts at Tel Aviv University, stopped the truck carting the archive to the dump and salvaged Brod's cards. They had all along lay dormant in unlabeled boxes at Tel Aviv University.

At a dinner party I joined one evening in Jerusalem, a German graduate student at Hebrew University suggested that the Marbach archivists would take better care of the Brod estate than the National Library. I asked him why. In 2013, he said, he chanced across a remarkable volume on the discarded books rack of the Hebrew University library on Mt. Scopus: Max Brod's own copy (*Handexemplar*, as the Germans call it) of his Heinrich Heine biography (1934). Inside, the astonished student found more than a hundred comments, corrections, and emendations in Brod's own hand. The librarian could not tell him why the book had been discarded. Another guest added that in 2014 he had spotted first editions of several of Brod's novels on the equivalent rack of decommissioned volumes at the National Library.

———

Ever faithful to his promise of promoting the memory of Kafka in the new country, Brod worked two days a week at the theater, and the rest on editing, transcribing, and publishing Kafka's manuscripts. So much so that Brod's name came in these years to be invariably invoked in the same breath as Kafka's. "In the eyes of the world," the New York literary critic Irving Howe wrote in 1947, "he has become a mere figure in the Kafka myth; he has lost independent existence."

In a letter to Salman Schocken, dated February 22, 1951, Brod writes: "My most urgent wish is to see the German biography I wrote about

Kafka distributed in Germany." Once in Tel Aviv, Brod added to his biography of Kafka three studies on Kafka, each written in German. The Czech writer Milan Kundera called the trilogy, which Brod fired off in rapid succession, "a veritable artillery attack."

The Israeli writer Aharon Appelfeld remembers an evening in which Brod arrived from Tel Aviv to address a study group in the Rehavia neighborhood of Jerusalem. Brod, Appelfeld says,

> argued that Kafka was a Jewish writer not only because his parents and his close friends were Jewish; and not only because he had deep yearnings toward Jewish creativity, a feeling for Yiddish, for poetry and theater in Yiddish, for the Hebrew language and for Jewish thinking, but beyond all this—he should be regarded as a Jewish writer because of the very essence of his work. After all, who was that person in *The Trial*, the person who stood accused, but had committed no crime—the person in the grip of anxiety, shunted back and forth between different courtrooms—who was this person, if not the persecuted Jew?

The young country's academic establishment, meanwhile, frowned on Brod's portrayal of Kafka as a modern saint. Prominent literary critic Baruch Kurzweil (1907–1972) of Bar-Ilan University censured Brod for "pseudo-religious readings of Kafka" that sought to turn the author "into a prophet of redemption and Zionism." Against Brod, Kurzweil claimed that Kafka "is a Jew for whom Judaism is meaningless." Gershom Scholem, then a formidable figure at Hebrew University, joined his friend Walter Benjamin in dismissing Brod's 1937 biography of Kafka as vacuous and sentimental hagiography, its authority undermined by Brod's dilettantish lack of detachment and smug middle-brow banality. Benjamin, a student of Kafka's works since the mid-1920s, had felt close affinities to their author. "His [Kafka's] friendship with Brod," Benjamin wrote to Scholem, "is to me above all else a question mark which he chose to ink in the margin of his life."

But then he gropes toward an answer. "Concerning friendship with Brod," Benjamin wrote to Scholem in 1939, "I think I am on the track of the truth when I say: Kafka as Laurel felt the onerous obligation to seek out his own Hardy." Kafka's fate, Benjamin added, "was to keep stumbling upon people who made humor their profession: clowns."

———

Despite his difficulties with his adopted country's language, literary climate, and cultural establishment, Brod explained to his old friend Hans-Joachim Schoeps (1909–1980), returning to Europe after the cataclysm was unthinkable. Schoeps was a German-Jewish historian of religion who had published several important essays during the 1930s on Kafka's Jewish-theological significance. He had briefly collaborated with Brod on editing the first posthumous collection of Kafka's short stories (*Beim Bau der chinesischen Mauer*, 1931). Although they agreed on reading Kafka's work in light of Jewish theology, they had parted ways over the question of Zionism. In August 1932, Schoeps wrote to Brod:

> And when it comes to Zionism, it is utterly impossible for us to come to an agreement. The experiential substance that one must possess in order to become a Zionist has never been granted me, and everything that has to do with national rootedness [*völkische Verwurzelung*] is foreign to me.... I have great reason to doubt that Zionism represents an objective return to Judaism. In fact, I see it as nothing else but a late-blooming of West-European imperialism, a product of the Occident's secularized realm of thought. Zionism is not a religious movement. Its conception of the Jewish people secularizes all that is religious, and turns the people of God into a worldly people, thereby distorting the Jewish reality.

Brod's reply was swift:

> I greatly regret that our differences are so great that they make it impossible for me to preserve the good feelings I had for you at the beginning. As far as Kafka is concerned, I ask that you return the manuscripts that are still in your possession. I plan to publish all of Kafka's works with Schocken Press. I can assure you that the new edition will acknowledge all of the editorial work you have undertaken up to this point.

A Prussian patriot, Schoeps had survived the war years in Sweden. Though his mother was murdered in Auschwitz and his father in Theresienstadt, Schoeps returned to Germany in 1945 to teach theology at the University of Erlangen. In June 1946, Brod wrote to Schoeps:

> It is the greatest crime in human history that the German nation a) let this murderous gang come to power, and b) put millions of collaborators at their service. This crime can never be atoned; it reached metaphysical depths. So I do not comprehend how you could have a desire to live and teach among that accursed nation [*verruchten Volk*].

A month earlier, on May 15, 1948, the armies of Iraq, Egypt, Jordan, and Syria invaded the state David Ben-Gurion had just declared. The outbreak of Israel's War of Independence caught Brod in Genoa; he was on his way back from Switzerland, his first return to Europe since fleeing in 1939. Fearful of imminent invasion and "annihilation" by Arab forces, he sent a plea to the writer Hermann Hesse on May 22. Brod asked the Nobel laureate, almost seventy-one at the time, to use his international reputation to "raise your voice in this tragic hour of Jewish history," and "wake the conscience of mankind from its deep slumber." Brod added that the war imperiled not just people, but also cultural treasures like Kafka's manuscripts. Three days later, Hesse replied from

Switzerland. He rebuffed Brod's call for help, "beautiful and noble" though it may be.*

In the months during and after Israel's War of Independence, Brod channeled his anxieties into a novel called *Unambo* (published in German in 1949 and in English in 1952). In the novel, a strange-looking "fat man" offers the amiable protagonist Helfin (or helper) a Faustian bargain: by means of a "doubling machine," he can live two lives at the same time, "equally present" in each: as a pioneer and soldier in Palestine, and as a film producer in Europe. (Brod took the novel's title, and the name of the contraption, from the words *uno*—one, and *ambo*—both.) Helfin is spared the either-or choice that his author had to make.†

Brod chose Tel Aviv. In July 1948, Brod wrote to Walter Berendsohn (1884–1984), a German-Jewish literary critic living in exile in Stockholm, and an old friend: "It is a good thing that we have to stand now on our feet and need no longer hanker after the judgment of others about Jewish character, Jewish peculiarities."

———

However little recognition Brod gained in the new country, in 1948, a decade after his arrival, he was awarded the annual Bialik Prize. Named for the poet H. N. Bialik, this was the first Hebrew literature prize and the country's most prestigious literary accolade. To be precise, the award

---

* "I consider every would-be intellectual action . . . on the part of intellectuals vis-à-vis the masters of the earth to be wrong, a further damaging and degrading of the spirit. . . . It is not for us either to preach or to command or to beg, but to stand steadfast in the thick of hell."

† *Unambo* came out to mixed reviews. "Whoever would see the new Israel in the light of both the criticism and longing of the old, departing Europe," Herbert Howarth wrote in his review in *Commentary*, "may see it best through this book." The *New York Times* reviewer noted the novel's "pleading of Israel's cause" and heard in it "a heavy and steady propagandist note."

recognized not Brod but his eight-hundred-page historical novel, *Galileo in Shackles*. According to the jury, "The whole book is permeated with the original Jewish spirit and eternal ideals of the people of Israel." The book was translated from the German into Hebrew by Dov Sadan (1902–1989), then a member of the editorial board at the Am Oved publishing house, later a Member of Knesset who himself would be awarded the Bialik Prize decades later (1980).

The awards ceremony took place on January 11, 1949, in the ornate ground-floor reception room of Bialik's former house in Tel Aviv. The room's walls were painted in royal blue, and its columns were tiled with colorful cartouches depicting the twelve tribes of Israel. The German-born actress Orna Porat, at twenty-four already a rising star of the Cameri Theater, opened the evening with a reading of excerpts of Bialik's essay "The Hebrew Book." Then Brod spoke:

> I told a friend that today is a great holiday for me; I have the impression that thanks to the Bialik Prize I've now been accepted into the family of Hebrew writers—and there is nothing in the world I value more highly than this honor. Tonight I'm given the opportunity to apply to myself the biblical verse "I dwell among my own people" [2 Kings 4:13]. . . . I dedicate this book, a book on the freedom of thought, which I have written as one of the "sons who have returned to their homeland," to my people, who are in these very days fighting for their full freedom.

The family of Hebrew writers, it turns out, did not unanimously gratify Brod's hopes of acceptance. Eight days after the awards ceremony, David Shimoni, head of the Hebrew Writers Association and later chairman of the Academy of Hebrew Language (and Bialik Prize winner the next year) registered a protest: a work written in German should under no circumstances be eligible for a prize reserved for genuine Hebrew literature, he said. Shimoni and the members of his association treated *Galileo* more as a corpus delicti than as a worthy novel.

Although Shimoni's polemics avoided ad hominem attacks on Brod, a public controversy ensued. In February, a translator named Isaac Loeb Baruch (Brocowitz) (1874–1953) took to the pages of the right-wing daily *Herut* to explain why he was scandalized. Baruch dismissed Sadan's translation of the novel from the German as "linguistic garbage." He worried that if Brod's award were allowed to stand, a slippery slope would lead to the appalling spectacle, before too long, of a Yiddish-speaking author claiming the prize.

To be sure, some defended Brod's award and took the episode as a study in the possibility of Jewish writing in a non-Jewish language. They argued for opening the Bialik Prize to all languages in order to infuse new blood into a Hebrew literature that some believed had curdled into provincial conformity.

But the damage had been done. Brod never commented publicly on the controversy, and conspicuously failed to mention the prize in his memoir.

———

For the next decade or so after the Bialik Prize episode, Brod and Esther Hoffe would take Dakota twin-engine planes from Tel Aviv to Germany, where Brod would speak to packed halls of German students. He would lecture either on Kafka (as he did in Berlin in 1954, on the thirtieth anniversary of Kafka's death), or on the importance of distinguishing German culture and language from the crimes of the Third Reich. He related how, in the years when he had unquestioningly seen himself as part of German literature, he had been moved to gratitude for the poetry of Goethe and Hölderlin. Again and again, he asked the young people, who still remembered the war years, to understand the difference between Nazism and Germanness (*Deutschtum*), and to see that German culture ought not be held responsible for Nazi crimes.

In 1964, during an interview for the newspaper *Maariv* on the occasion of Brod's eightieth birthday, the journalist Refael Bashan raised the subject again.

"Most of your books appear first in Germany, you go on lecture tours in Germany, you appear there on radio and television. Do you believe in a 'different Germany'?"

"Sir," Brod replies, "I have a special reckoning with Germany. For my fiftieth birthday, the Minister of Propaganda Joseph Goebbels presented me with a gift: an official manifesto calling for my books to be put on the pyre!*.... The Germans also murdered my beloved brother, Dr. Otto Brod.... So what can I tell you? That I don't know the Germans? But I also found decent ones among them, and if a German is decent then he is very decent!"

For the rest of his life, Brod used his writing to withdraw to familiar territory. He wrote forewords and afterwords to Hebrew editions of Heinrich von Kleist, Oskar Baum, and others, acting as a gatekeeper for reception of German-language authors in Israel. His adaptation of Kafka's novel *The Castle* for stage (translated by A. D. Shaphir) was performed at the Cameri Theater in Tel Aviv in 1954 (directed by Leopold Lindtberg, and starring Orna Porat and Michael Shilo). (Eva Hoffe told me that Brod was hurt that his own Habima theater declined to produce the play, which was "an unforgettable success," she said.)† Content to love at a distance, he revisited the carefree days of his youth in novels like *Jugend im Nebel* (Youth in the Fog, 1959), which Brod called "the story of my awakening," and *Die Rosenkoralle* (The Red Coral, 1961), about his gymnasium years. He spent the early 1960s writing *Der Prager*

---

* According to the U.S. Holocaust Museum, all of Brod's works except *The Redemption of Tycho Brahe* (*Tycho Brahes Weg zu Gott*) were burned in Nazi book burnings. "Although Max Brod's work might well have been banned from German libraries on racial grounds," the Czech-Jewish educator Max Lederer noted in 1944, "it exhibited in its pacifist tendencies another quality equally odious to the Nazi regime."

† Brod's dramatic adaptation of *The Castle*, translated by James Clark and produced by the Royal Academy of Dramatic Arts, premiered in London's Vanbrugh Theatre in June 1963.

Kreis (The Prague Circle), a semiautobiographical portrait of the writers (including Felix Weltsch, Hugo Bergmann, and Franz Werfel) who made the city on the Moldau a cultural mecca in the waning years of the Habsburg Empire. In the attempt to replicate such a circle in Tel Aviv, he continued to participate in a literary salon for German-speaking Jews hosted by his sister-in-law Nadja Taussig in her home on Mapu Street. (Some seventy letters Brod sent to Taussig were put up for sale by the Kedem Auction House in Jerusalem in March 2018.)

All the while, Brod was pursued by a deep need to be understood in Israel. In that 1964 *Maariv* interview, Brod was asked about his plans. "Plans? What plans can a man of eighty entertain? I dream that my autobiography, which has already appeared throughout the world, will be translated into Hebrew as well. That is my great dream. I so wish that Israeli youth would get to know me a bit more!"*

---

* Brod's memoir, *A Contentious Life*, came out in German in 1964, with the same publishing house that brought out the German translation of *Exodus*, the bestseller by Leon Uris. It would be published in Hebrew three years later, just before Brod's death. (*Chayei Meriva*, trans. Yosef Selee, Ha-Sifriya Ha-Tzionit, 1967.) Born in Stopnica, Poland, the translator Selee emigrated to Palestine in 1933, and published a collection of essays under the title *Max Brod: Iyyunim Bemishnato* [Max Brod: Studies in his Thought], Am Ha-Sefer, 1971.

Max Brod (right) with actors at the Habima Theater, Tel Aviv.
(Israel Government Press Office)

Max Brod (seated far right) with actors at the Habima Theater, Tel Aviv,
March 1942. (Zoltan Kruger, Israel Government Press Office)

13

Brod's Last Love

Max Brod's apartment, HaYarden Street 16, Tel Aviv
April 2, 1952

> Amalia smiled, and this smile, even though it was sad, illumi-
> nated her grimly drawn face, made her silence speak, made the
> foreignness familiar . . .
>
> —Kafka, *The Castle*

In 1942, Max Brod was devastated by three losses. In late February, he learned of the suicide of his old friend Stefan Zweig in Brazil. The news brought home to Brod the magnitude of the cultural catastrophe being visited on Jewish exiles not fortunate enough to have made it to Palestine. In his book *Prophets without Honor*, Frederic V. Grunfeld, who fled from Germany to New York with his family in 1938, asks his readers to imagine

> that T. S. Eliot had died in exile in Peru; that the aged Bernard
> Shaw committed suicide on a ship to South America; that Hem-
> ingway and Fitzgerald, as well as Rodgers and Hammerstein, had
> been compelled to live out their last days in a small community

in Guatemala . . . that William Faulkner had learned Spanish in order to teach in a school in Caracas. . . .

That imaginative exercise gives us some idea of Brod's devastation as he witnessed the land of Goethe and Schiller banishing his Jewish colleagues (no matter how vital their contributions to German culture) and scattering the last upholders of Central European humanism to the four corners of the earth.

Nearly a decade earlier, in March 1933, another literary refugee, the Austrian-Jewish novelist Joseph Roth, had written to his patron Stefan Zweig: "We stem from the 'Emancipation,' from Humanity, from the humane rather than from Egypt. Our ancestors are Goethe, Lessing, Herder, no less than Abraham, Isaac and Jacob." Roth died six years later in squalid exile in Paris, just after learning that the playwright Ernst Toller had hanged himself in New York. Brod, who had published Roth's essays in the *Prager Tagblatt* and put him in contact with the Paul Zsolnay publishing house, was burdened by their fates, too.

A second loss of 1942: in August of that year, Brod's wife, Elsa, died in Tel Aviv a day short of her fifty-ninth birthday. Elsa and Max had been married twenty-nine years. Even in Prague, the marriage had been beset by Brod's womanizing. Kafka biographer Ernst Pawel writes that Brod was "formally married and informally promiscuous." Brod had often confessed his extramarital adventures to Kafka—with a married woman in Brno, and with a Catholic chambermaid named Emmy Salveter (later an actress under the name Aenne Markgraf) in Berlin. Kafka took up the role of a tactful marriage counselor when the affairs threatened Brod's marriage.

Later that year, Brod suffered "the most tragic" of his disappointments, as he wrote to his close friend Shin Shalom: an aspiring, Czech-born Habima actress, Ella Berglass (Shalom described her as "stunningly beautiful"), had ended their affair without warning.* Brod

---

* Berglass, fictionalized in *Unambo*, also contributed stories in the 1940s to *Gazit*, a magazine of arts and literature. At Brod's funeral in December 1968, Berglass remorse-

feared she had used him to advance her career, and called her "egoistic and calculating." So strong was his hatred for her that Brod made Shalom promise never again to see her, even after Brod's death.

Brod was thrown into a turmoil of the spirit.

> A long-lasting and deep-churning revolution went on in me, particularly since the death of my wife. The great question, "Is the soul immortal?" . . . screamed for an answer. After the end of the war, when I received the news that my brother and his family had been killed in Auschwitz, another equally old question emerged with the same urgency: "How is the suffering of the world compatible with belief in an all-powerful, all-good God?"

Brod would find some measure of consolation from an unlikely direction. Kafka's uncanny presence, and his manuscripts, would bring him together with a woman twenty-two years his junior. She would serve as his secretary and intimate friend for twenty-six years.

———

Ilse Hoffe was born in 1906 to Josef (b. 1874) and Hedwig Reich (b. 1876) in Opava (Troppau, in German). Opava was the capital of Czech Silesia, but also a center of a brand of "greater Germany" anti-Semitism led by the far-right politician Georg Ritter von Schönerer. Soon after the birth of their two daughters, Ilse and Marion, the Reichs moved to Havlíčkovo Square in Prague's hilly working-class Žižkov district, a twenty-five-minute walk from the cemetery where Kafka would be buried in 1924. It was here that Ilse met her husband-to-be, Otto Hoffe.

Otto, twenty-one years older than Ilse, was born in Myslkovice

---

fully confessed to Shin Shalom "how deep and pure her love for Max Brod had been all these years."

(Miskowitz, in German), a village 170 miles west of Opava and today an hour-and-a-half drive south of Prague. Orphaned at age fourteen, Otto was taken in by the family of the Czech-Jewish industrialist Jindřich Waldes. After the marriage in 1930, Otto found work as a manager at the Koh-i-noor Company factory in the Vršovice district of Prague, founded by Waldes. In the early 1930s, he and Ilse had two children—Ruth and Eva. (After the war, members of the Waldes family who had escaped to America ensured that Otto received a pension.)

In early 1940, at Ilse's strenuous urging, the Hoffe family obtained permission from the German occupation authorities to take a two-week holiday to Germany. On the eve of departure, Gestapo men searched the apartment to verify that the Hoffes had packed only for a holiday. On the night train to Germany, Ilse and Otto did not tell their daughters that they would never be coming back to Prague. Eva says she remembers humming songs to herself to the gentle rhythms of the train.*

From Germany, the Hoffes fled to Vichy France. Otto was detained in an internment camp outside of Paris. Eva and Ruth found refuge in Villard-de-Lans, a town near Grenoble. For several months, Ilse shuttled back and forth, desperate both to protect her girls and to free her husband. At last, with help from relatives in the United States, Ilse obtained certificates permitting transit to Palestine. They purchased tickets from "Messageries maritimes" shipping company and took a French ocean liner, the SS *Patria*, from Marseilles to Haifa.

Eva told me that Otto Hoffe never uttered a word about his internment. "He hemmed himself into silence," she said. Ilse, radiant in public, would liberally scatter laughter around her. ("If she were to walk in to this café, all heads would turn," Eva told me.) But she bore the pangs

---

* Marion Reich, Ilse's sister, meanwhile fled to Rome, where she was taken in by a community of Catholics, and converted to Catholicism. After the war, Marion returned to Prague and was jailed by the Communist regime. With the help of Max Brod, she was released, and spent the rest of her life, until her death in 1977, in the convent of the Sisters of Our Lady of Zion (Notre Dame de Sion) in Ein Karem, Jerusalem.

of displacement in private. Eva remembers her mother pounding on the walls of their apartment in Tel Aviv, as if they could absorb her pain.

Once safe in Palestine, the Hoffes lived in a cramped three-room apartment on Tel Aviv's Spinoza Street shared with two other families. Otto found work as an accountant at a factory in nearby Ramat Gan that made dyes for clothing, his cubicle surrounded by boiling vats.

In 1942, Otto enrolled in an introductory Hebrew-language class, or *ulpan*, where he met a fellow émigré from Prague named Max Brod. Several days later, Otto introduced Brod to his wife Ilse. In their first conversation, Brod told Ilse that he had known her mother, Hedwig Reich, in Prague. A decade earlier, they had volunteered together on a campaign to offer help to the economically devastated region of the Ore Mountains (Erzgebirge) on the border between Saxony and Bohemia.

The three refugees found in one another what they could not find in their new environment. "My parents and Max were not Israelis," Eva tells me. "They didn't understand Israeli culture. They were internationalists in their ways of thinking." Brod, recovering from the death of his wife, Elsa, and the loss of his mistress Ella, began to join the Hoffes for Shabbat dinners. At their home, Brod's friend Shin Shalom said, "he at last found his familial nest." Brod invited the Hoffes for classical concerts at the Israel Philharmonic and opening nights at the Habima theater, and they invited Brod to come over and listen to the radio.

In December 1958, the pianist Glenn Gould gave a recital in Tel Aviv. Afterwards, he recalled, Brod

came backstage with an elderly lady, whom I took to be his secretary, and made a few nice sounds, and the lady in question, whose name I didn't catch, came up to me and in a rather heavy German accent said ... [conspiratorial half-whisper], "Mr. Gould, ve haf attended already several of your pairformances in Tel Aviv, but tonight's, zis was somehow, in some vay, somesing vas different, you vere not qvite one of us, you vere—you vere—your being was *removed*." And I bowed deeply and said, "Thank you, madam," realizing of course that she had in fact put her finger on something that was too spooky to talk about even, and I realized that with her obviously limited English there was no way I could convey what I'd really done.

Before long, Brod and the Hoffes were summering together in Flims, a Swiss spa town. "The only time my father laughed was when he was with his best friend Max," Eva told me.

The Hoffe girls, Eva and Ruthie, loved Brod, who had no children of his own, like "a second father," Eva said. (Childlessness runs like an undercurrent through this story: Kafka, Brod, Eva Hoffe.) Brod bought Eva her first piano. He would take Eva to classical concerts and put the score on their laps and show her the place with his finger. "Your musical ear is better even than mine," Brod once told Eva. He would send young Eva as his courier to Shimon Finkel, actor and artistic director of the theater (the first actor to play *Hamlet* on an Israeli stage). "Brod was her mentor, he was the person who interpreted the world for her," Eva's longtime friend Yoella Har-Shefi told *Haaretz* during the trial. "Her identification with him is total. Her actions over the years stem from her perception as the one who inherited her mother's authority. She is completely pure of heart in this matter. It's all about her soul, not her pocket." Yoella told me: "Eva is the most altruistic person I've ever known."

It was at Brod's suggestion that Ilse Hoffe took the Hebrew name Esther, and it was at his urging that Esther agreed to help him transcribe and organize the papers he had rescued from their hometown in his suitcase. He sensed that she could understand how the manuscripts served as the slackened cord that threaded together his present to the bygone world of his own former life.

Each morning, Esther Hoffe would come to his apartment on the third floor of a modest four-story walk-up building at HaYarden Street 16, two blocks from the beach. She would bring a paper bag of croissants when she arrived, and would heat the samovar before she left in the afternoon. Because he was growing hard of hearing, Brod relied on

Esther to repeat things he hadn't heard on the telephone. In his memoir, Brod calls Esther "my creative partner, my most stringent critic, my help-mate and ally," to whom he felt "infinitely indebted." To his friend Shin Shalom, Brod remarked that she had burst into his life "like a rescuing angel." (On some of Brod's letters to Shalom, Esther added postscripts at the bottom margin in German or in Hebrew: "Greetings and best wishes from me too. –Esther." Sometimes they jointly signed: "Esther und Max.")

Esther, in turn, grew fiercely protective of him. With Brod's encouragement and guidance, she published a slim forty-eight-page book of poems in German, *Gedichte aus Israel* (Poems from Israel). "They were a threesome," Eva recalls, though she insists that her mother's love for Brod "wasn't carnal, it was spiritual."

Kafka's manuscripts, which so vitally linked Brod to his former heyday in Prague, now began to link Brod with Esther—the currency of their relationship. According to Eva, Esther received no regular salary for her years of work with Brod. Instead, Brod formally gave all his Kafka papers to Esther.

———

One morning in the spring of 1952, after a decade of close friendship and collaboration, Max Brod invited Esther Hoffe into his book-lined study. She watched as he took a sheet of stationery from the drawer and put pen to paper. Brod wanted to express his wishes regarding the fate of Kafka's manuscripts in gift letters, and not just in his last will and testament.

"Dear Esther, In 1945 I gifted you all the Kafka manuscripts and letters in my possession."

Brod specified that the gift—intended to take effect immediately, not after his death—included: Kafka's letters to Brod and his late wife, Elsa; Kafka's original manuscripts of *The Trial*, "Description of a Struggle," and "Preparations for a Village Wedding"; Kafka's original typescript of his letter to his father; three notebooks of Kafka's Paris diaries; a draft of *Richard and Samuel*, a novel that Kafka and Brod had started to write together in Prague; Kafka's speech on Yiddish; aphorisms; a draft of a novella; photographs; and first editions of Kafka's publications. Brod added that he and Esther "jointly" deposited this material in a safe in 1948.

In the margin, Esther Hoffe wrote in German: "I hereby accept this gift" (*"Ich nehme dieses Geschenk an"*).

Brod wished to leave no doubts. Five years earlier, on April 22, 1947, Brod had signed another note:

"Kafka's letters addressed to me, which all belonged to me, are the property of Mrs. Hoffe."

Some sixty years later, Amnon Bezaleli, a court-appointed handwriting expert, would examine Brod's promissory notes and declare them authentic. (In 1987, as head of the Israeli police document identification laboratory, Bezaleli had verified the key piece of evidence in the Israeli prosecution of alleged concentration-camp guard John Demjanjuk— "Ivan the Terrible.") To some, the very existence of these notes came as a surprise. "Neither I nor my mother were aware of any such letters being produced until long after the Israeli litigation commenced," says Michael Steiner, son of Kafka's niece.

———

In December 1968, as Brod lay dying in Beilinson hospital, Esther and Eva took turns staying at Brod's bedside—Esther from 7 a.m. to 7 p.m., and Eva from 7 p.m. to 7 a.m. The hospital, located in the Petach Tikva suburb of Tel Aviv, was named for the director of Israel's General Health Fund and founding publisher of the newspaper *Davar*, where Brod had published his columns. It was a 45-minute bus ride each way from the Hoffe's home on Spinoza Street.

During one of his last nights, Eva said she arrived to find that nurses had put Brod's wrists in restraints to prevent him from plucking out his intravenous tubes. "If ever you loved me," she recalls Brod saying, "untie me." She did, and she held his hand as his chin drooped to his chest and he drifted to sleep.

Max Brod died on December 20, 1968. He once remarked to Esther that he would not like to live longer than Goethe, who died in his eighty-third year. Brod passed away a few weeks before he reached the age of eighty-five. He worked to the end—on a foreword to the English edition of his philosophical treatise, *Paganism, Christianity, Judaism*, and on an expanded second edition of his memoir, *A Contentious Life*. A month earlier, he had written to his old friend Robert Weltsch: "One must always to begin anew" (*man muss immer von vorn anfangen*).

Few mourners attended Brod's funeral in Tel Aviv's Trumpeldor cemetery, the final resting place of H. N. Bialik, Israel's national poet, and Ahad Ha'am, the visionary of cultural Zionism. To this day, Eva pays her respects at his grave twice a year: on his birthday in May and on the anniversary of his death in December.

In his first will, dated March 24, 1948, Brod named Esther Hoffe as his sole heir and executor, and expressed his desire that she should arrange to give his literary estate "to a public Jewish library or archive in Palestine." He did not mention Kafka's manuscripts.

In his last will, dated June 7, 1961 (written in German, and translated into Hebrew by his lawyer Simon Fritz Haas), Brod gave two instructions: On the one hand, he appointed Esther Hoffe as sole executor of his estate and bequeathed to her all his possessions. On the other, in paragraph 11 he instructed that after her death his literary estate should be placed "with the library of the Hebrew University of Jerusalem, the Municipal Library in Tel Aviv, or another public archive in Israel or abroad. . . . Mrs. Hoffe will determine which of these institutions will be chosen, and under which conditions." The paragraph does not mention Kafka's manuscripts. (Kafka biographer Reiner Stach calls Brod's last will—giving Esther the right to do with the estate as she wished but at the same time obligating her heirs to transfer the estate intact to a proper archive—"inadvisably vague.") As for the personal correspondence between Brod and Hoffe, Brod instructed in paragraph 13 of his will that these were not to be published until fifty years had elapsed from the death of whichever of them passes away last, unless Esther Hoffe decided otherwise.

On April 22, 1969, the Tel Aviv District Court granted probate to Brod's last will, and appointed Esther Hoffe as executor of his estate. The manuscripts Brod had rescued from Prague she now guarded in the home on Spinoza Street she shared with her daughter Eva, and in ten safe deposit boxes: six in a bank in Tel Aviv, and four at a UBS bank in Zürich, Switzerland. Thanks to Brod, Esther Hoffe literally and figuratively held the keys to part of the legacy of Kafka, a man who once described himself as "locked away within himself with a strange key."

———

In 1973, five years after Brod's death, the State of Israel, concerned about the prospect that Esther might sell Kafka's manuscripts abroad, sued for their possession. The case (mentioned earlier) was brought before Judge Yitzhak Shilo of the Tel Aviv District Court.

Kafka's niece Marianna Steiner, invited to take part in the 1973 trial, declined the chance to contest Hoffe's control of the manuscripts. Marianna's son, Michael Steiner, now the executor of the Kafka estate, seventy-nine at the time of this writing, wrote to me from London to explain why:

> My mother was approached in 1973 for assistance by the Attorney General for Israel and was in fact served by post with a summons to appear in the proceedings against Mrs. [Esther] Hoffe. My mother understood that the litigation concerned the construction

of Brod's will, as to which we considered she had no locus and no views, and my mother was unwilling to incur the potentially heavy costs in appearing by legal advisers in the proceedings. An equally powerful factor was her desire to facilitate access by scholars to any manuscripts held by Mrs. Hoffe and her consequent reluctance to adopt any adversarial position in the proceedings between the Attorney General and Mrs. Hoffe. My mother did not at that time have any inventory of what manuscripts were held by Mrs. Hoffe and assumed that they consisted only of those which Max Brod had claimed had been given to him by Franz Kafka in the latter's lifetime and which had been so asserted by Brod in a letter he wrote to my mother in April 1952.

In the end, the state's petition was rejected on January 13, 1974. Judge Shilo ruled that Brod's last will "allows Mrs. Hoffe to do with his estate as she pleases during her lifetime . . . The instructions to that end are clear, it does not seem to me that they can admit of a different interpretation."

According to Michael Steiner, "In 2010, I was approached by the National Library for information and it was mooted that the Kafka Estate might wish to be joined in the litigation that was in prospect. I was not able to understand how, after so many years, the construction of Max Brod's will determined by Judge Shilo could be relitigated."

On February 8, 1974, Paul Alsberg, a German Jew who served as Israel's state archivist from 1971–1990, wrote to Esther Hoffe in support of the ruling:

> I acknowledge that the Kafka manuscripts are not part of the inheritance of the writer Max Brod, but rather were given to you as a gift many years before his passing. I have therefore listed the Kafka manuscripts in the archive registry as private property.

Alsberg alluded to a crucial distinction between a gift (an asset received from a living person) and an inheritance (or bequest) received posthumously. Property acquired by way of gift is not subject to any future inheritance disputes.

The state chose not to appeal Judge Shilo's verdict, but authorities kept a watchful eye on Esther Hoffe. The Israeli Archives Law of 1955 stipulates that the state archivist can prevent the removal from Israel of privately owned records that are of "national" value and "which, irrespective of where they are found, are deemed relevant to the study of the nation's history, its people, the state, and society." The law also makes it a criminal offense to remove archival material from the country without the permission of the state archivist. On July 23, 1974, Esther was detained at Tel Aviv's airport under suspicion of attempting to smuggle handwritten documents abroad. A search of her luggage revealed six envelopes with photocopies of Kafka letters, but no originals.

At the time, a joke circulated in certain Israeli circles: What's the worst thing you can say when a security agent at the Tel Aviv airport asks whether you have packed your suitcase by yourself? "No, Esther Hoffe helped me."

On January 14, 1975, Hoffe signed an agreement with the state archivist: she was permitted to remove archival material from Israel if she allowed the state archivist to review the material and copy it at his discretion. The state, for its part, undertook not to make the material accessible for a period of fifty years without the express consent of Hoffe or her heirs.

During the first stage of the trial at the Tel Aviv Family Court, attorney Shmulik Cassouto had noted that the National Library, which was not party to the trial before Judge Shilo in 1973, could not explain why it had waited forty years to contest Hoffe's ownership of manuscripts given to her by Brod. Legally, the library was within its rights. Section 72 of Israel's succession law allows an interested party to apply to the registrar to ask for the amendment of a probate order given on the basis of facts or claims that have come to light since the time of the order.

This is true even for a party which did not participate in the discussion of the original probate order.

Yet Cassouto argued that the National Library had brought no new facts beyond those brought before Judge Shilo in 1973. Further, the National Library had brought its claims as part of its challenge of Esther Hoffe's will, rather than in the proper context: a challenge to *Brod's* will. Rather than directly challenging Judge Shilo's interpretation of that will, the library waited for Esther's death to submit an objection to the order for the fulfillment of her will. Yet the claims rejected by Shilo cannot now be accepted forty years later, Cassouto argued. "If the National Library was of the opinion that it has a right to get Kafka's manuscripts 'for free,' as it claims today, what prevented it from making such a claim in the 1970s?" Cassouto asked. "That it did not do so speaks for itself, and it must not be permitted now to revise a probate forty years after the fact." Cassouto suggested that the National Library had waited until neither Brod nor Hoffe could speak for themselves. "Now that the principal actors have passed away, it is all too easy for the National Library to infringe on the boundaries of imagination and claim itself as Dr. Brod's true heir."

14

The Last Heiress: Selling Kafka

Sotheby's, New Bond Street, London
November 17, 1988

Kafka did not know [Esther] Hoffe, never conversed with her, and never met her. She was not dear to his heart. There was no familial relationship. He did not know her daughters. Kafka and Hoffe lived and died in different countries. . . . Consider from Kafka's perspective the sale of his personal writings—the very writings he instructed to be destroyed—at public auction to the highest bidder by the secretary of his friend and by her daughters. Would this accord with justice?
—Tel Aviv District Court ruling, June 2015

Is someone who receives a Picasso as an inheritance and wants to sell it prohibited from doing so because he didn't know Picasso?
—Eva Hoffe, February 2017

On November 17, 1988, two decades after Max Brod's death, Esther Hoffe put the 316-page original 1914 manuscript of Kafka's *The Trial* up for auction at Sotheby's in the heart of London's Mayfair district. Kafka had written it in ten different notebooks shortly after breaking off his first engagement to Felice Bauer. In September 1914, he had read the first chapter to Brod. On deciding that the novel had failed, he ripped out the pages from the notebooks and kept them in his desk in sixteen bundles of loose sheets. In 1920, he gave them to Brod, and Brod had given them in turn to Esther.

The decision to auction *The Trial* "was a very dangerous move," said Mark Anderson, a leading Kafka scholar at Columbia University. "It could have disappeared into the safe of an internet billionaire, or a Japanese banker who had a wine collection and wanted to have a Kafka manuscript. It could have disappeared forever and never been available to scholars."

Germany's preeminent Kafka expert Klaus Wagenbach was aghast for the same reason—in putting it up for auction Esther risked the chance that it could be sold to a private collector who would once again lock it away. "Max Brod certainly did not risk his life to save Kafka's manuscripts from the Nazis so that they can now be sold off by Esther Hoffe with total contempt for literary obligations," Wagenbach said. "There was great anger with my mother after the Sotheby's sale," Eva Hoffe told me. "She used to be harassed by threatening phone calls at 2 a.m."

As long as Brod was alive, Esther had never attempted to sell a Kafka manuscript. After Brod's death, however, she changed course. In 1974, for example, twenty-two letters and ten postcards sent by Kafka to Brod, among other documents, were auctioned off for 90,000 Deutsche marks (€46,000). In 1981, Esther offered the autographed copy of Kafka's story "Wedding Preparations in the Country" to the German Literature Archive in Marbach for the large sum of 350,000 Deutsche marks. The Marbach archive declined.

The same year, Michael Krüger, publisher of Hanser Verlag, came from Munich to Tel Aviv to ask Esther about acquiring the rights to publish Kafka's sketches. Refusing to let him into her apartment, Esther insisted on talking with him in the stairwell. She referred Krüger to

Elio Froehlich, a Zürich lawyer (also executor of Robert Walser's estate), who told him that even to look at the sketches would cost Krüger 100,000 marks. Krüger declined.

In 1988, before the Sotheby's auction, Esther Hoffe concluded a contract with the Swiss publisher Artemis & Winkler. She ceded rights for the publication of Max Brod's diaries in exchange for a five-digit sum. She received the advance payment but never handed over the journals. Eva Koralnik, of the Zürich-based Liepman Literary Agency, mediated the deal. "For many years we tried to persuade her to honor the contract, but she always refused," Koralnik told *Haaretz*. Artemis & Winkler sued for breach of contract. "I went personally to Switzerland and met with the director of the publishing house," Eva Hoffe responded in an interview with *Haaretz*. "I explained to him that our only request was that the sections relating to the Hoffe family not be published. He agreed and allowed us to go through the diaries and send them back piecemeal. The suit against us was withdrawn and we planned to transfer the material as agreed. In the meantime, though, my mother's sight deteriorated, she could hardly read, and everything was delayed."

In the interim, Artemis & Winkler filed for bankruptcy, and Esther never returned the advance. "When we heard that the publishing house had gone bankrupt," Eva Hoffe said, "we consulted with attorney Mibi Moser about what to do and to whom we should return the advance. He said that if there was no publishing house, there was no one to return it to."

Given her previous miscues, would Esther come through this time at Sotheby's?

———

In the weeks before the auction, to create anticipation, Sotheby's exhibited Kafka's unfinished manuscript on a three-city tour in New York, Tokyo, and Hong Kong.

On the afternoon of the auction, a tense duel ensued among the bidders for *The Trial*. They had assembled from New York, Ottowa, Paris, Brussels, Amsterdam, Berlin, Rome, Zürich, Budapest, Moscow, Warsaw, Istanbul, even Tokyo; none came from Jerusalem. The forty-nine-year-old director of the Marbach archive, Ulrich Ott, sat in the center of the room. He wished to add *The Trial* to the archive's existing Kafka stock: Kafka's letters to Milena Jesenská (sold in 1981 by the heirs of Salman Schocken to the Federal Republic of Germany, which gave the letters as a permanent loan to Marbach), and the manuscript of Kafka's short story "The Village Schoolmaster" (purchased at an auction in Berlin in 1956).

The latter had been a gift from Max Brod to Hans-Joachim Schoeps, who in turn put the manuscript up for auction at the Galerie Gerd Rosen (founded by a Jewish bookseller in 1945). The buyer: Ott's predecessor and founding director of the Marbach archive, Bernhard Zeller. Zeller called the manuscript "the primal cell (*Urzelle*) of the Marbach Kafka collection," and planned to publish a facsimile. Salman Schocken sought a temporary restraining order on the grounds that Marbach's publication of the story would infringe on his rights to Kafka's works. Zeller could ill afford an international intellectual property rights battle with a Jewish publisher over Kafka, of all people, even if, as he believed, Marbach would win. In the end, Marbach published the text (but not a full facsimile) of Kafka's story in 1958, accompanied by a special note underlining Schocken's rights to the material.

Now faced with the chance to buy *The Trial*, Ott hesitated, for two reasons: first, the estimated price: £1 million. Second, Ott felt that *The Trial* might find a more appropriate home at the Bodleian Library in Oxford, which held the two manuscripts of Kafka's other unfinished novels. It was also home to the scholar Malcolm Pasley, who was then working on the critical edition of *The Trial*. "Pasley indeed tried to negotiate the purchase for Oxford," Ott told me by e-mail, "but informed us that he failed (this was the era of Prime Minister Margaret Thatcher, who was very parsimonious in affairs of culture). He and Kafka's niece Marianna Steiner urgently asked us to do everything possible to bring the manuscript to Marbach to prevent it ending up in private hands, which would likely render it inaccessible for the critical edition." Just then, an article by the prominent German journalist and essayist Frank Schirrmacher appeared in the *Frankfurter Allgemeine Zeitung*. Schirrmacher, who had written his doctoral thesis on Kafka, called for the newly created Cultural Foundation of the German Federal States (Kulturstiftung der Länder) to help fund Marbach to purchase the manuscript.

Ott had concocted a plan. Since everyone knew of Marbach's intense interest in acquiring Kafka's manuscript, he would stop bidding at £900,000. If the bidding went any higher, Ott would leave the field open to Heribert Tenschert, a little-known West German rare-books dealer who had founded an antiquarian book shop in the Bavarian village of Rotthalmünster in 1977. "Indeed," Ott recalls, "nobody knew that he was acting on Marbach's behalf."

The tactic worked. With Ulrich Ott, Marianna Steiner, and Malcolm Pasley looking on, Tenschert raised his green-and-white bidding paddle and clinched the sale on behalf of the Marbach archive for 1 million pounds sterling (about $2 million dollars, or 3.5 million German marks). "This is perhaps the most important work in twentieth-century German literature, and Germany had to have it," Tenschert said. It was the highest price ever paid for a modern manuscript, but half of what Sotheby's and Hoffe had hoped for. (The previous auction record for a literary work was also held by Kafka: in June 1987, Kafka's five hundred letters to Felice Bauer, dated 1912 to 1917, were sold at Sotheby's in New York for $605,000.)

Esther Hoffe was pleased that *The Trial* would find a home in Germany. She had a long history with the Marbach archive, which she had first visited together with Brod in 1965. Marianna Steiner, Kafka's seventy-five-year-old niece, said she, too, was pleased with the sale. "I'm very happy because it won't end up locked away in a drawer," she said.

———

Esther Hoffe died on September 2, 2007, at age 101. Her will (written in German and dated June 17, 1988) bequeaths the Kafka manuscripts given to her by Brod to her daughters Eva and Ruth: "The drafts, the letters, and the drawings by Kafka, given to me as a gift by the late Max Brod, I gave as a gift to my two daughters in 1970, in equal portions. Kafka's books from Brod's library remain in the possession of my two daughters." The letter she referred to reads as follows:

August 25, 1970

To my daughters Ruth Wiesler and Eva (Dorit) Hoffe:

To avoid any doubt, I hereby declare that I granted you as a gift, in equal portions, the letters and manuscripts and drawings by Kafka and other things given to me as a gift in 1947 and 1952 by Max Brod. . . . Kafka's manuscripts, as mentioned above, as well as the collection of documents Max Brod had of Kafka's, do not—I state explicitly—constitute a part of Brod's estate. . . .

As long as I live, I reserve to myself the rights to decide about the publication of Kafka's manuscripts, letters, drawings, etc., or if necessary, to sell some of them. . . . *

On July 5, 1978, Eva and Ruth signed a power of attorney authorizing their mother to handle the publishing of Kafka's manuscripts that she had gifted to them, as well as to make any disposition that it deems appropriate in these writings. According to the power of attorney, Esther would be entitled to a third of the receipts from any sale of the manuscripts, and Eva and Ruth would each receive a third.

As for Brod's literary and musical estate, published and unpublished

---

* Esther Hoffe neglected to mention this letter during her 1973 trial before Judge Shilo.

both, Esther instructed in paragraph 5 of her 1988 will that her daughters should arrange for it to be preserved intact in the National Library in Jerusalem, a library in Tel Aviv, or the German Literature Archive in Marbach. She added several conditions:

> Any publication of the papers must involve obtaining the consent of my daughters. Royalties and the payments shall be transferred directly to them. . . . The transfer of archival materials to one of the libraries listed above will be conditional upon the commitment of said institution to grant a Max Brod Scholarship and a Max Brod Prize for excellence in the field of literature every two years, at the library's expense, and from time to time to hold a symposium in memory of Max Brod. The institution that receives the Brod archive will be obliged to invest its efforts in publishing the writings of the estate and in publishing both unpublished material and new editions of books that have already been published.

15

The Last Judgment

Supreme Court of Israel, Jerusalem
August 7, 2016

Wrapped in a Torah scroll, Hananiah ben Teradion was placed
by the Romans on a pyre and set alight. His disciples asked:
"Master, what do you see?" He answered: "I see the parchment
burning while the letters of the Law soar upward."

—Talmud, Tractate Avoda Zara 18a

As Eva Hoffe awoke in Tel Aviv one morning in August 2016 from
uneasy dreams, she found herself transformed into a disinherited
woman. Six weeks after hearing her case, Israel's Supreme Court issued
its unappealable verdict. The panel of three judges unanimously upheld
the lower courts' decisions. It ruled that Eva Hoffe must hand the entire
Brod estate, including Kafka's manuscripts, to the National Library
of Israel, in return for which she would receive not a single shekel of
compensation.

Justice Elyakim Rubinstein wrote the twenty-one-page opinion. Citing the Talmudic injunction to fulfill the will of the deceased (Tractate Gittin 14b), he writes that Max Brod clearly wished Esther Hoffe to

choose a public archive to house his estate, and intended that the only rights Esther's daughters would enjoy are the rights to royalties from his literary estate. Rubinstein ruled that any royalties would go to Eva Hoffe, but that the National Library would decide what would be published.

According to Israeli estate law, Rubinstein continued, Esther was required to fulfill Brod's wish within a reasonable period of time. "For forty years, Hoffe delayed carrying out Brod's instruction, and there is no doubt that this constitutes an unreasonable period of time." Thus, he added, "the Court has the authority to choose the body to which Brod's estate ought to be transferred." The fact that in his will Brod listed the National Library first among the possible recipients of his estate signaled that "this is the option he most preferred."

Nor was this the high court's only consideration. Although Brod, "one of the great and celebrated cultural figures of the twentieth century," was a product of German-speaking culture, Rubinstein wrote, "without a doubt he pitched his tent and rooted his activities in Israel; this fact deserves to be given weight."

Following Sa'ar Plinner's arguments, Rubinstein then distinguished the manuscripts Kafka gave Brod during Kafka's lifetime from those Brod took from Kafka's desk after Kafka died.* The latter, the judge argued, had been in Brod's possession, but not his ownership. Therefore,

---

* Brod himself distinguished the two sets of Kafka manuscripts. On July 1, 1957, he wrote to Salman Schocken:

> I wish to make clear that Kafka's manuscripts belong to my heirs, with the exception of items given to me as a gift. Those of Kafka's manuscripts that were granted to me, and thus constitute my private property, have always been marked apart; I removed them many years ago from the archive and this was brought to the attention of the heirs, who gave their full consent.... When the time comes to prepare a complete edition of Kafka's works, I shall make sure that the manuscripts in my possession will be made available. The ownership rights to all other Kafka manuscripts belong to the heirs, as expressly stipulated in the December 6 contract between Mr. Gustav Schocken (of Schocken Publishing House Ltd.) and myself.

they cannot be said to belong to Brod's literary estate. "Yet for practical reasons, and in the absence of claims made by Kafka's heirs, they too must be transferred to the National Library along with the other materials." This was to be done on December 15, 2016.

Rubinstein concluded the judgment by invoking God's description of the biblical Joshua. Brod, the judge wrote, was "a man in whom is the spirit" (Numbers 27:18); as such, he hoped that as a result of this ruling, fifty years after his death, the National Library would at last grant Brod "a fitting literary resurrection."

———

Reactions to the verdict were as swift as they were polarized. "This is a celebratory day for any person of culture, in Israel and abroad," said David Blumberg, chairman of the board of the National Library. "The Supreme Court asked the National Library to do its utmost to reveal Brod's estate to the public. The National Library will follow the court's ruling and will preserve the cultural assets by keeping them in the country as well as making them accessible to the general public."

In Kafka's fictional world, the law is meant for us, and yet we are barred from fathoming its workings. "I don't know this law," says Joseph K. in *The Trial*. The warder is unimpressed: "So much the worse for you." Later on, the painter Titorelli informs Joseph K. that the court is impenetrable (*unzugänglich*) to argument or reason. It is both omnipresent and opaque, everywhere and nowhere.

In his parable "The Problem of Our Laws," Kafka writes:

Our laws are not generally known; they are kept secret by the small group of nobles who rule us. We are convinced that these ancient laws are scrupulously administrated; nevertheless it is an extremely painful thing to be ruled by laws that one does not know.

Like the man from the country in Kafka's parable "Before the Law," Eva Hoffe remained stranded and confounded outside the door of the law. There would be no redemptive revelation for her. She did not understand the law or the intricacies of legal reasoning, but she did understand the sentence. Her inheritance was the trial itself. Paradoxically, she had inherited her disinheritance, inherited the impossibility of carrying out her mother's will. She possessed only her dispossession.

Normally, a will establishes the heir's identity by acknowledging continuity and legally recognizing what she can consider her own. A will allows the heir to understand her place in the generational order of things. Eva insisted that the disputed manuscripts connected her as much with Brod as to her mother. "You must understand that Max was a member of our family," she told me.

She told me after the verdict that she felt "worse than despairing... as though I've been raped." She said that in her humiliation, she felt too ashamed even to meet her friends at their usual Thursday coffee klatch. Instead, she tended to her cats and went to matinee movies "to pass the time." She told me that because most of her teeth had fallen out and she couldn't afford dental work, she ate soup or bread with tahini or jam. When we met at a café on Dubnow Street, she poked at her potato purée.

A form of masochism or sublimated self-fury seemed to have awakened within her. She had instructed her hairdresser to shave her head. In a convulsion of mourning? In a debt to the dead? In the wish to appear the martyr? "If I went on hunger strike," she said, "they would just force feed me."

The next time we met, her hair had grown out somewhat, but a thin film of melancholy seemed to coat her blue eyes. Speaking as though she regarded herself as the sum of her legal misfortunes, she compared the endless deferrals and delays of her case to those encountered by Joseph K. in *The Trial*. In both cases, she felt, an arbitrary system had insinuated itself into places both public and private. "Well," the painter tells Joseph K., "everything belongs to the court." "I felt from the beginning of the trial like an animal being led to slaughter," she said.

The Supreme Court ruling, Eva insisted, represented "the will to appropriate, not the will to adjudicate." Still, she felt that Brod's gift to her mother, and her mother's to her, was unrevoked and unrelinquished. She held out the slim hope that the court would reverse itself and recognize that it had failed both to fulfill Brod's will and to respect her privacy. Because the ruling made no distinction between Brod's estate and Esther Hoffe's personal correspondence, Eva did not wish to ship off everything indiscriminately to the National Library.

During that conversation, I thought of the successive violations of intimacy that accompanied each chapter of the story: Joseph K. arrested in his bedroom in the opening scene of *The Trial*; Brod's decision to publish Kafka's diaries and letters (including the letter to his father); Esther selling off Kafka's manuscripts at public auction; and now a trial that had thrust Eva into the public eye.

I relayed Eva's concerns to Aviad Stollman, head of collections at the National Library. "For reasons both legal and moral," he replied, the library "has no desire to publish personal material" and remained "committed to return to Hoffe any material of a personal nature in the estate." The National Library has experience with such sensitivities in its treatment of the estates of living Israeli writers like A. B. Yehoshua and David Grossman, Stollman said. He added that the library has forged partnerships with the German publisher Suhrkamp to publish material from the Gershom Scholem estate, for example, and with YIVO (a research organization established in 1925 as the Yidisher Visnshaftlekher Institut) regarding the estate of Vilnius-born Yiddish writer Chaim Grade (1910–1982).*

---

* For more than two decades after Chaim Grade's death in 1982, his widow Inna (née Hecker) turned away researchers who requested access to his voluminous papers, threatened translators with cease and desist letters, and refused to allow the printing of her husband's works in Yiddish. After she died without immediate survivors in New York on May 2, 2010, the papers (including original manuscripts of Grade's fiction as well as correspondence) were transferred from the decrepit apartment they shared in the Amalgamated Housing Cooperative in the Bronx to the YIVO Institute for Jewish Research on West

Such assurances were cold comfort to Eva Hoffe, whose dejection deepened by the day. She feared the authorities would break into her apartment to seize the papers by force. If they did, she told me, she would kill herself.

Several days after the ruling, Eva passed the Green Brothers bookshop on Frishman Street not far from her home. In the display window was a copy of *J'Accuse*, the open letter Emile Zola published in January 1898 in the newspaper *L'Aurore* accusing the French government of anti-Semitism in its prosecution of alleged traitor Alfred Dreyfus. Eva bought it. "Zola didn't address the court," she told me. "He addressed the president of the Republic. Maybe I should do the same." She, too, hoped for exoneration, however belated.

Dan Miron, a leading authority on Hebrew literature, took to the pages of *Haaretz* to paint the Supreme Court verdict as the misguided choice of "nationalist sentiment and local interests over the universal and objective interests of literary culture." He noted that in the half century since Brod's death, no Israeli institution had bothered to publish his collected works. To do so would require a team of experts in German literature and resources that the National Library lacks. It was not realistic to expect, Miron wrote, "that the National Library of Israel, which made no effort at the time to raise the relatively modest funds necessary to prevent Yehuda Amichai's literary estate from being transferred from Jerusalem to the Beinicke Library at Yale, to now invest its resources in translating Brod's works into Hebrew.... or to take care of the materials in his estate." In Miron's view, the National Library feigned interest in Brod in order to get at the real prize: the Kafka manuscripts that it claimed were legally inseparable from the Brod estate. The Supreme Court, in his view, had bought into the pretense.

16th Street in Manhattan. In 2013, the Public Administrator of Bronx County awarded the YIVO Institute and the National Library of Israel rights to the estate. YIVO and the National Library agreed to digitize the archive and make it accessible online.

"What do I want from Kafka?" Eva had told me. "Years ago, I asked Michael Steiner [the son of Kafka's niece] to get involved. If anyone, he, and not the National Library, should have what remains of Kafka's papers. He wasn't interested. So Kafka for me has been a disaster. They mixed Kafka into Brod's estate in order to take it all away from me." Eva told me she was "absolutely convinced" that as soon as the publicity died down, the National Library in Jerusalem would cut a secret deal to sell Kafka's manuscripts from the Brod estate to Marbach.

Reiner Stach took to the pages of the German weekly *Die Zeit* to argue that journalists had used Kafka as a kind of flammable lighter fluid to ignite controversy. "Ofer Aderet spun the tale in the liberal daily *Haaretz* of a considerable amount of unpublished Kafka works hidden by Eva Hoffe." For this, and for obscuring the fact that many of Kafka's manuscripts are in the Bodleian Library in Oxford, Stach charged Aderet with journalistic sensationalism and "disinformation."

Still, Stach expressed relief at the verdict handed down in Jerusalem. The Hoffes, he said, "had for half a century literally no idea how to do justice to their cultural responsibility." Stach, among others, contended that Marbach, given its exemplary work with literary estates of other German-Jewish writers, would have made a more fitting home. But they could now be comforted that the question of the physical location of the Kafka and Brod estates had been rendered redundant by the National Library's pledge to digitize the material and put it all online.

"The presence of the original," Walter Benjamin said, "is the prerequisite to the concept of authenticity." What, if anything, can the trial in Israel tell us about the meaning of ownership in a digital age? Has the "aura of the original" become obsolete? Or do original manuscripts become more prized—and more fetishized—if they can be infinitely reproduced? Does modern technology destroy the aura of authenticity even as it creates an appetite for it?

"I would have preferred to have the papers preserved—with fair access to scholars—at the German Literature Archive at Marbach,"

Stanley Corngold, professor emeritus at Princeton and dean of American Kafkaists, told me. "But that is a practical impossibility."

> Of course, they have the manuscript of *Der Process* [*The Trial*]. It would be good to have all of Kafka's manuscripts together—in principle. For the rest, how could one disagree with what you quote Stach as saying? One is passionately glad that they are out of the hands of Ms. Hoffe and glad of the National Library's promise to digitize—and make them available—soon. In this case the practical outcome outweighs in importance the immense international brain-spill over the niceties of Kafka's philosophy of non-arrival. . . . Meanwhile, if it were not for the intrusions of the Library, many of the documents—being mere paper—may not have survived at all in the dubious care of Ms. Hoffe—or otherwise never seen the light of day.

Karl Erich Grözinger told me that, research considerations aside, from a moral perspective, the trove of manuscripts properly belongs in Israel. "It was only thanks to the Zionist enterprise and to the *yishuv* [the Jewish community in Palestine before the declaration of the state in 1948] that Brod was able to rescue the manuscripts," he said.

Others weren't so sure that Kafka's legacy—as elusive and enigmatic as ever, and nowhere at home—could be located on any earthly map. "From my perspective," Tel Aviv poet Lali Michaeli told me, "Kafka's manuscripts should be sent to the moon."

———

Eva Hoffe had one more chance: she had fifteen days from the date of the ruling to enter a request for another Supreme Court hearing. Despite the efforts of her lawyer, Eli Zohar, to contact her about next steps, she felt despondent and alone. In her desperation, she reengaged

Yeshayahu Etgar (a friend of Supreme Court Justice Rubinstein), whom she had retained and then dropped much earlier in the litigation. On the fifteenth day, August 22, 2016, she and Etgar submitted the request for a new hearing. It noted that the National Library did not formally exist as such when Brod wrote his will (either in its original form in 1948 or last form in 1961). It was incorporated only in 2007. The request also reiterated that since Esther explicitly gave her daughters the Kafka manuscripts—as formalized in a letter of August 1970—they belong neither to Brod's estate nor to Esther's, and should therefore not be subject to the ruling. On December 13, 2016, Justice Salim Joubran, the first Arab to receive a permanent appointment to Israel's Supreme Court, declined the request.

In a last-ditch effort, Etgar advised Eva to take offensive action and sue the Justice Ministry for negligence and misconduct in its handling of the case. To describe Eva's careening emotions that week, one of her close friends invoked a line from Goethe's *Egmont*, now a common German saying: *"Himmelhoch jauchzend, zu Tode betrübt"*—"heavenly joy, deadly despair."

On December 15, as ordered by the court, the first of Hoffe's red-brown safe deposit boxes was brought in a Brink's armored truck from Bank Leumi in Tel Aviv to the National Library in Jerusalem. On December 20, the boxes were to be opened for the first time. I watched as six boxes were wheeled under armed guard on a trolley into the library's Holtzman conference room next to the cafeteria.

I wondered whether the manuscripts they contained could be thought of as filaments, however frayed over the years. Though the words they carry remain unchanged, the meaning of the loose leaves and sheafs of paper in question had undergone its own metamorphosis. They had connected Kafka to Brod; Brod in exile in Tel Aviv to his prewar heyday in Prague; Brod to the intimate partner of the second half of his life, Esther Hoffe; Hoffe to her devoted daughters; and finally, Germany to Israel in a legal tug of war.

In the conference room, two archivists, Stefan Litt (a Berlin native who has made Israel his home since 1995 and has worked at the National Library since 2010) and Paul Maurer (a Riga-born specialist on German-Jewish material at the National Library who in 2002 conducted research in Marbach), sat on the right side of a long table. They were eager to begin the work of sifting through thousands of pages of material and checking it against Itta Shedletzky's inventory. Supervising them from the facing side of the table were Matan Barzilai, head of the library's archives department, and Yaniv Levi-Korem, head of its technical services department. None of them knew quite what to expect. Video cameras had been set up at the head of the table to record the occasion.

In the first few days, Litt and Mauer turned up private correspondence between Max Brod and Esther Hoffe that makes the intimacy of their relationship quite clear. They discovered letters between Kafka and members of his family, and three unknown aphorisms in Kafka's handwriting, written during World War I and intended for a book never published. Subsequent finds included a file of twenty-five of Brod's musical scores, thickly bundled handwritten drafts of his novels, and voluminous correspondence ("a who's who of Central European literary life," Maurer said.) Rusted paperclips had bled onto many of the papers. The files also confirmed Brod's instinct to keep mementos of all kinds: signed tickets from 1905 or so for Vienna's Casino de Paris nightclub, and illustrated postcards from the Wiener Werkstätte (the Vienna workshops of visual artists, established in 1903).

Part of their work involved separating papers belonging to Esther Hoffe's estate (letters to her from Brod, for example) from those belonging to the Brod estate (Esther's letters to him). The former would be returned to Eva Hoffe, they said. In the meantime, Eva Hoffe and Yeshayahu Etgar vowed to fight the "extradition" of the materials from Zürich.*

---

* As of this writing, despite Ehud Sol's attempts the National Library of Israel has not yet obtained an order from a Swiss court recognizing the Supreme Court's decision or

More than one of Eva's closest friends worried that she might succumb to despair and do something rash. In one of our conversations, Eva told me, apropos of nothing, about Ingeborg Bachmann, the Austrian writer who in 1973 ignited a blaze in her bedroom, apparently from a lit cigarette. Bachmann died in the hospital three weeks later. I could not help imagining a nightmarish scene: after her final defeat, Eva defiantly burns what remains of the manuscripts on Spinoza Street: at once a fulfillment of Kafka's last wish, a sacrifice of her most precious possession—like Abraham willing to sacrifice Isaac, like the offerings on the altar of the Temple in Jerusalem—and a belated acknowledgment that Kafka belongs to no one.

In the spring of 2018, Eva was diagnosed with intestinal cancer. During recovery from an operation to remove a tumor, she fell and broke her hip. Losing the will to live, she refused to eat. Eva Hoffe died in Tel Aviv on August 4, 2018, at age 84. She was buried the next day in the city's Kiryat Shaul cemetery. Lacking her own plot, she was buried atop her mother. "Her mother swallowed Eva up in death as in life," one of Eva's friends said.

"Art is never owned, neither by its patrons nor even by the artists themselves," the poet Joseph Brodsky wrote. The trial laid bare a possessiveness over the artistic legacy of the least possessive of men. Reiner Stach writes of Kafka: "There is not a single known episode in his life in which he displayed possessiveness." Not so Kafka's would-be heirs in Israel and Germany who forgot that Kafka is not theirs; if anything, they are his.

The trial also disclosed how unsettled these heirs seemed by what they sought to possess. Aware of the latent power of Kafka's imagination,

---

affirming that it can be executed in Switzerland. Under Swiss law, the Ministry of Culture can approve international transfer of cultural assets (as defined by UNESCO guidelines) only in cases in which a treaty governing the protection of those assets exists between Switzerland and the country to which the assets are to be transferred or repatriated. Since no such treaty has been concluded between Switzerland and Israel, no procedures for the transfer of the Hoffe manuscripts in Zürich are currently in place.

they wanted not just to possess but to contain and classify. Artistic affirmation and national affirmation, after all, are quite different things. In his 1987 Nobel lecture, Brodsky said: "The revulsion, irony, or indifference often expressed by literature towards the state is essentially a reaction of the permanent—better yet, the infinite—against the temporary, against the finite." The latter is the preserve of archivists. But which is more ethereal—words or states?

If the trial represents the apprehensive counterreaction of the finite (state interests) against the infinite (literature), it seems apt that the German word for trial, *Prozess*, suggests something in open-ended progress. "Only our concept of time," Kafka once wrote, "makes it possible for us to speak of the Day of Judgment by that name; in reality, it is a summary court in perpetual session." The judges in Jerusalem may have reached their verdict, but the symbolic trial over Kafka's legacy has yet to adjourn.

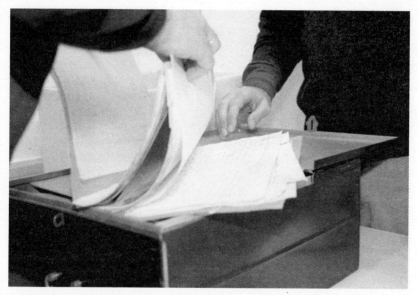

Esther Hoffe's bank deposit box, opened for the first time at the National Library, Jerusalem, December 2016. (Hanan Cohen, National Library of Israel)

Epilogue

And the heavens shall be rolled together as a scroll: and all their host shall fall down, as the leaf falleth off from the vine.

—Isaiah 34

Like a path in autumn: scarcely has it been swept clear when it is once more covered with leaves.

—Kafka, Aphorism 15

Viewed from a certain elevation, Kafka's writing appears to take its boundaries from the notion that messages are more often than not lost, misunderstood, perpetually postponed, or (which may come down to the same thing) garbled in transmission. They arrive too late, if at all. Kafka's novel *The Trial*—itself an unfinished message—tells the story of an increasingly baffled man who is tried by laws that remain shrouded in incomprehensibility. The accused is in the end executed without having been able to discover what it is all about.

In the parable "Before the Law," part of *The Trial*, Kafka's supplicant from the countryside receives the crucial message—that the door to the law before which he has waited for years is meant only for him—just before he dies, when it is too late to matter. He is never granted access to the radiant revelation behind the door.

In *The Castle*, the village mayor explains to K. that ten years earlier the village had sent a representative to the castle to request a land surveyor. When this was judged unnecessary, a second message canceled the first. But the second message was inexplicably lost, only to resurface just when K. arrived. (Kafka seems to leave open the question of whether the surveyor had been summoned at all.)

In Kafka's story "The Stoker," which Brod made the first chapter of Kafka's unfinished novel *Amerika*, our young hero is about to disembark from the ship that has taken him across the ocean when he meets the stoker. This man who fuels the ship has an urgent story to tell, and we are on the brink of hearing it, but in the end do not. Perhaps it is incommunicable.

Kafka's most unsettling story, "In the Penal Colony," features an "apparatus" of needles that inscribes a sentence into the prisoner's flesh in a kind of slow execution by exegesis. The observer cannot decipher the labyrinth of lines the cruel contraption carves; he finds it "incomprehensible" (*unbegreiflich*). Its macabre message—Kafka calls it a *Gebot*, or commandment—is intelligible only to the condemned man, if at all, and only at the point of death.

In Kafka's parable "An Imperial Message," the emperor—an image of paternal authority—whispers a message from his deathbed to a messenger who has no hope of emerging from the impenetrable chambers and thronged inner and outer courts to deliver and divulge it. He bears a message—as undeliverable as it is urgent—"from a dead man."

Consider, finally, one of Kafka's fragments:

They were given the choice of being kings or king's couriers. Like children, they all wanted to be couriers. So now there are only couriers; they dash through the world, and as there are no kings, shout their meaningless messages to one another. They would gladly put an end to their wretched lives, but they dare not because of their oath of loyalty.

Perhaps we might best understand our story as a series of messages that have been lost, deferred, went unheeded, left in abeyance, or arrived too late: Kafka's letter to his father, his last instruction to Brod, the unheeded calls beckoning Kafka to the Promised Land, the letter inviting Brod to the United States on the eve of the war, Brod's last will, and Esther Hoffe's last will.

In Kafka's imagination, intelligibility will not illuminate our messages until the Messiah comes. And yet the Messiah himself arrives too late. "The Messiah will come only when he is no longer necessary," Kafka writes.

———

What happens to the Law without a lawgiver? Another of Kafka's great motifs, returning like a refrain, is that the Law, radiant but inaccessible, is guarded by fallible, petty, even unscrupulous gatekeepers: seedy judges, lawyers, officials, priests, and clerks. The representatives of the Law, however powerful, are all of them fallen men. Guardians, however devoted, do not always understand what they are guarding. Walter Benjamin compared Kafka's students to "pupils who have lost the Holy Writ." Or at least they read the Holy Writ against the grain.

If the Israeli judges can be understood as the latest of Kafka's gatekeepers of interpretation, then their verdict might be read as another telling reading—or misreading; as the latest page in the long history of the uses and abuses of Kafka's literary afterlife at the hands of those who claim to be his heirs.

In centering on the question of who can claim to be Kafka's true heirs, the trial threw into stark relief the very different ways Israel and

Germany remain freighted by their ruptured pasts and by the noble lies on which their healing depended. Each attempted to connect a national "we" with Kafka's name. Seen through that aperture, the trial offered an object lesson in how Germany's claim on a writer whose family was decimated in the Holocaust is entangled with the country's postwar attempt to overcome its shameful past. As we have seen, the trial also reawakened a long-standing debate about Kafka's ambivalence toward Judaism and the prospects of a Jewish state—and about Israel's ambivalence toward Kafka and toward Diaspora culture.

Long before the trials in Israel, legion are those who have sought to claim Kafka. What is it about this writer, whose very name has become an adjectival cliché, that allows so many interpreters to appropriate and misappropriate Kafka's legacy?[*]

By design, Kafka's fictions—at once lucid and obscure, precise and dreamlike—both solicit and resist interpretation. They invite interpretation even as they evade it; even as they circle in eddies of ambiguity. Theodor W. Adorno once remarked that Kafka's fiction was like "a parable whose key has been stolen."[†] Kafka himself never supplied the key. "A story-teller cannot talk about story-telling," he said. "He tells stories or is silent."

---

[*] "The ugly word 'Kafkaesque' is an invention," Max Brod writes in *The Prague Circle*, "but it is precisely this 'Kafkaesque' which Kafka detested and fought most violently. Kafkaesque is that which Kafka was not! He loved the natural, pure, good, and constructive, not the oddly-eerie, hopeless, not the strange that he always perceives and notes as a given in the world and incorporates with grim humor without making it anywhere his focus. This tender yet steel-like soul was not turned to destruction but to blossoming. Alas, he had no illusions about the difficulty of this blossoming and building-up.... Away with the repulsive expression Kafkaesque!" Among others who expressed a Brod-like distaste for the term Kafkaesque, Philip Roth protested in 1974 that Kafka's name "is plastered indiscriminately on almost any baffling or unusually opaque event that is not easily translatable into the going simplifications."

[†] Adorno was especially wary of attempts to unlock Kafka's writing with a Zionist key. In a letter to Walter Benjamin, he categorically denied that Kafka "can be regarded as a poet of the Judaic homeland."

———

Kafka's Czech translator and lover Milena Jesenská once remarked on Kafka's "terrible clarity of vision." In what did his powers of seeing consist?

For Max Brod, Kafka saw the incommensurability of the human and divine—or of God's law and man's purpose. Kafka's motifs—revelation and redemption, law and commandment, guilt and sacrifice—fix Kafka's place as what Brod called a "saint of our time."

For psychoanalytically inclined interpreters, Kafka charts the dreadful, the incomprehensible and inscrutable beneath the prosaic; he is the herald of Freud's idea of the uncanny—the familiar re-presented to us in unfamiliar guise. Or he is crippled by an inferiority complex and an inability to assert himself vis-à-vis his father, an indecisive introvert who saw no farther than his own neuroses. Kafka's visions, the literary critic Edmund Wilson wrote, represent "the half-expressed gasp of a self-doubting soul trampled under."

For still others, Kafka is a forerunner of angst-ridden existentialists, a kind of Jewish Kierkegaard who stared into the abyss of amorality, absurdity, and the disorienting void of meaning left after the death of God. "Kafka spoke to us about ourselves," Simone de Beauvoir said. "He revealed to us our own problems, confronted by a world without God and where nonetheless our salvation was at stake." It is in this sense that Kafka is said to have shaped our conception of the crisis of traditional values in the twentieth century. (In 1941, the poet W. H. Auden said about Kafka: "Had one to name the artist who comes nearest to bearing the same kind of relation to our age that Dante, Shakespeare and Goethe bore to theirs, Kafka is the first one would think of.")

———

In the ever-expanding firmament of Kafka interpretation, Kafka's would-be heirs have looked to his writing as a guide to their own perplexities. In "The Prague Orgy," Philip Roth has a Czech writer tell Roth's alter ego Nathan Zuckerman: "When I studied Kafka, the fate of his books in the hands of the Kafkologists seemed to me to be more grotesque than the fate of Joseph K."

To navigate these hazards is to consult what Shimon Sandbank, one of Kafka's best Hebrew translators and interpreters, calls a "map of misreadings." The often contradictory interpretations—attempts to develop a usable notation adequate to Kafka's music—are hidden self-interpretations. Sandbank quotes a remark of the poet T. S. Eliot: "About anyone so great as Shakespeare, it is probable that we can never be right; and if we can never be right, it is better that we should from time to time change our way of being wrong." To which Sandbank adds: "Kafka, I feel, is great enough for these words to apply to him as well, great enough for us never to be right about him."

In an enigmatic five-paragraph sketch called "The Cares of a Family Man" ("Die Sorge des Hausvaters"), Kafka imagines an encounter between a paterfamilias, a "house-father," and a strange vagrant creature called Odradek, which "is extraordinarily nimble and can never be laid hold of." The family man asks the uninvited creature where he lives. " 'No fixed abode,' he says and laughs; but it is only the kind of laughter that has no lungs behind it. It sounds rather like the rustling of fallen leaves [*Blätter*]."

In a case not lacking in ironies, surely the last involves taking a proprietary attitude toward a writer so bound up in the refusal to belong to a fixed abode. Kafka's marginality, dislocation, and estrangement from life, what the Germans call his *Weltfremdheit*, are the alpha and omega of his imagination, the wellspring of its multiple metamorphoses. To use the American poet John Ashbery's phrase, Kafka was on the outside looking out, and he wasn't about to be conscripted by those on the inside.

Kafka writes in his diary of his "infinite yearning for independence and freedom in all things." In life and literature both, that yearning brought him into a stubborn homelessness and non-belonging. It is not just that the places in his fiction are not named (only the interior landscapes are recognizable). It is that he untethered both himself and his writing from the comforting anchors of national or religious belonging.

Does Kafka's beguiling writing belong to German literature or to the state that regards itself as the representative of Jews everywhere? In the end, is Kafka a German-language writer who happened to be Jewish, or a profoundly Jewish writer who honed German into a new Jewish language adequate to articulating a Jewish thinking in a world without God and without revelation? Or does Kafka's body of work resonate beyond any national canon, "obedient to its own laws of motion," to use his phrase?

Kafka himself, in a letter to his fiancée Felice Bauer in October 1916, seems to have had a premonition of the contradictory ways he would be claimed. He contrasts two recent articles about his work, one of them by Max Brod:

> Won't you tell me what I really am? In the last *Neue Rundschau* the writer says: "There is something fundamentally German about K's narrative art." In Max's article ["Our Writers and the Community," in *Der Jude*] on the other hand: "K's stories are among the most typically Jewish documents of our time."

"A difficult case," Kafka concludes. "Am I a circus rider on two horses? Alas, I am no rider, but lie prostrate on the ground."

Franz Kafka may have been long ago laid dormant in the ground, and the courtroom commotions long since calmed, but the fallen leaves and loose sheets of his writings, whatever their fixed abode, rustle with us still.

Acknowledgments

For graciously agreeing to speak with me and reply to my queries—in person, by phone, or in correspondence—I thank Shmulik Cassouto, Jan Eike Dunkhase, Karl Erich Grözinger, Eva Hoffe, Elad Jacobowitz, Caroline Jessen, Tom Lewy, Stefan Litt, Dafna Mach, Paul Mauer, Ariel Muzicant, Nurit Pagi, Sa'ar Plinner, Ulrich Raulff, Shimon Sandbank, Sebastian Schirrmeister, Tom Segev, Itta Shedletzky, Dimitry Shumsky, Danny Spitzer, Reiner Stach, Michael Steiner, Ulrich Ott, Sigrid Weigel, and A. B. Yehoshua.

For their discerning comments on drafts of the manuscript, I'm indebted to Tamar Abramov, George Eltman, Matti Friedman, Karina Korecky, Nicole Krauss, and Vivian Liska (and hasten to add that remaining flaws are mine alone).

I'm immeasurably grateful to Deborah Harris, literary agent extraordinaire, for her unfailing encouragement and unstinting faith in this book from the start; and to John Glusman of W. W. Norton and Ravi Mirchandani of Picador for their deft editing.

I also wish to thank the dedicated librarians and staff at the Van Leer Institute in Jerusalem, my home for the last several years.

Notes

1. The Last Appeal

6   "You spend your time at Kassit . . ." Quoted in Uri Dan, *Ariel Sharon: An Intimate Portrait*, Palgrave Macmillan, 2006, p. 22.

2. "Fanatical Veneration"

22   "Music is for me like the ocean . . ." Quoted in Leon Botstein, "The Cultural Politics of Language and Music: Max Brod and Leoš Janáček," in *Janáček and his World*, ed. Michael Beckerman, Princeton University Press, 2003.

22   "Men seeking salvation . . ." Letter to Milena Jesenská, June 20, 1920.

23   "Composing his love poems in bed . . ." Referring to the Viennese writer whose short-lived journal *Hyperion* was the first to publish work by a young Franz Kafka, Austrian satirist Karl Kraus dismissed Brod as Franz Blei's "erotic appendix." See Paul Raabe, "Franz Kafka und Franz Blei," in *F. Kafka: Ein Symposium. Datierung, Funde, Materialien*, Verlag Wagenbach, 1965, pp. 7–20.

24   "For every ten Germans . . ." Emil Faktor (1876–1942) reviewed Brod's first novel, *Nornepygge Castle*, in the daily paper *Bohemia* (December 23, 1908).

29 "The ninety-nine-page volume, called *Meditation* ..." Kafka's first vol-
    ume was not fated to sell well. "Eleven books were sold at André's store,"
    Kafka said. "I bought ten of them myself. I would love to know who has
    the eleventh." For an English translation of the book, see *Contemplation*,
    trans. Kevin Blahut, Twisted Spoon Press, 1996.
29 "Just because the friendship he feels for me ..." Letter to Felice Bauer, Feb-
    ruary 14–15, 1913. Quoted in Reiner Stach, *Kafka: The Decisive Years*, p. 342.

3. The First Trial

34 "The National Library was eager to add the Kafka collection to a long list
    of the papers of German-Jewish writers ..." These include the papers of
    Kafka's friends Hugo Bergmann, Felix Weltsch, Friedrich Thieberger, and
    Oskar Baum, but also those of Martin Buber, Anna Maria Jokl (1911–2001),
    Ludwig Strauss (1892–1953), Gershom Scholem, and Else Lasker-Schüler.
    Of German-Jewish writers who (like Kafka) never lived in Israel, the
    National Library also holds the archives of Leopold Zunz (1794–1886),
    the founder of academic Judaic Studies (*Wissenschaft des Judentums*),
    whose papers were brought here from Berlin in 1939 (though it remained
    unopened until the late 1950s); Stefan Zweig (who wrote in December 1933
    to Hugo Bergmann to offer parts of his correspondence—with Einstein,
    Freud, Herzl, Valéry, Rathenau, James Joyce, and Thomas Mann, among
    others—to the National Library on condition that it would remain sealed
    until ten years after his death); and Austrian-born German Expressionist
    poet Albert Ehrenstein (1886–1950), who died penniless in New York. (In
    December 2011, Sotheby's New York sold a letter from Kafka to Ehren-
    stein [ca. 1920], in which Kafka complains about his writer's block: "When
    worries have penetrated to a certain layer of inner existence, writing and
    complaining obviously cease." The single-page letter was sold for $74,500.)
    The National Library has a small archive (more than twenty letters) of the
    blind poet Oskar Baum (1883–1941), a friend of both Brod and Kafka. The
    letters may have been brought to Jerusalem by Baum's son. For more on the
    Prague Circle, see Margarita Pazi, *Fünf Autoren des Prager Kreises* (Peter
    Lang, 1978).
43 "Marbach would certainly be the proper place ..." Reiner Stach, "Kafkas
    letztes Geheimnis," *Tagesspiel*, January 26, 2010.
44 "Only in 2007 did the library establish ..." See Rachel Misrati, "48 Years
    of Personal Archives: A Historical User Study in the Jewish National and
    University Library's Archives Department," M.A. thesis, Bar-Ilan Univer-

sity, Ramat Gan, 2009. Mordechai Nadav's own estate was auctioned off in January 2013 by Winner's Auctions and Exhibitions in Jerusalem.

44 "As a native of Prague . . ." Ofer Aderet, "Professors Call for Max Brod's Archive, Including Unpublished Kafka Manuscripts, to Stay in Israel," *Haaretz*, February 8, 2010.

44 "We the undersigned . . ." Other signatories included Professors Mark Gelber, Yehuda Bauer, Dimitry Shumsky, Zohar Maor, Sergio DellaPergola, and David Bankier (head of the International Institute for Holocaust Research at Yad Vashem). The German version of the open letter can be found at www.hagalil.com/2010/02/brod-archiv/.

45 "The struggle to keep the Brod archive in Israel . . ." Nurit Pagi, "Brod und Kafkas Nachlass—und unsere Zukunft in Israel," *Yakinton*, 2011.

4. Flirting with the Promised Land

49 "He had been invited by the Bar Kochba Association . . ." Felix Weltsch, who had worked at the National University Library in Prague, had coauthored a philosophical book with Brod (*Anschauung und Begriff*, Perception and Concept, 1913), and had edited the Zionist newspaper *Selbstwehr* from 1919 to 1939. In March 1939, Weltsch, together with his wife and daughter, emigrated with Brod to Palestine, where he found work at the National Library in Jerusalem. He died in Jerusalem, age eighty, in 1964. See Weltsch's *Religion und Humor im Leben und Werk Franz Kafkas*, Herbig, 1957; and Carsten Schmidt's biography of Weltsch, *Kafkas fast unbekannter Freund*, Koenigshausen & Neumann, 2010.

50 "moved from an almost exclusive and deliberate preoccupation . . ." Robert Weltsch, *Max Brod and His Age*, Leo Baeck Institute, 1970. See also Maurice Friedman, "The Prague Bar Kochbans and the 'Speeches on Judaism,'" in *Martin Buber's Life and Work: The Early Years, 1878–1923*, Dutton 1981.

58 "The Three Phases of Zionism." Brod's 1917 essay put Ahad Ha'am's recently republished 1895 essay, "At the Crossroads," in conversation with Martin Buber's *The Jewish Movement* (Die jüdische Bewegung), a collection of Zionist speeches and essays published in 1916.

60 "A 78-minute silent documentary film, produced by Noah Sokolovsky . . ." On the reception and restoration of the film, see "For Czarist Russia's Jews, a Look at a Promised Land," J. Hoberman, *New York Times*, February 27, 2000. Eight years later, in 1921, Kafka attended a screening of the silent film *Shivat Zion* (A Return to Zion), which similarly depicted the pioneers and Zionist leaders in Palestine.

60 "What had they done…" Quoted in Wilma Iggers (ed.), *Die Juden in Böhmen und Mähren. Ein historisches Lesebuch*, C.H. Beck Verlag, 1986, p. 225.

61 "He read reports in Prague's Zionist weekly *Selbstwehr* about the Beilis blood libel in Kiev…" See Arnold J. Band, "Kafka and the Beilis Affair," *Comparative Literature*, Spring 1980.

61 "Hans Blüher's *Secessio Judaica*…" Hans Blüher, *Secessio Judaica: Philosophische Grundlegung der historischen Situation des Judentums und der antisemitischen Bewegung* (Berlin: Der Weiße Ritter, 1922). Blüher, a leading intellectual of the Wandervogel, the German youth movement, rejected the idea of a German-Jewish symbiosis and argued that the Jews' "corruptive patterns of thought" are antithetical to the "German essence." For Kafka's comments on the book, see his diary entries for June 16 and 30, 1922. Felix Weltsch, friend of Kafka and Brod, responded to *Secessio Judaica* in a letter to Hugo Bergmann. Since anti-Semitism is inflamed by the Jews' disproportionate influence on German society, Weltsch says, segregation is desirable (*Max Brod: Ein Gedenkbuch 1884–1968*, ed. Hugo Gold [Tel Aviv: Olamenu, 1969], p. 102). See also the exchange between Blüher and Hans-Joachim Schoeps, published in 1933 as *Streit um Israel: Ein jüdisch-christliches Gespräch*.

62 "A popular textbook by Moses Rath…" *Hebrew Grammar for Schools and Self-Instruction* (*Lehrbuch: Der Hebräischen Sprache für Schul und Selbstunterricht*).

63 "Yes. Kafka spoke Hebrew…." Langer, "Something about Kafka" [*Mashehu al Kafka*], in the Tel Aviv journal *Hegeh*, Issue 256, February 23, 1941. Langer played a role in introducing Kafka to Hassidic life and leaders. In September 1915, Langer took Kafka and Brod to see the Grodeker Rebbe, and the following July Langer took Kafka to meet the Rebbe of Belz in Marienbad. According to Shaun J. Halper, who wrote a doctoral dissertation about Langer (University of California, Berkeley, 2013): "When Langer died his estate passed to Max Brod, who donated his small collection of books to the municipal library in Tel Aviv, which is today's Beit Ariella (the library, however, has no record or further information about this donation)." Halper also notes that Brod helped to arrange the posthumous publication of Langer's volume of poetry: *Me'at Tzori* [A Bit of Balm], Tel Aviv, 1943. See also Milan Tvrdík, "Franz Kafka und Jiří (Georg) Langer: Zur Problematik des Verhältnisses Kafkas zur tschechischen Kultur," in *Moderne in der deutschen und der tschechischen Literatur*, ed. K. Schenk (Tübingen, 2000).

65 "How could I think of such a thing…" Franz Kafka, *Briefe 1902–1924*,

Gesammelte Werke, Taschenbuchausgabe in acht Banden, ed. Max Brod, S. Fischer Taschenbuch Verlag, 1998, pp. 403–4. Paul Mendes-Flohr, former director of the Franz Rosenzweig Research Center for German-Jewish Literature and Cultural History at the Hebrew University, writes that "under Buber's deft stewardship, *Der Jude* became not only the most sophisticated journal within the Jewish community, but one of the most engaging periodicals in the Weimar Republic." (*Divided Passions: Jewish Intellectuals and the Experience of Modernity*, Wayne State University Press, 1991, p. 211.)

66   "Y. H. Brenner's bleak last novel *Breakdown and Bereavement...*" Brenner's novel was written in Palestine in 1913–14 and published in 1920, a year before the author was killed on the outskirts of Jaffa by Arab rioters. He was buried in a mass grave in Tel Aviv's Trumpeldor cemetery, steps away from where Max Brod would be buried forty-seven years later. Hillel Halkin's excellent English translation appeared as *Breakdown and Bereavement*, Cornell University Press, 1971 (republished in 2004 by Toby Press). "Without knowing that Kafka had ever read Hebrew," Harvard professor Ruth Wisse reports, "the Hebrew critic Baruch Kurzweil called *Breakdown and Bereavement* the terrifying counterpart of Kafka's *The Trial*." (See Kurzweil's introduction to the Hebrew reissue of the novel by Am Oved, 1972.)

68   "In her forthcoming novel, *Forest Dark...*" See my interview with Nicole Krauss in the 2018 edition of *Paper Brigade*, the Jewish Book Council's annual literary magazine. Like Krauss, Philip Roth imagined that Kafka had survived both his tuberculosis and the Shoah. Roth brings the writer not to Palestine but to New Jersey, a "Jewish refugee arriving in America in 1938 ... a frail and bookish fifty-five-year-old bachelor." Finding employment as a Hebrew-school teacher, this Kafka instructs a nine-year-old Philip Roth and dates Philip's Aunt Rhoda, with whom he converses in Yiddish about gardening (" 'I Always Wanted You to Admire My Fasting'; or, Looking at Kafka," originally published in *American Review*, May 17, 1973). Harold Bloom called "Looking at Kafka" Roth's "best and most revealing critical performance." See also Peter Demetz, "Mit Franz Kafka in den Strassen von Newark," *Frankfurter Allgemeine Zeitung*, March 23, 2002. Another recent fictional treatment is *Kafka's Cats* (*Kafka macskái* in Hungarian), a novel by Hungarian writer Gábor T. Szántó, which chronicles a Budapest professor's obsession with finding Kafka's missing manuscripts. Two chapters of the novel, both translated by Ivan Sanders, appeared in *Moment* (July/August 2016) and *Tablet* (March 2016).

5. First and Second Judgments

72 "Brod's obsession with collecting everything . . ." In 2011, for example, Jerusalem art dealer Meir Urbach, son of eminent Hebrew University scholar E. E. Urbach, summoned Shedletzky to a hotel in Wiesbaden, in western Germany, to evaluate a trove of Brod ephemera—from school notebooks to shopping lists—that Esther Hoffe had apparently sold in 1982.

73 "Two-dozen unknown drawings by Kafka . . ." Sometime around 1980, Esther Hoffe had told Unseld that she had fifty unpublished sketches and drawings by Kafka. French researcher Jacqueline Sudaka-Bénazéraf says she saw fifty drawings at Hoffe's apartment in Tel Aviv, of which twenty-six had been published, and twenty-four had not. Two of Kafka's sketches have been housed at the Albertina Museum in Vienna since 1952; it is unclear how they got there. For more on these drawings, see Frederike Fellner, *Kafkas Zeichnungen*, Fink Verlag, 2014.

78 "Ottla, the youngest and most vivacious of the Kafka sisters . . ." Ottla Kafka, together with Max Brod's wife, Elsa, was active in Prague's Zionist Club of Jewish Women and Girls, founded in 1912. A plaque affixed to the bottom of Kafka's tombstone in Prague carries an inscription in Czech: *To the memory of the sisters of the renowned Prague Jewish writer Franz Kafka murdered during the Nazi occupation in 1942–1943.* See H. Zylberberg, "Das tragische Ende der drei Schwestern Kafkas," *Wort und Tat*, 1946–47, Heft 2. According to Hélène Zylberberg (1904–92), who met Kafka's sisters in late 1936, Ottla "never accepted the fact that Kafka's works had been published as the result of someone's indiscretion. Franz had left a will and his deepest and most sacred wish that all he had written be burned ought to have been obeyed. For this reason, she was angry with Max Brod." Zylberberg later translated Brod's biography of Kafka into French (Gallimard, 1945).

83 "In June 2015, the Supreme Court upheld that decision . . ." Israelitische Kultusgemeinde Wien v. Central Archives for the History of the Jewish People, file 9366/12.

6. Last Son of the Diaspora

85 "Kafka was one of ours. . . ." Weltsch, "Freiheit und Schuld in Franz Kafkas Roman *Der Prozeß*," in *Franz Kafka: Kritik und Rezeption 1924–1938*, ed. Jürgen Born, Fischer, 1983, pp. 122–128. See also Weltsch's essay from three

decades later, "The Rise and Fall of the Jewish-German Symbiosis: The Case of Franz Kafka," *Leo Baeck Institute Yearbook*, vol. 1 (1956), pp. 255–76.

86 "Kafka's nameless heroes, Hannah Arendt wrote..." In his epilogue to Kafka's novel *The Castle*, Brod reports on the enthusiasm with which Kafka told him the story of Flaubert's visit to a simple, normal family with many children. "*Ils sont dans le vrai* (those folks are right)," Flaubert exclaimed. "It was the perception of this truth," Hannah Arendt argued in 1944, "that made Kafka a Zionist. In Zionism he saw a means of abolishing the 'abnormal' position of the Jews, an instrument whereby they might become 'a people like other peoples.'" (Arendt, *The Jew as Pariah*, ed. Ron Feldman, Grove Press, 1978, p. 89.)

Kafka's readers in the Arab world, however, insisted otherwise. During the brief Damascus Spring of 2000, the Syrian writer Nayrouz Malek, for instance, brought out a novel called *Kafka's Flowers*. The protagonist, Jamal al-Halabi, is sent to Paris, where he immerses himself in Kafka's works to the point that he begins to converse with a statue of the writer.

> The bronze statue smiled: "I am sorry, I have not introduced myself; my name is Franz Kafka."
>
> I stopped, perplexed. I did not believe what the statue said.... True, that was Kafka, or someone who looks a lot like him and has assumed his personality. I protested: "But Kafka has been dead for sixty-five years; moreover, Kafka does not know Arabic." The Kafka statue smiled back. "Forgive me, please, I ask you not to speak of death. As for the Arabic in which I addressed you, I learned it recently and I was forced to learn it because, in their feverish fight against Zionism, some Arab critics accused me of being a Zionist and a writer who serves Zionist ideology. I had to learn Arabic so that I could tell them that my position is the opposite of what they think. I don't deny that I believe in Judaism that I am Jewish even though my relationship to religion and God was never compatible. As for the accusation of Zionism, it is utterly false."

In the end, Jamal returns home and checks into a mental asylum, where he goes by the name Kafka.

For a review of Kafka's reception in Arabic since 1939, see Atef Botros's study *Kafka—Ein jüdischer Schriftsteller aus arabischer Sicht*, Reichert Verlag, 2009.

86 "*Representative Man...*" Frederick R. Karl, Ticknor & Fields/Houghton Mifflin, 1991. "His was the voice of Europe well before Europe began to close in on its Kafkas," Karl writes.

87   "Although the word 'Jew' never appears . . ." Brod might have added that
the word "God" is similarly absent from Kafka's writing. In a dissertation
called *Kafka's German-Jewish Reception as Mirror of Modernity* (City University of New York, 2014), Abraham A. Rubin remarks: "Brod's recovery of Kafka's writing for a Jewish-national agenda illustrates the ways in
which his political and ideological convictions shaped his literary analysis.
The underlying irony of all this is that Brod's vision of Jewish particu-
larity is taken directly from an intellectual tradition whose influence he
would most likely disavow, German Romanticism. His conception of Kafka's Jewishness is deeply indebted to the Herderian idea that an author's
work expresses a *Volksgeist* unique to the nation to which he or she belongs.
His interpretation imposes an ideological coherence on Kafka that never
existed there in the first place. . . . The terms he uses to portray Kafka's
Judaism are meant to convey the idea that 'Jewish' and 'German' represent
mutually exclusive cultural entities."

87   "has said more about the situation of Jewry as a whole today . . ." In May
1927, Franz Rosenzweig, then translating the Hebrew Bible into German
with Martin Buber, remarked to his cousin Gertrud Oppenheim: "The
people who wrote the Bible indeed thought like Kafka. I have never read
a book that reminded me as powerfully of the Bible as his novel, *The Castle*." In a 1953 essay on Kafka, one of the earliest in Hebrew, the Israeli
poet Leah Goldberg (1911–1970), an immigrant from Königsberg (today
Kaliningrad), made a similar observation. "Kafka desired, desired greatly,
a solution and liberation from his current feelings and awareness. The
symbol of that liberation was a homeland. He repeats 'homeland' several
times [in *The Castle*]. This spells out the Land of Israel." Roberto Calasso,
one of the preeminent authors in Italy, regards *The Castle* and *The Trial*
as twin reflections on the election and condemnation of the Jews. "To be
chosen, to be condemned: two possible outcomes of the same process,"
Calasso writes. "Kafka's relationship to Judaism . . . emerges most clearly
on this point."

  For a contrasting view, see Jakob Michalski's 1935 review of *The Castle*:
"The only thing incomprehensible to the author of this review is the excess
of literary propaganda that dares to designate Kafka's art as specifically
'Jewish' and continues to celebrate him as a Jewish prodigy! His writings
are as un-Jewish as the novels of his friend and editor Max Brod . . . One
may celebrate Kafka as an artist, yet his accomplishments have nothing to
do with Jews or Judaism, and we reject the notion that a Jewish essence
[*jüdischen Wesen*] emanates from his work." (Jakob Michalski, "Das

Schloß." *Franz Kafka: Kritik und Rezeption 1924–1938*, ed. Jürgen Born, Fischer, 1983, p. 398.)

In writing *The Castle* in the first half of 1922, Kafka seems to have put his Hebrew to use. The protagonist's profession, *Landvermesser*, for instance, might play on the similarity of two Hebrew words: *maschoah* (land surveyor) and *mashiach* (messiah). See Rashi's commentary on Babylonian Talmud, Tractate Sanhedrin 98b.

88   "For Kafka knew better than anyone else . . ." Gershom Scholem, *Judaica* 3, p. 271 (Suhrkamp, 1973). See also Scholem, *Walter Benjamin: The Story of a Friendship* (Jewish Publication Society, 1981), pp. 170ff. It is worth noting that Scholem's disagreement with Walter Benjamin turns on just this point. In a letter from August 1, 1931, Scholem comments about a talk Benjamin gave called "Franz Kafka: Beim Bau der Chinesischen Mauer": "How, as a critic, you could manage to say anything about the world of this man without putting the doctrine, what Kafka called the law, into the center, is an enigma for me." For more on Scholem's appreciation of Kafka, see Stéphane Moses, "Zur Frage des Gesetzes. Gershom Scholems Kafka-Bild," in *Kafka und das Judentum*, eds. K. E. Grözinger, S. Moses, and H. D. Zimmermann (Athenaeum, 1987); Harold Bloom, *The Strong Light of the Canonical: Kafka, Freud and Scholem as Revisionists of Jewish Culture* (CCNY, 1987); David Biale, "Ten Unhistorical Aphorisms on Kabbalah, Text and Commentary," in *Gershom Scholem: Modern Critical Views*, ed. Harold Bloom (Chelsea House, 1987); and Robert Alter, *Necessary Angels: Tradition and Modernity in Kafka, Benjamin and Scholem* (Harvard University Press, 1991).

88   "According to his colleague Alexander Altmann . . ." Alexander Altmann, "Gershom Scholem, 1897–1982," *Proceedings of the American Academy for Jewish Research*, vol. 51 (1984). In 1916, Scholem had met Kafka's fiancée Felice Bauer while both were involved with the Jüdisches Volksheim, the Jewish community center in Berlin.

89   "In a 1929 essay, German-Jewish thinker Margarete Susman . . ." Margarete Susman, "Das Hiob-Problem bei Franz Kafka," *Der Morgen*, vol. 5 (1929); trans. Theodore Frankel, "Franz Kafka," *Jewish Frontier*, vol. 23 (1956). Max Brod also alluded to the ways Kafka addressed "the old Job-question." See Brod, "Franz Kafkas Grunderlebnis," *Die Weltbühne*, May 15, 1931. After reading *The Trial* in 1926, Gershom Scholem wrote: "Essentially, this work is without parallel, apart from the Book of Job. The situation of the hidden trial, within the framework of whose rules human life occurs, is developed in these two works to the very highest level. One may conjec-

ture that never did any Jew attain such a fashioning of his world from such an inner and profound center of Judaism." And in a 1931 letter, Scholem advised Walter Benjamin "to begin any inquiry into Kafka with the Book of Job, or at least with a discussion of the possibility of divine judgment." For more on Susman's association of Job with Kafka, see Mark Larrimore, *The Book of Job: A Biography*, Princeton University Press, 2013, pp. 236–39.

89 "Had Kafka lived a century or two earlier . . ." Robert Alter, "Kafka as Kabbalist," *Salmagundi*, Spring 1993. In his book *Canon and Creativity* (2000), Alter refers to Kafka's "midrashic adroitness" in his handling of the Tower of Babel story told in Genesis and underscores Kafka's "assumption that the Bible can provide him a resonant structure of motifs, themes, and symbols to probe the meaning of the contemporary world." (Kafka's reflections on that text can be found in *Parables and Paradoxes*, Schocken, 1961.) In an earlier book, *After the Tradition* (1969), Alter writes: "No Jew who has contributed so significantly to European literature appears so intensely, perhaps disturbingly, Jewish in the quality of his imagination as Kafka." British literary critic John Gross, in his review of the book, remarks that "Alter is rewarding, too, on the subject of critics who talk gaily about the 'talmudic' qualities of Kafka's prose without giving any sign that they know the difference between an *aleph* and a *bet*" (*Commentary*, April 1969). Like Alter, the literary critic George Steiner similarly sees Kafka as heir to Jewish styles of reading and interpretation. "The principal code" of his parables, Steiner writes, "is, self-evidently, that of the biblical and Talmudic legacy."

93 "I prefer another approach over psychoanalysis . . ." For more on Kafka's views on psychoanalysis, see "Kafka's Ambivalence towards Psychoanalysis," by Leena Eilittä, *Psychoanalysis and History* 3:2, 2001; and "Kafka, Freud, and 'Ein Landarzt,' " by Eric Marson and Keith Leopold, *The German Quarterly*, 37:2, March 1964.

99 "An overt or covert, or possibly self-tormenting usurpation . . ." Franz Kafka to Max Brod, June 1921 (quoted in Hannah Arendt, *Men in Dark Times*, p. 185). In a 1913 essay, "Der jüdische Dichter deutscher Zunge" [The Jewish Poet of the German Tongue], Brod argued that the Jewish poet merely safeguarded the German language as "foreign property" [*da es nicht das Erbe seiner Ahnen ist, das er verwaltet, sondern fremder Besitz*]. "Der jüdische Dichter deutscher Zunge," in *Vom Judentum: Ein Sammelbuch*, ed. Verein Jüdischer Hochschüler Bar Kochba, Kurt Wolff Verlag, 1913, pp. 261–63.

99 "Speech on the Yiddish Language." The critical edition more accurately titles Kafka's talk "Einleitungsvortrag über Jargon" (Introductory Lecture

on Jargon). For a more detailed discussion of Kafka's encounter with Yiddish theater, see Evelyn Torton Beck's groundbreaking study, *Kafka and the Yiddish Theater*, University of Wisconsin Press, 1971. "Kafka's abiding concern with the themes of justice, authority, and law, and his exploration of the relationship between the individual and the absolute and between the individual and the community may be seen as abstract formulations of the specifically Jewish problems raised by the Yiddish plays," Beck concludes. "By reinforcing his personal concerns, the plays of the Yiddish theater exercised a lasting influence on Kafka's style and helped to give shape to the problems that tormented Kafka the man."

7. The Last Ingathering

104 "In Berlin, hundreds of thousands more volumes were kept in the Reich Security Main Office . . ." See Dov Schidorsky, "The Library of the Reich Security Main Office and Its Looted Jewish Book Collections," *Libraries & the Cultural Record* 42, no. 1 (2007). In 1942, Johannes Pohl, a Nazi "expert" on the Jews, was dispatched to Vilna by the Nazi looting agency, Einsatzstab Reichsleiter Rosenberg, to organize the seizure of the city's great collections of Jewish books. Pohl and his staff planned to ship the most valuable materials to Germany and incinerate the rest. The Germans used forty ghetto inmates as slave-laborers to sort, select, pack, and transport the materials, either to Germany or to nearby paper mills. They ordered Herman Kruk, head of the Vilna ghetto library, to collect Jewish books in preparation for a "selection." Some 70 percent, Kruk reported, were to go "into the trash as scrap paper." "The Jewish workers employed on the project are literally weeping," he said. Between March 1942 and September 1943, Kruk organized a "paper brigade" which at great risk succeeded in rescuing thousands of Jewish books and manuscripts (including two hundred Torah scrolls, documents by H. N. Bialik, and a volume of Theodor Herzl's diaries). See Herman Kruk, *The Last Days of the Jerusalem of Lithuania: Chronicles from the Vilna Ghetto and the Camps 1939–1944*, trans. Barbara Harshav, Yale University Press, 2002; and David E. Fishman, *The Book Smugglers: Partisans, Poets, and the Race to Save Jewish Treasures from the Nazis*, University Press of New England, 2017.

105 "The Commission on European Jewish Cultural Reconstruction." See Cecil Roth, "The Restoration of Jewish Libraries, Archives, and Museums," *Contemporary Jewish Record* 7:3 (1944); Salo W. Baron, "The Spiritual Reconstruction of European Jewry," *Commentary* 1:1 (1945); Noam

Zadoff, "Reise in die Vergangenheit, Entwurf einer neuen Zukunft: Gershom Scholems Reise nach Deutschland im Jahre 1946," *Münchner Beiträge zur Jüdischen Geschichte und Kultur* 2 (2007); and Elisabeth Gallas, "Locating the Jewish Future: The Restoration of Looted Cultural Property in Early Postwar Europe," *Nahariam* 9 (2015). For a report of his rescue mission, see Scholem, "On the Question of Looted Jewish Libraries," *Haaretz*, October 5, 1947, pp. 5–6 [Hebrew].

106 "Comparatively few Israeli literary critics have written about Kafka..." Gabriel Moked (born Munwes), a survivor of the Warsaw ghetto who emigrated from Poland to Tel Aviv in 1946, published a book-length Hebrew commentary on "The Metamorphosis" in 1956. "Kafka's status as a Jewish author," Moked remarked, "is of major significance, since he expresses a certain continuity of Jewish spiritual affinities and thoughts, and not merely as an individual Jewish genius." The literary critic Mordechai Shalev (1926–2014) addressed the Jewish elements in Kafka's writing in a series of three essays in the Israeli newspaper *Haaretz* (October 15, 1997; April 10, 1998; and May 29, 1998). Yoram Bar David wrote a book about Kafka in 1998 (see also his article "Kafka's Paradise: His Hasidic Thought," in *Kafka's Contexuality*, ed. Alan Udoff, Gordian, 1986, pp. 235–86); as did Nathan Ofek (1942–2006) in 2002. See also *Kafka: New Perspectives*, a collection of essays in Hebrew edited by Ziva Shamir, Yochai Ataria, and Chaim Nagid (Safra, 2013). To be sure, this is by no means an exhaustive list, and some Israeli critics have addressed Kafka's work without stressing the author's Jewishness. See, for example, *The Way of Wavering: Forms of Uncertainty in Kafka* [*Derech Ha-Hissus*] by Shimon Sandbank (Ha-Kibbutz Ha-Meuchad, 1974), and *Kafka's Wound* by Galili Shahar (Carmel, 2008).

108 "A short-lived local German-language weekly called *Orient*...." See *Orient. Haifa 1942–1943: Bibliographie einer Zeitschrift*, ed. Volker Riedel, Aufbau Verlag, 1973. Arnold Zweig wrote one novel in Palestine: *Das Beil von Wandsbek* (*The Axe of Wandsbek*). It was published in Hebrew translation in 1943 as *Ha-Kardom shel Wandsbek* (trans. Avigdor Hameiri, Mervavia Publishing). Other postwar authors who lived in Israel but wrote in German included Werner Kraft, Ilana Shmueli, Manfred Winkler, and Schalom Ben-Horin.

109 "My mother tongue, as stated, was German..." Appelfeld, "First Years, Mother Tongue, and Other Pains," *Maariv*, April 18, 1997 [Hebrew].

109 "There is no question that Jews tried to enter into a dialogue with Germans..." See Gershom Scholem, "Wider den Mythos vom deutschjüdischen Gespräch," in *Auf gespaltenem Pfad: für Margarete Susman*,

ed. Manfred Schlösser (1964), pp. 229–33; and "Against the Myth of the German-Jewish Dialogue," in *On Jews and Judaism in Crisis: Selected Essays* (1976). See also "The 'German-Jewish Dialogue' and its Literary Refractions: The Case of Margarete Susman and Gershom Scholem," Abraham Rubin, *Modern Judaism*, February 2015, pp. 1–17.

111 "In his book *Old Worlds, New Mirrors...*" See Vivian Liska's review of Moshe Idel's book: "On Getting It Right," *Jewish Quarterly Review*, Spring 2012, pp. 297–301. See also Idel's discussion of Kafka's parable "Before the Law," in *Kabbala: New Perspectives* (Yale University Press, 1988), p. 271.

112 "Kafka was on the side of the mice or the moles..." Dan Miron, *From Continuity to Contiguity: Toward a New Jewish Literary Thinking*, Stanford University Press, 2010.

114 "Kafka's premonitions..." In his book *The Conflagration of Community*, J. Hillis Miller, professor at the University of California, Irvine, writes that "what Kafka foresaw was a wholesale destruction of the Jewish people." Miller further contends that Kafka's writing not only foretold the future but shaped it; Kafka, fearing his writings "might be prophetic or might have the force to bring about on a large scale the individual sufferings and catastrophes they dramatize," instructed Brod to destroy them to prevent them "from having their magic performative effect." Dissenters from this view include Robert Alter, who calls the making of Kafka into a prophet of the Holocaust "the ultimate vulgarity." For counterarguments and explanations for why "striking parallels do not a prophet make," see Lawrence Langer's 1986 essay, "Kafka as Holocaust Prophet: A Dissenting View," in *Admitting the Holocaust: Collected Essays*, Oxford University Press, 1995.

115 "Israeli allegorical fiction..." In his novel *The Retrospective* (2013), A. B. Yehoshua adapts Kafka's fragmentary story "In Our Synagogue" ("In unserer Synagoge," written in 1922 and translated into Hebrew by Dan Miron in 2009), about a timorous animal who takes up residence in a synagogue. Left untitled by Kafka, the story was given its title by Brod when he published it in 1937. For a discussion of "the omnipresence of Kafka" in Aharon Appelfeld's fiction, and the "heavy debt" Appelfeld's Hebrew owed to Kafka's German, see David Suchoff, "Kafka and the Postmodern Divide: Hebrew and German in Aharon Appelfeld's *The Age of Wonders*," *The Germanic Review* 75:2 (2000).

117 "Agnon consistently refused to recognize Kafka's paternity..." Vienna-born scholar of comparative literature Lilian Furst writes: "In spite of certain undeniable affinities between them, Kafka and Agnon are related only as black is to white." Among contemporary Israeli novelists, David Grossman (b. 1954) acknowledges his debt to Kafka but denies that the

Prague writer can be pinned to any single national tradition. "I think Kafka would be Kafka even if he were born in America, or England, or Australia," Grossman says. For a comparison of Kafka and Agnon, see Hillel Barzel, *Agnon and Kafka: A Comparative Study*, Bar-Ilan University Press, 1972 [Hebrew]; and Gershon Shaked, "After the Fall: Nostalgia and the Treatment of Authority in Kafka and Agnon," in *The New Tradition: Essays on Modern Hebrew Literature*, Hebrew Union College Press, 2006. "Both Kafka and Agnon," Shaked concludes, "were shaped by the trauma of World War I. Their works predict the greater cataclysm to follow, as well as the catastrophe awaiting Europe's Jewry, while they reflect the despair felt by residents of the disintegrating Habsburg Empire, who could find no viable substitute for the emperor/father/ 'former commandant.'" For Brod's views on Agnon, see his article, "Zwei Jüdische Bücher," *Die neue Rundschau* 29:2, 1918, where Brod writes of the way in which Agnon expressed "the atmosphere of his native land."

117 "A newfound fascination with German culture..." For more on the subject, see *The Slopes of a Volcano*, Amos Oz's collection of three essays in Hebrew on the normalization of relations between Israel and Germany (Keter, 2006); Fania Oz-Salzberger, *Israelis in Berlin*, Jüdischer Verlag im Suhrkamp Verlag, 2001; Dani Kranz, *Israelis in Berlin. Wie viele sind es und was zieht sie nach Berlin?* Bertelsmann, 2015; and sociologist Gad Yair's 2015 study of Israeli migration to Germany, *Love is Not Praktish: The Israeli Look at Germany*, Ha-Kibbutz Ha-Meuchad, 2015 [Hebrew]. Israeli writer Yoram Kaniuk (1930–2013) records his encounters in Germany between 1984 and 2000 in *Ha-Berlinai Ha-Acharon* [*The Last Berliner*], Yediot Acharonot, 2004; *Der letzte Berliner*, List, 2002.

8. Kafka's Last Wish, Brod's First Betrayal

126 "He wanted to burn everything that he had written..." Quoted in J. P. Hodin, "Memories of Franz Kafka," *Horizon*, January 1948. Before ill health forced him to leave Berlin for the last time, Kafka left with Dora some twenty notebooks. These, together with some thirty-five of his letters to her, were seized from her apartment by the Gestapo in March 1933 and have never resurfaced. Later in the '30s, Brod asked his friend the Czech-Jewish poet Camill Hoffmann, then press attaché at the Czech embassy in Berlin, to look for this material. The search was in vain, and Hoffmann himself, a close friend of President Masaryk, was arrested by the Gestapo. He perished in Auschwitz in October 1944.

127 "Brod was neither the first nor the last to confront such a dilemma...."
For a discussion of these and other examples, see *On the Burning of Books*
by Kenneth Baker, University of Chicago Press, 2017. For the Albee case,
see Michael Paulson, "Edward Albee's Final Wish: Destroy My Unfinished Work," *New York Times*, July 4, 2017. "I have often thought about
Brod's dilemma," the literary critic Lionel Trilling wrote in 1970, "and
have never been able to conclude that he was anything but right in resolv-
ing it as he did ... I think that in Brod's position I would have acted as
he did, though with qualms. Brod's knowledge of the nature and quality
of the literary manuscripts does of course bear decisively upon the right-
ness of his action. I am rather more hesitant about confirming Brod's
preservation of the private papers. But in the event, the private papers
being what we now know them to be, I believe he was right." *Life in
Culture: Selected Letters of Lionel Trilling*, ed. Adam Kirsch, Farrar, Straus
and Giroux, 2018, p. 385.

128 "The two notes forbidding the publication of Kafka's works..." For one of
the earliest defenses of Brod along these lines, see Walter Benjamin "Kava-
liersmoral," *Literarischen Welt*, October 10, 1929. Brod printed Kafka's two
notes in the German magazine *Weltbühne* a month after Kafka's death.

9. Kafka's Creator

133 "In his lecture on 'The Metamorphosis,' Vladimir Nabokov writes..."
Vladimir Nabokov, *Lectures on Literature*, ed. Fredson Bowers, Harcourt
Brace Jovanovich, 1980.

133 "We read Kafka Brodly." The phrase is borrowed from the English novelist and essayist Zadie Smith ("F. Kafka, Everyman," *New York Review of
Books*, July 17, 2008).

134 "William Phillips, coeditor of *Partisan Review*..." In a retort to William
Phillips, Austrian-Jewish writer Friedrich Torberg, who had been mentored
by Brod, writes: "There seems to be in this country a general critical tendency
to discard Brod's insistence on Kafka's Jewishness as a kind of sectarian queer-
ness, and it seems particularly outspoken among Jewish critics—obviously as
part and parcel of that glorious Jewish attitude which refuses to look at a
problem, be it ever so Jewish, from a 'merely' Jewish standpoint" ("Kafka the
Jew," *Commentary*, August 1947).

135 "In Israel, the small number of his books translated into Hebrew..."
Wallstein Verlag in Göttingen, Germany, is currently putting out
Brod's "Selected Works" (edited by Hans-Gerd Koch and Hans Dieter

Zimmermann). For a review of the first two publications of the twelve-volume series, see Nikolaus Stenitzer, "über *Ausgewählte Werke* von Max Brod," *konkret*, May 2013.

136 "He persuaded the Munich publisher Kurt Wolff..." Kurt Wolff founded his publishing house in 1912. After fleeing to the United States in 1940, Wolff and his wife, Helen, founded Pantheon Books in 1942. The Beinecke Rare Book and Manuscript Library at Yale University holds the Kurt Wolff Archive, 1907–1938, which includes Wolff's correspondence with Kafka, Brod, Rilke, Hermann Hesse, Karl Kraus, Else Lasker-Schüler, Heinrich and Thomas Mann, and Franz Werfel, among others. For an informed discussion of Jewish readings of *Amerika*, see Joseph Metz, "Zion in the West: Cultural Zionism, Diasporic Doubles, and the 'Direction' of Jewish Literary Identity in Kafka's *Der Verschollene*," *Deutsche Vierteljahrsschrift* 78:4 (2004).

136 "To end *The Trial* with Joseph K.'s execution..." In the critical edition published by S. Fischer Verlag, Malcolm Pasley resequenced the chapters of *The Trial*. (See Kafka, *Der Proceß. Roman in der Fassung der Handschrift*, ed. Malcolm Pasley, S. Fischer, 1990.) Herman Uyttersprot blames much of the interpretive difficulties in *The Trial* and *Amerika* on Brod's clumsy editing. See his book *Eine neue Ordnung der Werke Kafkas?*, de Vries-Brouwers, 1957. For a contrasting view, see Ronald Gray, "The Structure of Kafka's Works: A Reply to Professor Uyttersprot," *German Life and Letters*, 13 (1959).

138 "He was urged by one of his editors..." Quoted in "Publisher's Note," *The Trial: A New Translation Based on the Restored Text*, trans. Breon Mitchell, Schocken, 1998.

139 "The last bastion of culture in Germany..." Schocken Verlag issued the first of six volumes of Kafka's *Collected Works* in 1935. Other German reviews that greeted Schocken's publication of the first volume that year appeared in *Magdeburger Zeitung*, May 17, 1935; and *Schweinfurter Tagblatt*, May 31, 1935.

139 "Spitzer fled to Jerusalem..." Once settled into his home on Radak Street in Jerusalem's upscale Rehavia neighborhood, Spitzer founded Tarshish Books, a publishing house renowned for its innovative typography and high production values. It would publish 119 titles between 1940 and 1979, including Yosl Bergner's *Illustrations to Franz Kafka* (published in English in 1959 and in Hebrew in 1970); the poems of Avraham Ben-Yitzhak (Abraham Sonne); *Kelev Hutzot* (A Stray Dog) by S. Y. Agnon (with illustrations by Avigdor Arikha); and *Mein Blaues Klavier* [My Blue Piano] by Else Lasker-Schüler. Spitzer also brought out Hebrew translations of *Waiting for Godot* by Samuel Beckett, Bertolt Brecht (lithographs by Gershon

Knispel), the poems of Rilke (illustrations by Avigdor Arikha), and Heinrich von Kleist's *Michael Kohlhaas*. For more, see *Moshe Spitzer: Books-Typography-Design* (catalogue of an exhibition at the National Library of Israel), Jerusalem, 1981; Ada Wardi, ed., *Spitzer Book*, Mineged Publications, 2016; Israel Soifer, "The Pioneer Work of Maurice Spitzer," *Penrose Annual* 63, 1970; and Hilit Yeshurun's interview with Spitzer, "Unfinished Conversations," *Hadarim*, Winter 1982–83.

139   "Heinrich Heine's manuscripts and letters..." David Suchoff, author of *Kafka's Jewish Languages* (2012), calls Heine "the greatest—we could say the most universally loved—German-Jewish writer before Kafka." In late 1966, Gideon Schocken, a son of Salman Schocken, sold the family's Heine collection to the Bibliothèque Nationale, the French National Library, for an undisclosed price. (The Schocken Library in Jerusalem had put some of them on display ten years earlier, in 1956.) President Charles de Gaulle lent his personal support during the negotiations. Israeli authorities registered no objection. Once in Paris, the manuscripts were studied by a team of French and German scholars led by Louis Hay. In 1960, the auction house Hauswedell sold Schocken's Novalis collection to the Freie Deutsches Hochstift in Frankfurt am Main. Later in the decade, these were edited as volumes 2 and 3 of Novalis' *Complete Works*. (See "Ernst L. Hauswedell: Ein Arbeitsbericht," in *Ernst Hauswedell 1901–1983*, ed. Gunnar A. Kaldewey, Maximilian-Gesellschaft, 1987.)

10. The Last Train

148   "I have known and admired Dr. Brod..." *The Letters of Thomas Mann, 1889–1955*, trans. Richard and Clara Winston, University of California Press, 1975, pp. 237–38. See also Peter F. Neumeyer, "Thomas Mann, Max Brod, and the New York Public Library," *MLN* (*Modern Language Notes*), April 1975.

150   "The Schocken Library on Balfour Street..." For a detailed description of the Schocken Library in Jerusalem, see Adina Hoffman, *Till We Have Built Jerusalem: Architects of a New City*, Farrar, Straus & Giroux, 2016.

11. The Last Tightrope Dancer

156   "Several novels of Dostoyevsky..." In Kafka's copy of a German translation of Dostoyevsky's *The Brothers Karamazov*, Felice Bauer wrote a dedication dated 1914: "Perhaps we will read it soon together." For a detailed

account, see Jürgen Born, *Kafkas Bibliothek: Ein beschreibendes Verzeichnis*, S. Fischer Verlag, 1990.

156 "The Lutheran writer of Alemannic folktales Johann Peter Hebel..." Kafka's interest in Hebel's writings is perhaps particularly interesting in view of the attraction they would hold for an admiring Nazi readership. In 1933, the Nazi mayor of Freiburg, Franz Kerber, claimed that given "his deeply rooted love of the homeland... today Hebel too would support the National Socialist party." For Martin Heidegger's admiration for Hebel's "rootedness" in Alemannic dialect and landscape, see Heidegger's essays "Sprache und Heimat," in *Über Johann Peter Hebel*, Rainer Wunderlich Verlag, 1964; and "Hebel, der Hausfreund," G. Neske, 1957. The latter appeared in English as "Hebel—Friend of the House," translated by Bruce V. Foltz and Michael Heim, in *Contemporary German Philosophy*, Volume III, Pennsylvania State University Press, 1983.

156 "Goethe was his Bible..." Compare with the sentiments of Gershom Scholem, who emigrated from Weimar Germany to British Mandate Palestine in 1923, a year before Kafka's death: "Goethe has never spoken to me, which must mean something very important, perhaps that the Jewish genius in me demarcates itself somehow from the German world." *Lamentations of Youth: The Diaries of Gershom Scholem*, translated and edited by Anthony David Skinner, Harvard University Press, 2002, p. 212.

160 "German philosopher Wilhelm Dilthey..." See Wilhelm Dilthey, "Archive für Literatur," (address delivered on the occasion of the founding of the Gesellschaft für deutsche Literatur, January 16, 1889, *Deutsche Rundschau* 58 (1889); and Adolf Landguth, "Zur Frage der 'Archive für Literatur,'" *Centralblatt für Bibliothekswesen* 6:10 (1889).

160 "The National Socialists both commandeered German-language literature and called it into question..." The most trenchant treatment of the subject is Victor Klemperer's *LTI—Lingua Tertii Imperii: Notizbuch eines Philologen* (1947); translated into English by Martin Brady as *The Language of the Third Reich: A Philologist's Notebook* (2000). "If a piece of cutlery belonging to Orthodox Jews has become ritually unclean," Klemperer writes, "they purify it by burying it in the earth. Many words in common usage during the Nazi period should be committed to a mass grave for a very long time, some forever."

160 "The loose-knit circle of German writers known as Gruppe 47..." Many of the Gruppe 47 writers bore affinities, direct or indirect, with Kafka's work, including Ilse Aichinger (1921–2016), awarded the Kafka Prize in 1983, and Siegfried Lenz (1926–2014), whose short stories were unmistakably haunted by Kafka's influence. See Klaus Briegleb, *Missachtung und Tabu. Eine Streitschrift zur Frage: Wie antisemitisch war die Gruppe 47?* Philo-Verlag, 2003.

Briegleb disparaged the group's "deep malaise" (*"tiefe Befangenheit"*) vis-à-vis Jews writing in German and its "anti-Jewish affect" (*"antijüdische Affekte"*). Maxim Biller, a German-Jewish *provocateur*, went so far as to call the group a "de-nazified Chamber of Literature" (*"entnazifizierte Reichsschrifttumskammer"*). (*Brauchen wir eine neue Gruppe 47? Interviews mit Joachim Kaiser und Maxim Biller: 55 Fragebögen zur deutschen Literatur*, eds. Joachim Leser and Georg Guntermann, Reinhard Nenzel Verlag, 1995.)

161   "Hitler Youth, looking to Schiller as a standard-bearer of National Socialism . . ." For more on the Nazi appropriation of the poet, see *Schiller als Kampfgenosse Hitlers* (*Schiller Fighting at Hitler's Side*), by the National Socialist politician Hans Fabricius (published in 1932, reprinted in 1934 and 1936); and Lesley Sharpe, "National Socialism and Schiller," *German Life and Letters* 36 (1983). During the Second World War, the Schiller Museum in Marbach was directed by Georg Schmückle (1880–1948). A member of the Nazi Party since 1931, he also served as chairman of the right-wing anti-Semitic political society called the Militant League for German Culture (*Kampfbund für deutsche Kultur*).

165   "In his notorious essay 'Judaism in Music' . . ." Wagner, *Judaism in Music and Other Essays*, trans. William Ashton Ellis, University of Nebraska Press, 1995.

167   "West Germans pressed Kafka into service . . ." In East Germany, by contrast, Kafka was written out of the curriculum and literary canon. Angelika Winnen, in a study of his reception in the GDR, writes that the literary establishment of the 1950s, committed to socialist realism since the First All-Union Congress of Soviet Writers in August 1934, denounced Kafka's works were as "decadent" and "useless." Angelika Winnen, *Kafka-Rezeption in der Literatur der DDR: Produktive Lektüren von Anna Seghers, Klaus Schlesinger, Gert Neumann und Wolfgang Hilbig*, Königshausen & Neumann, 2006.

167   "Those who were guilty of and complicit in the excessive crimes of the Hitler regime . . ." Günther Anders, "Einleitung," in *Mensch ohne Welt. Schriften zur Kunst und Literatur*, C. H. Beck, 1984. See also Günther Anders, *Kafka, Pro und Contra: die Prozess-Unterlagen*, C. H. Beck, 1963; and "Kafka: Ritual Without Religion," *Commentary*, December 1949. "Ironically," writes Kata Gellen of Duke University, "Anders transforms Kafka from a prophet into an agent of historical delusion, from someone who sees into someone who prevents others from seeing." See "Kafka, Pro and Contra: Günther Anders's Holocaust Book," in *Kafka and the Universal*, eds. Arthur Cools and Vivian Liska, de Gruyter, 2016.

170   "Both are pariahs." Quoted in Marcel Reich-Ranicki, *Über Ruhestörer: Juden in der deutschen Literatur*, Piper 1973, p. 55; and in Amos Elon, *The Pity of it All: A History of Jews in Germany 1743–1933*, Metropolitan, 2002, p. 10.

12. Laurel & Hardy

173 "The flagship Habima theater..." Yfaat Weiss, professor at the Department of the History of the Jewish People and Contemporary Jewry of the Hebrew University in Jerusalem, points out that a considerable part of Habima's administrative archive from the first decade and a half of its existence is written in German. Why is this so, she asks, "given that the theater was founded in Moscow in 1917, and from its inception performed solely in the Hebrew language? Because Weimar Berlin, capital of European theater during the initial third of the twentieth century, was the city in which Habima was enthusiastically welcomed when it repeatedly visited there between 1926 and 1931. It was there that Habima shaped its professional profile and evolved from being just one of a number of eastern-European Jewish theater troupes that frequented the city to become a genuinely modernistic repertory theater." ("German or in German? On the Preservation of Literary and Scholarly Collections in Israel," *Transit: Europäische Revue*, Institut für die Wissenschaften vom Menschen, March 2, 2015.)

175 "I was invited by the universities in Zürich and Basel..." Gnazim archive, 97/24606.

176 "He created a two-act libretto for the first Hebrew opera in history..." Seventy years later, in May 2015, the opera would be revived and staged by the National Library of Israel. Shin Shalom was introduced to Brod by Anna and Meinhold Nussbaum in 1939. Anna, the sister of the German-Jewish poet Jakob van Hoddis, had translated one of Shalom's novels into German (*Galiläisches Tagebuch*). Brod's other musical compositions include a piano quintet, Israeli dances, and *Requiem Hebrascum* (words by Shin Shalom). Brod claimed to have "discovered" the Czech composer Leoš Janáček, whose libretti Brod translated into German. See Charles Susskind, *Janáček and Brod*, Yale University Press, 1985. For Brod's own views on his role in Hebrew theater, see "From the Notebook of a Dramaturg," *Bamah*, December 1940, and "From the Diary of a Dramaturg," *Bamah* 48, 1946 (both in Hebrew). For more on Brod's Habima archive, see Ofer Aderet, "Where Are the Missing Index Cards?" *Haaretz*, September 22, 2008.

177 "I've read your play..." Gnazim archive, 273/ 98884.א.

178 "*King Lear.*" See Yair Lipshitz, "Biblical Shakespeare: King Lear as Job on the Hebrew Stage," *New Theatre Quarterly* 31:4, November 2015.

180 "Three studies on Kafka . . ." *Franz Kafkas Glauben und Lehre* (Franz Kafka's Faith and Teaching, 1948); *Kafka als wegweisende Gestalt* (Kafka as Guide, 1959); and *Verzweiflung und Erloesung im Werk Kafkas* (Despair and Redemption in Kafka's Work, 1959).

181 "Hans-Joachim Schoeps." See Schoeps, *Der vergessene Gott: Franz Kafka und die tragische Position des modernen Juden*, ed. Andreas Krause Landt, Landt Verlag, 2006. See also Schoeps' memoir, *Ja, Nein und Trotzdem: Erinnerungen, Begegnungen, Erfahrungen*, Hase & Koehler, 1974. Brod and Schoeps began corresponding in the early 1920s after Schoeps reviewed Brod's book *Paganism, Christianity, Judaism* (*Heidentum, Christentum, Judentum*) in the *Christliche Welt*, a Protestant magazine founded in 1887, and met in Marienbad in 1929. Brod was by no means the only Zionist to denounce Schoeps. In 1933, Gershom Scholem wrote to Walter Benjamin: "As far as Kafka is concerned, in my estimation you *cannot* count on seeing the book you are awaiting from Herr Schoeps. The young man—I must have written you that I also made his acquaintance in Berlin and have little interest in its continuation, since he is bursting with vanity and the desire to be on everybody's lips—is so busy trying to connect up with German fascism in every way, *sans phrase* [without further ado], that he will not have time for any activities in the foreseeable future. . . . I confess that one did not expect such a spectacle from the editor of Kafka's papers, even if he is but a lad of 23, who was by no means selected by the deceased." In his postwar memoir, German-American rabbi and civil-rights leader Joachim Prinz described Schoeps and his followers as "fanatic, super-patriots, passionate anti-Zionists, and in a very real sense anti-Semitic. They were self-hating Jews who thought they could save themselves by making common cause with the Nazis" (*Rebellious Rabbi: An Autobiography*, ed. Michael A. Meyer, Indiana University Press, 2008). See also Scholem's denunciation of Schoeps' book *Jewish Belief in This Epoch*, "Offener Brief an den Verfasser der Schrift, 'Jüdischer Glaube in dieser Zeit,'" *Bayerische Israelitische Gemeindezeitung*, August 15, 1932; reprinted in Scholem, *Briefe*, I:466–71, C.H. Beck, 1994–99.

184 "Bialik's essay 'The Hebrew Book' . . ." Bialik delivered his talk "The Hebrew Book" at the Conference of Hebrew Language and Culture, held in Vienna in 1913, and published it in 1914 in the monthly review *Hashiloah*. The essay was included in the Jubilee edition of Bialik's *Collected Works* (1923) and appeared in the English translation of Minnie Halkin in 1951.

13. Brod's Last Love

193   "They had volunteered together ..." See Max Brod, "Erzgebirge schreit um Hilfe," *Prager Tagblatt*, April 8, 1932; and Hilfe für das Erzgebirge," *Prager Tagblatt*, April 14, 1932.

195   "Book of poems in German, *Gedichte aus Israel* (Poems from Israel) ..." Published with illustrations by Felix Gluck, Starczewski Verlag, 1967, reprinted 2004.

198   "The Tel Aviv District Court granted probate to Brod's last will ..." Tel Aviv District Court, file 245/69.

200   "The Israeli Archives Law of 1955 ..." For a detailed review of the drafting and history of the archives law, see Paul Alsberg, "The Israel Archives Law, History and Implementation," *Arkhyon: Reader in Archives Studies and Documentation* 1 (1987), pp. 7–29 [Hebrew].

Epilogue

225   "Had one to name the artist who comes nearest ..." W. H. Auden, "The Wandering Jew," in *The Complete Works of W.H. Auden. Prose: Volume II, 1939–1948*, ed. Edward Mendelson, Princeton University Press, 2002, 2:110.

Bibliography

Works by Max Brod

Arnold Beer: Das Schicksal eines Juden. Axel Juncker, 1912 [reprinted Wallstein, 2013].

"Axiome über das Drama." *Schaubühne*, September 21, 1911.

Beinahe ein Vorzugsschüler oder Pièce touchée. Manesse, 1952.

"Der Dichter Franz Kafka." *Die neue Rundschau* 32, 1921; reprinted in *Juden in der deutschen Literatur: Essays über zeitgenössische Schriftsteller,* ed. Gustav Krojanker. Welt Verlag, 1922, 55–62.

Diesseits und Jenseits. Mondial Verlag, 1947 (2 volumes).

"Die Dritte Phase des Zionismus." *Die Zukunft*, January 20, 1917.

Franz Kafka. Eine Biographie. Mercy Verlag, 1937 [English translation by G. Humphreys Roberts and Richard Winston, Schocken, 1960; Hebrew translation by Edna Kornfeld, Am Oved, 1955].

"Franz Kafkas Grunderlebnis." *Die Weltbühne*, May 15, 1931.

Die Frau, nach der man sich sehnt. Paul Zsolnay, 1927 [*Three Loves*, trans. Jacob Wittner. Knopf, 1929].

Das gelobte Land (Promised Land: Poems). Kurt Wolff, Leipzig, 1917.

Gustav Mahler: Beispiel einer deutsch-jüdischen Symbiose. Ner Tamid, 1961.

Heinrich Heine: The Artist in Revolt, 1934 [trans. Joseph Witriol, New York University Press, Valentine Mitchell 1956; Collier, 1962].

Jüdinnen. Axel Juncker, 1911 [reprinted Kurt Wolff, 1915; Wallstein, 2013].

"Der jüdische Dichter deutscher Zunge." In *Vom Judentum: Ein Sammelbuch.* Verein Jüdischer Hochschüler Bar Kochba in Prag, 1913.

"Die jüdische Kolonisation in Palästina." *Die Neue Rundschau* 28, 1917.

Eine Königin Esther. Drama in einem Vorspiel und drei Akten. Kurt Wolff, 1918.

"Macbeth through the Ages." *Davar*, May 21, 1954 [Hebrew].

Der Meister. Bertelsmann, 1952 [*The Master*, trans. Heinz Nordau. Philosophical Library, 1951].

Die Musik Israels. Sefer, 1951 [reprinted Kassel, 1976].

"Nachwort zur ersten Ausgabe." In Franz Kafka, *Das Schloß*. S. Fischer, 1951.

Paganism, Christianity, Judaism: A Confession of Faith, trans. William Wolf. University of Alabama Press, 2010 [*Heidentum, Christentum, Judentum: Ein Bekenntnisbuch*. Kurt Wolff, 1921].

Der Prager Kreis. Kohlhammer, 1966 [reprinted Suhrkamp, 1979; Wallstein, 2016].

Rassentheorie und Judentum. Barissia, 1934 [republished with an afterword by Felix Weltsch, R. Löwit, 1936].

Rebellische Herzen. Herbig, 1957.

Rëubeni, Fürst der Juden. Ein Renaissanceroman. Kurt Wolff, 1925 [*Reubeni: Prince of the Jews*, trans. Hannah Wallter. Knopf, 1928].

Die Rosenkoralle. Eckart, 1961.

Schloss Nornepygge: Der Roman des Indifferenten. Juncker, 1908.

Sozialismus im Zionismus. R. Löwit, 1920.

Streitbares Leben (A Contentious Life). Kindler, 1960 [expanded edition, F.A. Herbig, 1969; Insel, 1979; Hebrew: *Chayei Meriva*, trans. Y. Slaee. Ha-sifriya Ha-tzionit, 1967].

Tod und Paradies Chamber Works. Supraphon Records CD 1121882931, 1994.

Tycho Brahes Weg zu Gott. Wallstein, 2013 [*The Redemption of Tycho Brahe*, trans. Felix Warren Crosse. Knopf, 1928; reissued as *Tycho Brahe's Path to God*. Northwestern University Press, 2007].

Über Franz Kafka. S. Fischer, 1974.

Unambo: Roman aus dem jüdisch-arabischen Krieg. Steinberg, 1949 [English translation by Ludwig Lewisohn, Farrar, Straus & Young, 1952].

"Unsere Literaten und die Gemeinschaft." *Der Jude* 1, 1916.

"Ungedrucktes zu Franz Kafka." *Die Zeit*, October 22, 1965.

Die verkaufte Braut: Der abenteuerliche Lebensroman des Textdichters Karel Sabina. Bechtle, 1962.

Zauberreich der Liebe. Paul Szolnay, 1928 [*The Kingdom of Love*, trans. Eric Sutton, Secker, 1930].

Max Brod, ed. *Arkadia. Ein Jahrbuch für Dichtkunst.* Kurt Wolff, 1913.

Works by Franz Kafka

Abandoned Fragments: The Unedited Works of Franz Kafka 1897–1917, trans. Ina Pfitzner. Sun Vision Press, 2012.

Amerika. Kurt Wolff Verlag, 1927 [trans. Willa and Edwin Muir. Schocken, 1962].

Amtliche Schriften, ed. Klaus Hermsdorf and Benno Wagner. S. Fischer, 2004.

Beim Bau der chinesischen Mauer. Gustav Kiepenhauer Verlag, 1931.

Betrachtung. Kurt Wolff Verlag, 1915.

The Blue Octavo Notebooks, ed. Max Brod, trans. Ernst Kaiser and Eithne Wilkins. Exact Change, 1991.

Briefe, 1902–1924, ed. Max Brod. Schocken, 1959.

Briefe an Felice und andere Korrespondenz aus der Verlobungszeit, ed. Erich Heller and Jürgen Born. Fischer, 1967 [*Letters to Felice*, trans. James Stern and Elisabeth Duckworth. Schocken, 1988].

Briefe an Milena, ed. Jürgen Born and Michael Müller. S. Fischer, 1986 [*Letters to Milena*, trans. Philip Boehm. Schocken, 1990].

The Complete Stories, trans. Willa and Edwin Muir, ed. Nahum N. Glatzer. Schocken, 1976.

The Diaries of Franz Kafka, 1910–1913, ed. Max Brod, trans. Joseph Kresh. Schocken, 1948.

The Diaries of Franz Kafka, 1914–1923, ed. Max Brod, trans. Martin Greenberg and Hannah Arendt. Schocken, 1949.

Franz Kafka: Briefe. 1900–1912, ed. Hans-Gerd Koch. S. Fischer Verlag, 1999.

Franz Kafka: Briefe. 1913–1914, ed. Hans-Gerd Koch. S. Fischer Verlag, 2001.

Franz Kafka: Briefe. 1914–1917, ed. Hans-Gerd Koch. S. Fischer Verlag, 2005

Franz Kafka: Briefe. 1918–1920, ed. Hans-Gerd Koch. S. Fischer Verlag, 2013.

Franz Kafka: The Office Writings, eds. Stanley Corngold, Jack Greenberg, and Benno Wagner. Princeton University Press, 2009.

Hebrew letter to Puah Ben-Tovim, June 1923, reprinted in *Hayim U-Ma'As B'Mifalenu Ha-Khinukhim: Sefer Zikaron L'Dr. Yosef Shomo Menzel Zikhrono Livrakha, Leben und Wirken: Unser Erzieherisches Werk: In Memoriam Dr. Josef Schlomo Menczel 1903–1953*, ed. Puah Menczel-Ben-Tovim. Menczel Memorial Foundation, 1981.

I Am a Memory Come Alive: Autobiographical Writings, ed. Nahum Glatzer. Schocken, 1974.

Kafka Kritische Ausgabe, eds. Jürgen Born et al. S. Fischer, ongoing.

Ein Landarzt und andere Drucke zu Lebzeiten, ed. Hans-Gerd Koch. S. Fischer Taschenbuch, 1994.

Letters to Friends, Family, and Editors, trans. Richard and Clara Winston. Schocken, 1977.

Letter to His Father, trans. Ernst Kaiser and Eithne Wilkins. Schocken, 1953.

"The Metamorphosis," trans. Susan Bernofsky. W. W. Norton, 2014.

Nachgelassene Schriften und Fragmente I, ed. Malcolm Pasley. S. Fischer, 1993.

Nachgelassene Schriften und Fragmente II, ed. Jost Schillemeit. S. Fischer, 1992.

Parables and Paradoxes, ed. Nahum N. Glatzer. Schocken, 1961.

Der Prozess. Die Schmiede, 1925.

Der Prozess, trans. Melech Ravitch. Der Kval, 1966 [Yiddish].

Das Schloss. Kurt Wolff Verlag, 1926.

Selected Stories, ed. and trans. Stanley Corngold. W. W. Norton, 2007.

Tagebücher, eds. Hans-Gerd Koch, Michael Müller, and Malcolm Pasley. S. Fischer, 1990.

The Trial: A New Translation Based on the Restored Text, trans. Breon Mitchell. Schocken, 1998.

Vor dem Gesetz. Schocken, 1934.

Wedding Preparations in the Country and Other Posthumous Prose Writings, trans. E. Kaiser and E. Wilkins (notes by Max Brod). Secker & Warburg, 1954.

The Zürau Aphorisms of Franz Kafka, eds. Roberto Calasso, Geoffrey Brock, and Michael Hofmann. Schocken, 2006.

General Bibliography and Works Cited

Adorno, Theodor W. "Notes on Kafka." In *Franz Kafka*, ed. Harold Bloom. Chelsea House, 1986.

Allemann, Beda. "Kafka et l'histoire." In *L'endurance de la pensée. Pour saluer Jean Beaufret*, eds. René Char et al. Plon, 1968.

Alt, Peter-André. *Franz Kafka: Der ewige Sohn*. Beck, 2005.

Alter, Robert. *After the Tradition: Essays on Modern Jewish Writing*. Dutton, 1969.

——. *Canon and Creativity.* Yale University Press, 2000.

——. "Franz Kafka: Wrenching Scripture." *New England Review* 21.3, 2000.

——. "Kafka as Kabbalist." *Salmagundi*, Spring–Summer 1993.

——. *Necessary Angels: Tradition and Modernity in Kafka, Benjamin, and Scholem.* Harvard University Press, 1991.

Anderson, Mark. *Kafka's Clothes: Ornament and Aestheticism in the Habsburg Fin de Siècle.* Oxford University Press, 1992.

——, ed. *Reading Kafka: Prague, Politics, and the Fin de Siècle.* Schocken, 1989.

Appelfeld, Aharon. "A Conversation with Philip Roth." In *Beyond Despair: Three Lectures and a Conversation with Philip Roth*, trans. Jeffrey M. Green. Fromm International, 1994.

Arendt, Hannah. "Franz Kafka: A Revaluation." In *Essays in Understanding, 1930–1954*, ed. Jerome Kohn. Harcourt Brace & Co., 1994 [originally published in *Partisan Review* 11:4, 1944].

Arnold, Hannah. "Brod's Case." *TLS*, October 17, 2014.

Bahr, Ehrhard. "Max Brod as a Novelist: From the Jewish Zeitroman to the Zionist Novel." In *Von Franzos zu Canetti: Jüdische Autoren aus Österreich*, ed. Mark H. Gelber. Niemeyer, 1996.

Bahr, Hermann. "Max Brods Bewusstsein vom Judentum: Ethik in der Spannung von Diesseits und Jenseits." In *Messianismus zwischen Mythos und Macht: jüdisches Denken in der europäischen Geistesgeschichte*, eds. Eveline Goodman-Thau and Wolfdietrich Schmied-Kowarzik. Akademie Verlag, 1994.

Baioni, Giuliano. *Kafka: Literatur und Judentum.* Metzler, 1994.

Balint, Benjamin. "Kafkas letzter Prozess." *Die Zeit*, September 12, 2016.

——. "Kafka's Own Metamorphosis." *Wall Street Journal*, November 18, 2016.

Bärsch, Claus-Ekkehard. *Max Brod im Kampf um das Judentum. Zum Leben und Werk eines deutsch-jüdischen Dichters aus Prag.* Passagen Verlag, 1992.

Barzel, Hillel. *Agnon and Kafka: A Comparative Study.* Bar-Ilan University Press, 1972 [Hebrew].

Bashan, Refael. "Max Brod." In *I Have an Interview: New and Selected Interviews.* Am Oved, 1965 [Hebrew].

Batuman, Elif. "Kafka's Last Trial." *New York Times Magazine*, September 22, 2012.

Beck, Evelyn Torton. *Kafka and the Yiddish Theater.* University of Wisconsin Press, 1971.

Begley, Louis. *The Tremendous World I Have Inside My Head—Franz Kafka: A Biographical Essay.* Atlas & Co., 2008.

Benjamin, Walter. *Benjamin über Kafka: Texte, Briefzeugnisse, Aufzeichnungen*, ed. Hermann Schweppenhäuser. Suhrkamp, 1981.

——. "Franz Kafka: On the Tenth Anniversary of His Death." *Illuminations*, trans. Harry Zohn, ed. Hannah Arendt. Schocken, 1969.

——. "Review of Brod's Franz Kafka." In *Selected Writings: 1935–1938*, eds. Howard Eiland and Michael W. Jennings. Harvard University Press, 2002.

Bennett, Alan. *Two Kafka Plays.* Faber & Faber, 1987.

Binder, Hartmut. "Franz Kafka and the Weekly Paper *Selbstwehr*." *Leo Baeck Institute Yearbook* 12 (1967).

——. *Kafka-Kommentar: zu sämtlichen Erzählungen.* Winkler Verlag/Patmos, 1975.

——. "Kafka's Hebräischstudien." In *Jahrbuch der deutschen Schillergesellschaft* 11. Alfred Kroner Verlag, 1967.

——. *Motiv und Gestaltung bei Franz Kafka.* Bouvier, 1966.

Blanchot, Maurice. "Kafka and the Work's Demand." In *The Space of Literature*, trans. Ann Smock. University of Nebraska Press, 1982.

Bloom, Cecil. "Max Brod, Polymath." *Midstream*, January 1997.

Bloom, Harold, ed. *Franz Kafka*. Bloom's Literary Criticism/Infobase, 2010.

Born, Jürgen, ed. *Franz Kafka: Kritik und Rezeption 1924–1938*. S. Fischer Verlag, 1983.

———. *Kafkas Bibliothek: Ein beschreibendes Verzeichnis*. S. Fischer Verlag, 1990.

Bornstein, Sagi, writer and director. *Kafka's Last Story*. 53 minutes. 2011.

Botros, Atef. *Kafka: Ein jüdischer Schriftsteller aus arabischer Sicht*. Reichert Verlag, 2009.

Brenner, David A. *German-Jewish Popular Culture before the Holocaust: Kafka's Kitsch*. Routledge, 2008.

Brenner, Michael. *The Renaissance of Jewish Culture in Weimar Germany*. Yale University Press, 1998.

Brod, Max, and Hans-Joachim Schoeps. *Im Streit um Kafka und das Judentum: Der Briefwechsel zwischen Max Brod und Hans-Joachim Schoeps*, ed. Julius Schoeps. Jüdischer Verlag bei Athenäum, 1985.

Bruce, Iris. *Kafka and Cultural Zionism*. University of Wisconsin Press, 2007.

Buber, Martin. *Drei Reden über das Judentum*. Rütten & Loening, 1916.

Buber, Martin, et al. *Das jüdische Prag: eine Sammelschrift*. Verlag der Selbstwehr, 1917 [reissued 1978].

Butler, Judith. "Who Owns Kafka?" *London Review of Books*, March 3, 2011.

Calasso, Roberto. *K*. Knopf, 2005.

Canetti, Elias. *Kafka's Other Trial: The Letters to Felice*, trans. Christopher Middleton. Schocken, 1974.

Caputo-Mayr, Marie Luise, and Julius M. Herz, eds. *Franz Kafka: International Bibliography of Primary and Secondary Literature*. Saur, 2000 [three volumes].

Carmely, Klara. "Noch Einmal: War Kafka Zionist?" *The German Quarterly* 52:3, May 1979.

Carrouges, Michel. *Kafka versus Kafka*, trans. Emmett Parker. University of Alabama Press, 1968.

Caygill, Howard. *Kafka: In Light of the Accident*. Bloomsbury, 2017.

Cohen, Nili. "The Betrayed(?) Wills of Kafka and Brod." *Law and Literature* 27:1, 2015.

Cools, Arthur, and Vivian Liska, eds. *Kafka and the Universal*. de Gruyter, 2016.

Corngold, Stanley. *Franz Kafka: The Necessity of Form*. Cornell University Press, 1988.

———. *Lambent Traces: Franz Kafka*. Princeton University Press, 2004.

Cott, Jonathan. "Glenn Gould: The Rolling Stone Interview." *Rolling Stone*, August 15, 1974.

Dahm, Volker. *Das jüdische Buch im Dritten Reich* (Zweiter Teil: Salman Schocken und sein Verlag). Buchhändler-Vereinigung, 1982.

Dannof, Brian. "Arendt, Kafka, and the Nature of Totalitarianism." *Perspectives on Political Science* 29:4, 2000.

David, Anthony. *The Patron: A Life of Salman Schocken*. Metropolitan Books, 2003.

Dehne, Doris. *The Formative Years of Kafka Criticism: Max Brod's Interpretation of Franz Kafka*. PhD diss., Vanderbilt University, 1977.

Deleuze, Gilles, and Felix Guattari. *Kafka: Toward a Minor Literature*. University of Minnesota Press, 1986.

Demetz, Peter. "Speculations about Prague Yiddish and its Disappearance: From its Origins to Kafka and Brod." In *Confrontations/Accommodations: German-Jewish Literary and Cultural Relations from Heine to Wassermann*, ed. Mark H. Gelber. Niemeyer Verlag, 2004.

Derrida, Jacques. *Archive Fever*, trans. Eric Prenowitz. University of Chicago Press, 1998.

———. "Before the Law," trans. Avital Ronell. In *Kafka and the Contemporary Critical Performance*, ed. Alan Udoff. University of Indiana Press, 1987.

Diamant, Kathi. *Kafka's Last Love*. Basic Books, 2003.

Dietz, Ludwig. *Franz Kafka*. Metzler, 1975.

Dorn, Anton Magnus. *Leiden als Gottesproblem. Eine Untersuchung zum Werk von Max Brod*. PhD diss., Katholisch-Theologische Fakultät, Ludwig-Maximilians-Universität München, 1981.

Dowden, Stephen D. *Kafka's* The Castle *and the Critical Imagination*. Camden House, 1995.

Duttlinger, Carolin, ed. *The Cambridge Introduction to Franz Kafka*. Cambridge University Press, 2013.

Einhorn, Talia. "The Rights to the Kafka Manuscripts." *Wealth Management Law Review* 2, 2016 [Hebrew].

Eisner, Pavel. *Franz Kafka and Prague*. Griffin Books, 1950.

Emrich, Wilhelm. *Franz Kafka*. Athenäum Verlag, 1958. [*Franz Kafka: A Critical Study of His Writings*, trans. Sheema Zeben Buehne. Ungar, 1968 and 1981.]

Eshel, Amir. *Futurity: Contemporary Literature and the Quest for the Past*. University of Chicago Press, 2013.

———. "Von Kafka zu Celan: Deutsch-Jüdische Schriftsteller und ihr Verhältnis zum Hebräischen und Jiddischen." In *Jüdische Sprachen in deutscher Umwelt*, ed. Michael Brenner. Vandenhoeck & Ruprecht, 2002.

Fenves, Peter. "Introduction to the New Edition," *Tycho Brahe's Path to God*, Max Brod. Northwestern University Press, 2007.

Flores, Angel, ed. *The Kafka Debate: New Perspectives for Our Time*. Gordian Press, 1977.

———, ed. *The Kafka Problem*. New Directions, 1946.

Friedländer, Saul. *Franz Kafka: The Poet of Shame and Guilt*. Yale University Press, 2013.

Geissler, Benjamin, director. *Finding Pictures*. 107 minutes. 2002.

Gelber, Mark H. "The Image of Kafka in Max Brod's *Zauberreich der Liebe* and its Zionist Implications." In *Kafka, Zionism, and Beyond*, ed. Mark H. Gelber. Niemeyer Verlag, 2004.

———. "Max Brod's Zionist Writings." In *Leo Baeck Institute Yearbook*, 1988.

———. *Melancholy Pride: Nation, Race, and Gender in the German Literature of Cultural Zionism*. Niemeyer Verlag, 2000.

———, ed. *Kafka, Zionism, and Beyond*. Niemeyer Verlag, 2004.

Geller, Jay. *Bestiarium Judaicum: Unnatural Histories of the Jews*. Fordham University Press, 2017.

Gilman, Sander. *Franz Kafka: The Jewish Patient*. Routledge, 1995.

Glatzer, Nahum N. "Franz Kafka and the Tree of Knowledge." In *Between East and West: Essays Dedicated to the Memory of Bela Horovitz*, ed. Alexander Altmann. East and West Library, 1958.

Glazer, Hilo. "A Final Note from Kafka, a Trove of Manuscripts, and a Trial that Left an Israeli Heiress Destitute." *Haaretz*, February 18, 2017.

Gold, Hugo, ed. *Max Brod: Ein Gedenkbuch*. Olamenu, 1969.

Goldberg, Lea. *Yomanei Lea Goldberg* (The Diaries of Lea Goldberg), eds. Rachel and Arie Aharoni. Sifriat Poalim, 2005 [Hebrew].

Goldschmidt, Georges-Arthur. *Meistens wohnt der den man sucht nebenan. Kafka lesen*. S. Fischer, 2010.

Goodman, Paul. *Kafka's Prayer*. Vanguard, 1947.

Goldstein, Bluma. *Reinscribing Moses: Heine, Kafka, Freud, and Schoenberg in a European Wilderness*. Harvard University Press, 1992.

Gordon, Adi. *In Palestine. In a Foreign Land: The Orient. A German-Language Weekly between German Exile and Aliyah*. Magnes Press, 2004 [Hebrew].

Gray, Ronald. *Franz Kafka*. Cambridge University Press, 1973.

Grözinger, Karl Erich. *Franz Kafka und das Judentum*. Eichborn, 1987.

———. *Kafka and Kabbalah*, trans. Susan Hecker Ray. Continuum, 1994.

Grunfeld, Frederic V. *Prophets without Honour: A Background to Freud, Kafka, Einstein and Their World*. Holt, Rinehart & Winston, 1979.

Haas, Willy. "Der junge Max Brod." *Tribüne* 3, 1964.

Halbertal, Moshe. *People of the Book: Canon, Meaning, and Authority*. Harvard University Press, 1997.

Halper, Shaun J. "Mordechai Langer (1897–1943) and the Birth of the Modern Jewish Homosexual." PhD diss., University of California, Berkeley, 2013.

Hanssen, Jens. "Kafka and Arabs." *Critical Inquiry*, Autumn 2012.

Hayman, Ronald. *Kafka: A Biography*. Oxford University Press, 1981.

Heidsieck, Arnold. *The Intellectual Contexts of Kafka's Fictions: Philosophy, Law and Religion*. Camden House, 1994.

———. "Max Brods Kritik an der christlichen Kultur im Anschluß an den ersten Weltkrieg." In *Allemands, Juifs et Tchèques à Prague. Deutsche, Juden und Tschechen in Prag 1890–1924*, eds. Maurice Godé, Jacques Le Rider, and Françoise Mayer. Université Paul-Valéry, 1996.

Heinrich, Eduard Jacob. "Achtzig Jahre Max Brod." *Frankfurter Allgemeine Zeitung*, March 23, 1964.

Heller, Erich. *The Disinherited Mind: Essays in Modern German Literature and Thought*. Mariner Books, 1975.

———. *Franz Kafka*. Penguin, 1975; Princeton University Press, 1982.

———. "Kafka's True Will." *Commentary*, June 1973.

Hesse, Hermann. "Versuch einer Rechtfertigung: Zwei Briefe wegen Palaestina." *Neue Schweizer Rundschau* 16, 1948.

Hoffmann, Werner. "Kafkas Aphorismen und die jüdische Mystik." In *Kafkas Aphorismen*. Francke, 1975.

Hofmann, Martha. "Dinah und der Dichter. Franz Kafkas Briefwechsel mit einer Sechzehnjährigen." *Die österreichische Furche* 10, 1954.

Horwitz, Rivka. "Kafka and the Crisis in Jewish Religious Thought." *Modern Judaism* 15.1, 1995.

Howarth, Herbert. "The Double Liberation." *Commentary*, May 1952.

Howe, Irving. "Brod on Kafka." *The Nation*, July 12, 1947.

Jessen, Caroline. "Spuren Deutsch-Jüdischer Geschichte: Erschliung und Erforschung von Nachlässen und Sammlungen in Israel." *Archivar*, July 2013.

———. "Der Kanon im Archiv: Chancen und Herausforderungen für die Erforschung von Nachlässen deutsch-jüdischer Autoren in Israel." *Naharaim* 7, 2013.

Kayser, Werner, and Horst Gronemeyer. *Max Brod*. Hans Christians Verlag, 1972.

Kermani, Navid. "Was ist deutsch an der deutschen Literatur?" *Vortrag*, Konrad-Adenauer-Stiftung, December 13, 2006.

Kieval, Hillel J. *Languages of Community: The Jewish Experience in the Czech Lands*. University of California Press, 2000.

——. *The Making of Czech Jewry: National Conflict and Jewish Society in Bohemia, 1870–1918*. Oxford University Press, 1998.

Kilcher, Andreas B. *Franz Kafka*. Suhrkamp, 2008.

——. "Wie kommt Kafka aus dem UBS-Safe?" Tachles, March 2, 2018.

——. "Kafka im Betrieb. Eine kritische Analyse des Streits um Kafkas Nachlass." In *Literaturbetrieb. Zur Poetik einer Produktionsgemeinschaft*, eds. Philipp Theisohn and Christine Weder. Fink, 2013.

Klingsberg, Reuven, ed. *Exhibition Franz Kafka 1883–1924*. Catalogue: Jewish National and University Library, 1969.

Koch, Hans-Gerd, ed. *Als Kafka mir entgegenkam . . . Erinnerungen an Franz Kafka*. Wagenbach Verlag, 1995.

——. "Kafkas Max und Brods Franz: Vexierbild einer Freundschaft." In *Literarische Zusammenarbeit*, ed. Bodo Plachta. Tübingen 2001.

Koelb, Clayton. *Kafka's Rhetoric: The Passion of Reading*. Cornell University Press, 1989.

Kraft, Werner. *Franz Kafka: Durchdringung und Geheimnis*. Suhrkamp, 1968.

Kremer, Detlev. *Kafka: Die Erotik des Schreibens*. Athenäum, 1989.

Krojanker, Gustav. "Max Brods Weg zum Leben." *Der Jude* 1, 1916–17.

Kuehn, Heinz R. "Max Brod." *The American Scholar*, Spring 1993.

Kundera, Milan. "Rescuing Kafka from the Kafkaologists." *Times Literary Supplement*, May 24, 1991.

——. *Testaments Betrayed*, trans. Linda Asher. HarperCollins, 1995.

Lamping, Dieter. *Von Kafka bis Celan. Jüdischer Diskurs in der deutschen Literatur des 20. Jahrhunderts*. Vandenhoeck & Ruprecht, 1998.

Langer, Georg Mordechai. "Mashehu al Kafka" (A Kafka Anecdote). In *Me'at Tza'ari*, ed. Miriam Dror. Agudat Ha-Sofrim Ha-Ivrim, 1984 [Hebrew].

——. *Poems and Songs of Love*, trans. Elana and Menachem Wolff. Guernica Editions, 2014.

Langer, Lawrence. "Kafka as Holocaust Prophet: A Dissenting View." In *Admitting the Holocaust: Collected Essays*. Oxford University Press, 1995.

Leader, Zachary. "Cultural Nationalism and Modern Manuscripts." *Critical Inquiry*, Autumn 2013.

Leavitt, June O. *The Mystical Life of Franz Kafka: Theosophy, Cabala, and the Modern Spiritual Revival*. Oxford University Press, 2011.

Liehm, Antonin J. "Franz Kafka in Eastern Europe." *Telos* 23, Spring 1975.

Liska, Vivian. "As If Not: Giorgio Agamben Reading Kafka." In *Messianism and Politics: Kabbalah, Benjamin, Agamben*, eds. Vittoria Borsò, Claas Morgenroth, Karl Solibakke, and Bernd Witte. Königshausen & Neumann, 2010.

——. "Neighbors, Foes, and Other Communities: Kafka and Zionism." *Yale Journal of Criticism* 13:2, 2000.

——. *When Kafka Says We: Uncommon Communities in German-Jewish Literature*. Indiana University Press, 2009.

Meissner, Frank. "German Jews of Prague: A Quest for Self-Realization." *Publications of the American Jewish Historical Society* 50:2, 1960.

Menczel (Ben-Tovim), Puah. "Ich war Kafkas Hebräischlehrerin." In *Als Kafka mir entgegenkam . . . Erinnerungen an Franz Kafka*, ed. Hans-Gerd Koch. Wagenbach Verlag, 1995.

——. "Interview with Aviva Limon." Jerusalem, June 8, 1988, transcribed and edited by Ehud Netzer.

Mirecka, Agata. "Die Idee des Messianismus und Zionismus bei Max Brod." *Brücken: Germanistisches Jahrbuch Tschechien-Slowakei*, 2006.

Miron, Dan. *From Continuity to Contiguity: Toward a New Jewish Literary Thinking*. Stanford University Press, 2010.

Moked, Gabriel. *Kafka: Critical Essays on the Metamorphosis*. Mehadir, 1956 [Hebrew].

Moses, Stephane, and Albrecht Schöne, eds. *Juden in der deutschen Literatur*. Suhrkamp, 1986.

Murray, Nicholas. *Kafka*. Yale University Press, 2004.

Nagel, Bert. *Kafka and World Literature*. 1983.

Neumeyer, Peter F. "Thomas Mann, Max Brod, and the New York Public Library." *MLN (Modern Language Notes)* 90:3, April 1975.

North, Paul. *The Yield: Kafka's Atheological Reformation*. Stanford University Press, 2015.

Ofek, Natan. *Kafka ve-Hakiyum ha-Yehudi* (Kafka and Jewish Existence). 2002 [Hebrew].

———. *Sichot al Kafka Ve'od* (Conversations on Kafka and More). 2004 [Hebrew].

O'Neill, Patrick. *Transforming Kafka: Translation Effects*. University of Toronto Press, 2014.

Oppenheimer, Anne. *Franz Kafka's Relation to Judaism*. D.Phil. thesis, Oxford University, 1977.

Ozick, Cynthia. "How Kafka Actually Lived." *New Republic*, April 11, 2014.

———. "The Impossibility of Being Kafka." *New Yorker*, January 11, 1999.

Pasley, Malcolm, ed. *Max Brod, Franz Kafka: eine Freundschaft. Briefwechsel*. S. Fischer, 1989.

Pasley, Malcolm, and Hannelore Rodlauer, eds. *Max Brod, Franz Kafka: Eine Freundschaft. Reiseaufzeichnungen*. S. Fischer, 1987.

Pawel, Ernst. "Kafka's Hebrew Teacher." *New York Times*, August 16, 1981.

———. *The Nightmare of Reason: A Life of Franz Kafka*. Farrar, Straus & Giroux, 1984.

Pazi, Margarita. "Das Problem des Bösen und der Willensfreiheit bei Max Brod, Ernst Weiss und Franz Kafka." *Modern Austrian Literature* 18:1, 1985.

———. *Fünf Autoren des Prager Kreises*. Lang, 1978.

———. "Max Brod." *Modern Austrian Literature*, 20:3/4, 1987.

———. "Max Brod: Unambo." In *Turn of the Century Vienna and its Legacy: Essays in Honor of Donald G. Daviau*, eds. J. B. Berlin, J. B. Johns, and R. H. Lawson. Edition Atelier, 1993.

———. *Max Brod: Werk und Personlichkeit*. H. Bouvier, 1970.

———, ed. *Max Brod, 1884–1984: Untersuchungen zu Max Brods literarischen und philosophischen Schriften*. Lang, 1987.

———, ed. *Nachrichten aus Israel. Deutschsprachige Literatur in Israel*. Olms, 1981.

Politzer, Heinz. *Franz Kafka: Parable and Paradox*. Cornell University Press, 1966.

Preece, Julian. *Cambridge Companion to Kafka*. Cambridge University Press, 2002.

Preston, John. "Raiders of the Lost Archive." *Sunday Times* (London), August 12, 2012.

Raabe, Paul. "Die frühen Werke Max Brods." *Literatur und Kritik* 11, 1967.

———. *Zu Gast bei Max Brod: Eindrücke in Israel 1965*. Niedersächsische Landesbibliothek, Niemeyer, 2004.

Reich-Ranicki, Marcel. "Juden in der deutschen Literatur." *Die Zeit*, May 2, 1969.

Reitter, Paul. "Misreading Kafka." *Jewish Review of Books*, Fall 2010.

Robert, Marthe. *Seul, comme Franz Kafka*. Calmann-Lévy, 1979 [*As Lonely as Franz Kafka*, trans. Ralph Manheim, Harcourt Brace Jovanovich, 1982].

Robertson, Ritchie. "*Antizionismus, Zionismus*: Kafka's Responses to Jewish Nationalism." In *Paths and Labyrinths: Nine Papers from a Kafka Symposium*, eds. J. P. Stern and J. J. White. Institute of Germanic Studies, 1985.

———. "The Creative Dialogue between Brod and Kafka." In *Kafka, Zionism, and Beyond*, ed. Mark H. Gelber. Niemeyer, 2004.

———. *Kafka: Judaism, Politics, Literature*. Oxford University Press, 1985.

———. "Kafka's encounter with the Yiddish theatre." In *The Yiddish Presence in European Literature*, eds. Joseph Sherman and Ritchie Robertson. Legenda, 2005.

———. "Kafka's Writings: Private Confessions or Public Property?" *Bodleian Library Record* 25, 2012.

———. "Max Brod's novel *Tycho Brahes Weg zu Gott*: A Tale of Two Astronomers." In *Kafka, Prag und der Erste Weltkrieg*, eds. Manfred Engel and Ritchie Robertson. Königshausen & Neumann, 2012.

———. "Sex as Sin or Salvation: Max Brod's *Heidentum Christentum Judentum* and Kafka's *Das Schloß*." In *Kafka und die Religion in der Moderne*, eds. Manfred Engel and Ritchie Robertson. Königshausen & Neumann, 2014.

Rokem, Freddie."Max Brod as Dramaturg of Habima." In *Max Brod 1884–1984: Untersuchungen zu Max Brods literarischen und philosophischen Schriften*, ed. Margarita Pazi. Lang, 1987.

Rosenfeld, Isaac. "Kafka and His Critics." *New Leader*, April 12, 1947.

Roth, Philip. " 'I Always Wanted You to Admire My Fasting;' or, Looking at Kafka." In *Reading Myself and Others*. Penguin, 1985.

———. "In Search of Kafka and Other Answers." *New York Times Book Review*, February 15, 1976.

Rosenzweig, Franz. "Apologetic Thinking." In *Philosophical and Theological Writings*, eds. Paul W. Franks and Michael L. Morgan. Hackett Publishing, 2000 [originally published in *Der Jude*, 1923].

Rubin, Abraham A. *Kafka's German-Jewish Reception as Mirror of Modernity*. PhD diss., Graduate Center, City University of New York, 2014.

———. "Max Brod and Hans-Joachim Schoeps: Literary Collaborators, Ideological Rivals." *Leo Baeck Institute Yearbook*, June 2015.

Sandbank, Shimon. *After Kafka: The Influence of Kafka's Fiction*. University of Georgia Press, 1989.

———. *Derekh Ha-Hisus: al I-Hoda'ut Ve-Giluyah Bi-Yetsirat Kafka* (The Way of Wavering: Forms of Uncertainty in Kafka). Ha-Kibbutz Ha-Meuchad, 1974 [Hebrew].

Schirrmeister, Sebastian. *Begegnung auf fremder Erde. Narrative Deterritorialisierung in deutsch- und hebräischsprachiger Prosa aus Palästina/Israel nach 1933*. PhD diss., Universität Hamburg, 2017.

———. "On Not Writing Hebrew: Max Brod and the 'Jewish Poet of the German Tongue' between Prague and Tel Aviv." *Leo Baeck Institute Yearbook*, 2015.

Schoeps, Hans-Joachim. *Der vergessene Gott: Franz Kafka und die tragische Position des modernen Juden*, ed. Andreas Krause Landt. Landt Verlag, 2006.

Scholem, Gerhard (Gershom). "Das hebräische Buch: Eine Rundfrage." *Jüdische Rundschau*, April 4, 1928.

———. "Against the Myth of the German-Jewish Dialogue." In *On Jews and Judaism in Crisis*, ed. Werner J. Dannhauser. Schocken, 1976.

———, ed. *The Correspondence of Walter Benjamin and Gershom Scholem 1932–1940*, trans. Gary Smith and Andre Lefevere. Harvard University Press, 1992.

Shahar, Galili. "Fragments and Wounded Bodies: Kafka after Kleist." *German Quarterly* 80:4, Fall 2007.

——. "Kafka in Israel." In *Der Nahe Osten—Ein Teil Europas: Reflektionen zu Raum- und Kulturkonzeptionen im modernen Nahen Osten*, ed. Atef Botrus. Verlag Ergon, 2006.

——. *Kafka's Wound*. Carmel, 2008 [Hebrew].

Shahar, Galili, and Michal Ben-Horin. "Franz Kafka und Max Brod." In *Franz Kafka: Leben-Werk-Wirkung*, eds. Oliver Jahraus and Bettina von Jagow. Vandenhoeck & Ruprecht, 2008.

Shaked, Gershon. "Kafka, Jewish Heritage, and Hebrew Literature." In *The Shadows Within: Essays on Modern Jewish Writers*. Jewish Publication Society, 1987. [Published in German as "Kafka: Jüdisches Erbe und hebräische Literatur," *Die Macht der Identität—Essays über jüdische Schriftsteller*. Jüdischer Verlag, 1992.]

Shalom, S. *Im Chaim Nachman Bialik v'Max Brod: Pegishot* (with H. N. Bialik and Max Brod: Encounters). Aked, 1984 [Hebrew].

Shumsky, Dmitry. *Between Prague and Jerusalem*. Merkaz Shazar. 2010 [Hebrew].

Singer, Isaac Bashevis. "A Friend of Kafka." *New Yorker*, November 23, 1968.

Sokel, Walter H. "Kafka as a Jew." *New Literary History* 30, 1999.

——. *The Myth of Power and the Self: Essays on Franz Kafka*. Wayne State University Press, 2002.

Spector, Scott. *Prague Territories: National Conflict and Cultural Innovation in Franz Kafka's Fin de Siècle*. University of California Press, 2000.

Spitzer, Moshe. "Responses of German Jews to the Nazi Persecutions (Internal Life, 1933–1939)." Transcript of interview with Otto Dov Kulka, [undated] 1964, Department of Oral Documentation, Institute of Contemporary Jewry, Hebrew University of Jerusalem.

——. "Youth Movements in Czechoslovakia." Transcript of interview with Otto Dov Kulka (reel 312), April 20, 1964, Department of Oral Documentation, Institute of Contemporary Jewry, Hebrew University of Jerusalem.

Šrámková, Barbora. "Max Brod und die tschechische Kultur." In *Juden zwischen Deutschen und Tschechen, Sprachliche und kulturelle Identitäten in Böhmen, 1800–1945*, eds. Marek Nekula and Walter Koschmal. R. Oldenbourg, 2006 [republished Arco, 2010].

Stach, Reiner. *Kafka: The Decisive Years*, trans. Shelley Frisch. Harcourt, 2005; paperback ed. Princeton University Press, 2013.

——. *Kafka: The Early Years*, trans. Shelley Frisch. Princeton University Press, 2016.

——. "Kafkas letztes Geheimnis." *Tagesspiel*, January 26, 2010.

——. "Kafkas Manuskripte: Der Process gehört uns allen." *Frankfurter Allgemeine Zeitung*, August 7, 2010.

——. *Is that Kafka? 99 Finds*, trans. Kurt Beals. New Directions, 2016.

——. *Kafka: The Years of Insight*, trans. Shelley Frisch. Princeton University Press, 2013.

Stähler, Axel. "Zur Konstruktion einer 'zionistischen' Ethik in Max Brods Romanen *Rëubeni, Fürst der Juden* und *Zauberreich der Liebe*." In *Die Konstruktion des Jüdischen in Vergangenheit und Gegenwart*, eds. Alexandra Ponten and Henning Theissen. Ferdinand Schöningh, 2003.

Starobinski, Jean. "Kafka's Judaism." *European Judaism: A Journal for the New Europe* 8:2 (Summer 1974).

Steiner, George. "K." In *Language and Silence: Essays on Language, Literature, and the Inhuman*. Yale University Press, 1998.

Steiner, Marianna. "The Facts about Kafka." *New Statesman*, February 8, 1958.

Stern, J. P. "On Prague German Literature." In *The Heart of Europe: Essays on Literature and Ideology*. Blackwell, 1992.

Suchoff, David. "Kafka and the Postmodern Divide: Hebrew and German in Aharon Appelfeld's *The Age of Wonders*." *The Germanic Review* 75:2, 2000.

———. *Kafka's Jewish Languages: The Hidden Openness of Tradition*. University of Pennsylvania Press, 2011.

Sudaka-Bénazéraf, Jacqueline. *Le regard de Franz Kafka: Dessins d'un écrivain*. Maisonneuve & Larose, 2001.

Susman, Margarete. "Franz Kafka," trans. Theodore Frankel. *Jewish Frontier* 23, 1956.

Swales, Martin. "Why Read Kafka?" *Modern Language Review* 76, 1981.

Taussig, Ernst F., ed. *Ein Kampf um Wahrheit: Max Brod zum 65. Geburtstag*. ABC-Verlag, 1949.

Teller, Judd L. "Modern Hebrew Literature of Israel." *Middle East Journal* 7:2 (Spring 1953).

Thieberger, Friedrich. *Erinnerungen an Kafka*, ed. Hans-Gerd Koch. 1995.

Unseld, Joachim. *Franz Kafka: Ein Schriftstellerleben*. Hanser, 1982 [*Franz Kafka: A Writer's Life*, trans. Paul F. Dvorak. Ariadne, 1994].

Vassogne, Gaëlle. *Max Brod in Prag: Identität und Vermittlung*. Max Niemeyer Verlag, 2009.

———. "Max Brod, Tomáš G. Masaryk et la reconnaissance de la nationalité juive en Tchécoslovaquie." *Tsafon* 52, 2006–2007.

Vogl, Joseph. *Der Ort der Gewalt: Kafkas literarische Ethik*. Fink, 1990.

Wallace, David Foster. "Laughing with Kafka." *Harper's*, July 1998.

Warshow, Robert. "Kafka's Failure." *Partisan Review*, April 1949.

Weidner, Daniel. "Max Brod, Gershom Scholem Und Walter Benjamin: Drei Konstellationen Theologischer Literaturkritik im Deutschen Judentum." In *Literatur im Religionswandel der Moderne: Studien zur christlichen und jüdischen Literaturgeschichte*, eds. Alfred Bodenheimer, Georg Pfleiderer, and Bettina von Jagow. Theologischer Verlag, 2009, 195–220.

Weinberger, Theodore. "Philip Roth, Franz Kafka, and Jewish Writing." *Journal of Literature and Theology* 7, 1993.

Weingrad, Michael. "A Rich 1925 Novel about the Recurring Dilemmas of Jewish Existence." *Mosaic*, September 19, 2016.

Weltsch, Felix. "Der Weg Max Brods." *Bulletin des Leo-Baeck-Instituts*, 1963.

———. "Max Brod: A Study in Unity and Duality," trans. Harry Zohn. *Judaism*, Winter 1965.

———. *Max Brod and His Age*. Leo Baeck Institute, 1970.

———. *Religion und Humor im Leben und Werk Franz Kafkas*. Herbig, 1957 (Bialik Institute, 1959) [Hebrew].

———, ed. *Dichter, Denker, Helfer: Max Brod zum fünfzigsten Geburstag*. Julius Kittls Nachfolger, Keller & Co., 1934.

Wessling, Berndt W. *Max Brod: Ein Portrait*. Kohlhammer, 1969 (rev. ed. 1984).

Wilk, Melvin. *The Jewish Presence in Two Major Moderns: Eliot and Kafka*. PhD diss., University of Massachusetts Amherst, 1978.

Wilson, Edmund. "A Dissenting Opinion on Kafka." In *Classics and Commercials*. Farrar, Straus and Cudahy, 1950.

Wisse, Ruth. "The Logic of Language and the Trials of the Jews: Franz Kafka and Y. H. Brenner." In *The Modern Jewish Canon*. University of Chicago, 2003.

Wlaschek, Rudolf M. *Juden in Böhmen. Beiträge zur Geschichte des europäischen Judentums im 19. und 20. Jahrhundert*. Oldenbourg, 1990.

Wolff, Kurt. *Autoren, Bücher, Abenteuer. Betrachtungen und Erinnerungen eines Verlegers.* Wagenbach Verlag, 1965.

Woods, Michelle. *Kafka Translated: How Translators Have Shaped our Reading of Kafka.* Bloomsbury, 2013.

Yerushalmi, Yosef Hayim. "Series Z. An Archival Fantasy." *Psychomedia: Journal of European Psychoanalysis,* Spring 1997/Winter 1997.

Yildiz, Yasemin. "The Uncanny Mother Tongue: Monolingualism and Jewishness in Franz Kafka." In *Beyond the Mother Tongue.* Fordham University Press, 2012.

Yudkin, Leon I. *In and Out: The Prague Circle and Czech Jewry.* L. Marek, 2011.

Zabel, Hermann, ed. *Stimmen aus Jerusalem: zur deutschen Sprache und Literatur in Palästina/Israel.* Lit Verlag, 2006.

Zeller, B. "Fünf Jahre Deutsches Literaturarchiv in Marbach. Ergebnisse, Erfahrungen, Planungen." In *In Libro Humanitas. Festschrift für Wilhelm Hoffmann zum 60 Geburtstag.* Ernst Klett, 1962.

——. *Marbacher Memorabilien. Vom Schiller-Nationalmuseum zum Deutschen Literaturarchiv 1953–1973.* Deutsche Schillergesellschaft, 1995.

Zeller, B., et al. *Klassiker in finsteren Zeiten, 1933–1945. Eine Ausstellung des Deutschen Literaturarchivs im Schiller Nationalmuseum, Marbach am Neckar.* Deutsche Schillergesellschaft Marbach, 1983.

Zimmermann, Moshe. "The Chameleon and the Phoenix: Germany in the Eyes of Israel." In *Avar Germani—Zikaron Israeli.* Am Oved, 2002.

Zinger, Miriam. "Kafka's Hebrew Teacher." *Orot* 6, 1969.

Zohn, Harry. "Max Brod at Seventy-Five." *Jewish Frontier,* October 1959.

Zweig, Stefan. Foreword to *The Redemption of Tycho Brahe* by Max Brod, trans. Felix Waren Crosse. Knopf, 1928.

Zylberberg, H. "Das tragische Ende der drei Schwestern Kafkas." *Wort und Tat,* 1946/1947, Heft 2.

Archives

Hugo Bergmann archives, National Library, Jerusalem (ARC. 4* 1502)

Max Brod archives, National Library, Jerusalem (Schwad. 01 02)

Papers of Franz Kafka, Bodleian Library, Oxford (MSS. Kafka 1–55), including Kafka's German-Hebrew vocabularies and Hebrew exercises (shelfmarked MS. Kafka 24; 26, fols. 28v–29v; 29–33; 46, fols. 5–8; and 47, fols. 4–15)

Shin Shalom-Esther Hoffe correspondence, Gnazim: Asher Barash Bio-Bibliographical Institute, Tel Aviv (file 97)

Court Rulings

Tel Aviv District Court 1169/73, State Legal Advisor Kerem v. Esther Hoffe, January 17, 1974 [Hebrew].

Tel Aviv Family Court 105050/08, Eva D. Hoffe v. General Custodian Tel Aviv, October 12, 2012 [Hebrew].

Tel Aviv District Court 47113-11-12, Eva D. Hoffe v. Shmulik Cassouto (executor of the estate of Esther Hoffe), Ehud Sol (executor of the estate of Max Brod), the National Library of Israel, and the German Literary Archive in Marbach. June 29, 2015 [Hebrew].

Supreme Court of Israel 6251/15, Eva D. Hoffe v. Shmulik Cassouto (executor of the estate of Esther Hoffe), Ehud Sol (executor of the estate of Max Brod), the National Library of Israel, the German Literary Archive in Marbach, and General Custodian, August 7, 2016 [Hebrew].

Index

Note: Page numbers in *italics* refer to illustrations.

Ackermann, Theodor, bookseller, 155
Adenauer, Konrad, 108
Aderet, Ofer, 215
Adorno, Theodor W., 142, 144, 148, 224
Agnon, S. Y., 44, 115, 117, 174
Aichinger, Ilse, 246n
Albee, Edward, 127
Aleichem, Sholem, 97, 178
Alfried Krupp von Bohlen und Halbach
    Foundation, 163
Alsberg, Paul, 199
Alter, Robert, 89, 238n, 241n
Alterman, Natan, 11, 174
Altmann, Alexander, 88
Amichai, Yehuda, 11, 46, 214
Amis, Kingsley, 11–12
Am Oved, 107n, 184
Anders, Günther, 88n, 167, 168
Ansky, S., 178
Appelfeld, Aharon, 109, 114–15, 116, 175, 180
Ardon, Mordecai, 103
Arendt, Hannah, 41n, 86, 105, 133, 140n,
    148, 157, 167, 235n
Artemis & Winkler, 204
Ashkenazi, Yossi, 10

Ashman, Aharon, 178
Ashwall, Harel, 74
Auden, W. H., 86, 107n, 225
Auerbach, Erich, 41n
Auschwitz concentration camp, 78, 115,
    182, 191
Austro-Hungarian Empire:
    dissolution of, 52, 61
    Kafka's father in army of, 91
Avnery, Uri, 6

Bachmann, Ingeborg, 218–19
Balfour Declaration, 87
Bankier, David, 231n
Bank Leumi, Tel Aviv, 71, 73, 217
Bar Kochba Association, 23, 49, 51–52,
    58–59, 95, 99, 146n, 156
Baron, Salo W., 105
Baruch, Isaac Loeb (Brocowitz), 185
Barzilai, Matan, 218
Bashan, Refael, 186
Bauer, Felice, 30, 41n, 54–57, 58, 61, 62, 67,
    94, 95, 206, 227
Bauer, Yehuda, 231n
Baum, Oskar, 30n, 186, 230n

Beardsley, Aubrey, 22
Beauvoir, Simone de, 225
Beck, Evelyn, *Kafka and the Yiddish Theater*, 239n
Beckett, Samuel, 115
Beethoven, Ludwig van, 140
Begin, Menachem, 108
Bellow, Saul, 89, 96
ben Abuya, Elisha, 95
Ben-Gurion, David, 59, 182
ben Hama, Pinchas, 121
Ben-Horin, Schalom, 174, 240n
Benjamin, Walter, 38, 113, 145, 180–81, 215, 223, 224n, 237–38n, 249n
Benn, Gottfried, 41n
Ben-Tovim, Puah, 64–65
Ben-Yehuda, Eliezer, 59
Berdichevsky, M. Y., 156, 175
Berendsohn, Walter, 183
Berglass, Ella, 190–91
Bergmann, Elsa (née Fanta), 67
Bergmann, Hugo, 49, 52, 58–59, 62, 64, 67, 104, 105, 115, 187, 230n
Bergner, Yosl, 6
Bezaleli, Amnon, 196
Bialik, H. N., 97, 183, 184, 197
Binder, Hartmut, 169
Birnbaum, Nathan, 59
Blei, Franz, 29
Bloch, Grete, 41n, 56
Bloom, Harold, 67, 107n
Blüher, Hans, *Secessio Judaica,* 61
Blumberg, David, 211
Blumenfeld, Kurt, 59
Böll, Heinrich, 160, 171n
Bondy, Fritz, 147
Born, Jürgen, 156
Bornstein, Sagi, 165
Botstein, Leon, 21
Bowie, David, 3
Brahe, Tycho, 27–28
Brandeis, Louis D., 51
Brecht, Bertolt, 145, 178
Brenner, Hagai, 78, 79, 81
Brenner, Y. H., 66, 175
Breton, André, 131n
Briegleb, Klaus, 160
Brod, Adolf [father], 17

Brod, Elsa [wife], 126, 142, 149, 190, 191
Brod, Fanny (née Rosenfeld) [mother], 17
Brod, Henri [oboist; no relation], 21
Brod, Max, 7, *154*
    and anti-Semitism, 61, 62, 82
    birth and early years of, 17
    death of, 6, 9, 33, 35, 106, 196–97
    diaries of, 73
    estate of, 4, 10, 11, 13, 33–48, 72, 75–77, 78, 80–81, 84, 162, 164, 179, 197–99, 204, 207–8, 209–11, 213–15, 217–18
    and Esther Hoffe, 10, 33, 34, 36, 47, 75–77, 79, 80, 185, 191, 193–201, 207–8, 209, 213, 218
    family members killed in Holocaust, 78, 186, 191
    finances of, 173
    flight from Prague to Palestine, 6, 45, 142–44, 145–49
    friendship of Kafka and, 17–20, 24, 28, 29–30, 42, 62, 124, 126, 133–34, 181, 225
    and Germany, 48, 81, 82, 185–86
    grave of, *15*
    and Habima, 173–74, 176, 177–79, 186, *188*, 193
    and Hebrew language, 63–64, 174–77, 181
    honors and awards to, 134, 183–85
    influences on, 26–27
    in Israel, 108, 173–80, 181–83, 187
    on Kafka as genius, 25–26, 27, 68, 133, 225
    and Kafka's illness and death, 122, 123–24
    and Kafka's last wish, 80n, 81, 122, 124–31, 132–37, 213, 223, 234n, 241n
    Kafka's letters to, 28, 38, 41n, 55, 66, 67, 70, 93, 99, 118, 127, 151, 155, 158, 161, 172, 195, 227
    as Kafka's literary agent, 28–30, 54, 97, 132–38, 140, 152, 165n, 179–81, 182, 213
    as Kafka's literary executor, 4, 34, 43, 81, 129, 203
    and Kafka's papers, 4, 9, 10, 11, 34, 39, 40, 42–43, 46–47, 72–73, 75–77, 79–80, 128–29, 132–40, 144, 149–53, 170n, 195–96, 199, 213, 215
    Kafka's works edited/interpreted by, 7, 57, 87, 107n, 132, 133, 136–37, 140, 179, 244n

letters of, 41n, 43–44, 82
literary legacy of, 28n, 34–35, 44–45,
  47–48, 77, 81, 133, 135
literary output of, 24–25, 26–27, 37
losses sustained by, 189–91
and National Library of Israel, 59, 80
personal traits of, 20, 21, 22–23
in Prague, 16–19, 113, 144
reputation of, 24–25, 45, 174, 179, 183
and Schopenhauer, 16, 18
street in Tel Aviv named for, 106n
travels with Kafka, 22, 38, 90, 156–57
U.S. refuge sought by, 148–49
will of, 33, 34, 36, 37, 46–47, 72, 77, 80,
  152, 197–99, 213, 217, 223
and women, 22–23, 24, 35, 190–91
and Yiddish theater, 95, 97n, 173–74
and Zionism/Judaism, 44, 45, 48,
  50–54, 58, 60, 62, 86, 92, 133, 134, 166,
  174, 216, 236n
as *Zwischenmensch*, between cultures,
  24, 43–44
Brod, Max, works:
  Abschied von der Jugend (*Farewell to
    Youth: A Romantic Comedy in Three
    Acts*), 26
  Achot Ketanah, 177
  Arkadia, 30
  Armer Cicero, 71
  Arnold Beer, 27, 30
  autobiography: *A Contentious Life* (*Stre-
    itbares Leben*), 17, 135, 149, 187n, 197
  A Czech Servant Girl (*Ein tschechisches
    Dienstmädchen*), 23
  Dan the Guard (opera libretto), 176–77
  "Der jüdische Dichter deutscher Zunge"
    ("The Jewish Poet of the German
    Tongue"), 238n
  Der Meister (*The Master*), 177
  Diary in Verse (*Tagebuch in Versen*), 26
  Die Musik Israels, 177
  Die Rosenkoralle (*The Red Coral*), 186
  Diesseits und Jenseits (*Here and Beyond*),
    177
  "Franz Kafka the Writer," 30
  Galileo in Shackles, 184
  "Hebrew Lesson" (Hebräische Lektion),
    64

Judinnen (*Jewesses*), 87
Jugend im Nebel (*Youth in the Fog*), 186
Kafka biography, 14, 80n, 107, 133, 134,
  135, 179–81
Kafka's opinions of, 26, 28
The Kingdom of Love (*Zauberreich der
  Liebe*), 113–14, 129–31
in later years, 186
*The Miracle on Earth; or the Jewish Idea
  and Its Realization*, 175
musical compositions, 248n
*Nornepygge Castle; Novel of the Indiffer-
  ent Man*, 26
"Our Writers and the Community," 227
Paganism, Christianity, Judaism, 23, 54,
  143, 156, 175, 197, 249n
Pinkas Katan (Small Ledger) [newspaper
  column], 177
The Prague Circle (*Der Prager Kreis*), 145,
  170n, 186–87, 224n
Rassentheorie und Judentum (*Race
  Theory and Judaism*), 143
The Redemption of Tycho Brahe, 27–28,
  139, 147, 174, 186n
Reubeni: Prince of the Jews, 134, 176
Richard and Samuel (with Kafka, unfin-
  ished joint novel), 26, 196
"Selected Works," 243n
Socialism in Zionism, 62
Three Loves (*Die Frau Nach der Man Sich
  Sehnt* or *The Woman One Longs For*), 23
"The Three Phases of Zionism," 58
Tod den Toten!, 41n
Unambo, 183, 190n
Brod, Otto [brother], 17, 78, 186, 191
Brod, Sophia [sister], 17
Brodsky, Joseph, 219
Buber, Martin, 28n, 29, 34, 35, 44, 49–50,
  65, 95, 104, 113, 138, 165, 166, 174, 230n
Bülow, Ulrich von, 42
Butler, Judith, 56, 118

Cafe Kassit, Tel Aviv, 6
Café Savoy, Prague, 95
Camus, Albert, 107, 115
Canetti, Elias, 14, 106
Carmel, Abraham (Kreppel), 107n
Casanova, 22

Cassouto, Shmulik, 36, 47, 77, 79, 200–201
Celan, Paul, 41n, 107n, 160, 168
Chmurzyński, Wojciech, 101n
Clemens, Samuel, 127
Coe, Peter, 178
Coetzee, J. M., 133
Cohen, Margot, 34–36, 46
Cohen, Oded, 9
Commission on European Jewish Cultural
    Reconstruction, New York, 105
Corngold, Stanley, 97n, 216
Czechoslovakia, creation of, 52

Dante Alighieri, 176, 225
Danziger, Yoram, 8
Das gelobte Land (Promised Land), 63–64
Davar, 177, 196
Dayan, Moshe, 6
de Gaulle, Charles, 245n
DellaPergola, Sergio, 231n
Der Jude, 53, 65, 138, 165, 227, 233n
Derrida, Jacques, 65n
Diamant, Dora, 61, 66–67, 73, 121, 126,
    131n, 170, 242n
Die Jüdische Rundschau, 45, 98
Die Schmiede, publisher, 136
Dietrich, Marlene, 23
Die Zeit, 169, 215
Dilthey, Wilhelm, 160
Dolejs, Svatopluk, 171n
Dostoyevsky, Fyodor, 156
Dreyfus, Alfred, 214
Dumesnil, René, 18
Dvořák, Antonín, 21

Echte, Bernhard, 71
Edelstein, Jacob, 143
Ehrenburg, Ilya, 114
Ehrenstein, Albert, 230n
Einstein, Albert, 21, 28n, 148, 230n
Eisner, Pavel, 23, 51
Eliot, T. S., 37–38, 189, 226
Eliot, Valerie, 37–38
Emrich, Wilhelm, 169
Erhard, Ludwig, 109
Eshkol, Levi, 109
Etgar, Yeshayahu, 9, 46, 217, 218

Faktor, Emil, 24
Faynman, Zygmund, 95
Feierberg, M. Z., 111
Fenves, Peter, 28n
Finkel, Shimon, 194
Fischer, Gottfried, 140n
Flaubert, Gustave, 18, 21, 24, 94
Flores, Angel, 107n
Franz Josef I, Kaiser, 92
Freud, Sigmund, 225, 230n
Freud, Victor Mathias, 146–47n
Friedländer, Saul, Franz Kafka: The Poet of
    Shame and Guilt, 136–37
Friesel, Evyatar, 11n
Frisch, Shelley, 39
Fritsch, Werner, 155–56
Froehlich, Elio, 204
Fromer, Jakob, 98

Gabrieli, Arnan, 46
Galerie Gerd Rosen, 205
Garel, Georges, 34
Geissler, Benjamin, 101n
Gelber, Mark, 40, 77, 147, 168, 231n
Gellner, Julius, 178
George, Stefan, 161
German Literature Archive, see Marbach
Germany:
    Brod's manuscripts seized in, 82, 186
    cultural heritage protection law, 12
    cultural legacy of, 12, 13, 46, 132, 138, 158,
        160–70, 224
    Czechoslovakia annexed by, 143–44, 146
    and Holocaust, 42, 78–79, 108, 224
    and Israel, 108–10, 117, 165, 184
    and Kafka's Jewishness, 168–70
    Kafka's move to, 66–67, 170
    Kafka's works published in, 107–8, 167
    language and literature of, 10, 79, 93,
        97n, 98–100, 108–10, 114, 117, 131n,
        132, 156–61, 166–69, 174, 184–85, 227,
        238n
    and Munich Agreement, 143
    national identity of, 159–60, 164, 185
    and Prussia, 159
Gershuni, Gershon K., 177
Gluzman, Michael, 116

Goethe, Johann Wolfgang von, 21, 140, 156–57, 159, 161, 163, 165, 185, 190, 197, 225
Goethe Archive, 160
Goldfaden, Avrom, 95
Goldstein, Moritz, "The German-Jewish Parnassus," 166
Gordin, Jacob, 95
Gordon, A. D., 138
Gould, Glenn, 193–94
Grade, Chaim, 213–14
Graetz, Heinrich, 98
Grafton, Anthony, 24
Grass, Günter, 109, 160
Graves, Robert, 12
Greenberg, Clement, 88n
Greene, Graham, 12n
Grillparzer, Franz, 156
Gross, John, 238n
Grossman, David, 213, 241–42n
Grözinger, Karl Erich, 216
　Kafka and Kabbalah, 169
Gruenberg, Abraham, 61
Grunfeld, Frederick V., 189
Gruppe 47, 160, 246n
Grütters, Monika, 12
Guthrie, Tyron, 178

Ha'am, Ahad, 55, 166, 197
Haaretz, 44, 45, 72, 74, 104, 194, 204, 214, 215
Haas, Simon Fritz, 197
Haas, Willy, 26, 51, 170
Habima theater, 173–74, 176, 177–79, 186, *188,* 193, 247–48n
Habsburg Empire, 53, 116, 187, 242n
Hácha, Emil, 142
Hachavazelet, 59
Halper, Shaun J., 232n
Hammerman, Ilana, 107n
Hanser Verlag, 203–4
Harati, Ilan, 72
Harel, Zvi, 35
Ha-Reubeni, David, 134n
Harshav, Benjamin, 88n
Har-Shefi, Yoella, 194
Hauptmann, Gerhart, 166

Hauschner, Auguste, 53
Hay, Louis, 245n
Hazaz, Haim, 174
Hebbel, Friedrich, 156
Hebel, Johann Peter, 156
Hebrew language, 63–64, 166, 174–77, 180, 181, 237n
Hebrew University, 42, 110, 175
　and Brod's estate, 197
　and National Library, 103; *see also* National Library of Israel
Hedeyat, Sadeq, 107n
Hefer, Haim, 6
Heidegger, Martin, 41n
Heine, Heinrich, 21, 134, 139, 159, 176, 179, 244–45n
Heinrich Mercy Verlag, 139
Heller, Erich, 113
Heller, Meir, 10–11, 13, 33–34, 40, 47, 78–79, 152
Hermann, Gerti, 80
Hermann, Leo, 23
Herzl, Theodor, 45, 52, 58, 60, 156, 230n
Hess, Moses, 155
Hesse, Hermann, 25, 41n, 138, 166, 182–83
Hillel, teachings of, 85
Hilsner, Leopold, 61
Hitler, Adolf, 114, 142, 145, 149
Hoffe, Esther (Ilse) [mother]:
　and access to Brod's and Kafka's papers, 38–39, 45, 73, 199–200, 206
　birth and background of, 191
　and Brod's estate, 7, 9–10, 34–38, 40–41, 46–47, 77, 80, 81, 197–200, 204, 207–8, 209–10, 213
　Brod's relationship with, 47, 185, 191, 193–201, 213, 218
　death of, 34, 74, 201, 207
　estate of, 47, 79, 218
　financial gain from sales of papers, 38n, 39, 40, 70, 76, 79, 81, 202–6, 213, 234n
　Gedichte aus Israel (Poems from Israel), 195
　inventory of manuscripts in possession of, 71–73
　Israel's suit against, 9–10, 46, 75, 76, 79, 198–201, 207n

Hoffe, Esther (Ilse) [mother] (*continued*)
  and Kafka's papers, 10–11, 36, 38, 40, 47,
    70–74, 75–77, 194, 195, 198, 200, 206,
    207, 213, 217
  and National Library of Israel, 34–37,
    162
  reparations from Germany to, 74
  safe-deposit boxes of, 198, 217–18, *220*
  will of, 32–34, 40, 41, 74–77, 201, 207,
    212, 223
Hoffe, Eva, *15*
  birth and early years of, 5–7
  and Brod's estate, 4, 10, 34, 42, 43,
    76–77, 198, 204, 209–10, 213, 218
  and Esther's will, 32–33, 34, 74–77, 212
  finances of, 73–74
  and first appeal, 77–78
  and first trial, 35–36, 46–48
  and inventory of manuscripts, 73
  and Kafka's papers, 8, 10, 71, 73, 137, 151,
    152, 203, 207, 215–17
  and last appeal, 3–5, 7–10, 13–14, 82, 84,
    202, 209–11, 212–15
  memories of Brod, 194–95, 197, 212
  and request for new hearing, 216–17
  and safe-deposit boxes, 71–72, 198,
    217–18, *220*
  and sales of manuscripts, 77, 79, 164
  in Tel Aviv, 6–7, 45, 67–68
Hoffe, Otto [father], 5, 6, 191–93, 194
Hoffe, Ruth (Weisler) [sister], 194
  and Brod's estate, 34, 43, 210
  death of, 74
  and Esther's will, 32, 34, 74, 77
  and first trial, 46
  and Kafka's papers, 10, 207, 217
Hoffe family, 82, 191–94
  and Brod's estate, 40, 215
  escape from Prague, 5, 192
  and Kafka's papers, 4, 40, 42, 215
  safe-deposit boxes of, 71–73, 198, 217–18,
    220
Hoffmann, Camill, 242n
Hoffmann und Campe Verlag, 41n
Hofmannsthal, Hugo von, 18, 25, 50, 140,
  156
Hölderlin, Friedrich, 140, 185

Holocaust:
  Brod's family members murdered in, 78,
    186, 191
  and German language, 108–9, 114
  guilt connected to, 42
  horrors of, 114–15
  and Jewish cultural legacy, 83–84, 89,
    101–2n, 103
  Kafka's family members murdered in,
    44, 78–79, 224, 234n
  postwar writings on, 168
  survivors of, 80, 114, 117
  and Yad Vashem, 101–2n
  see also Nazi Party
Horkheimer, Max, 148
Howarth, Herbert, 183n
Howe, Irving, 134, 179
Hughes, Ted, 38
Hugo, Victor, 176
Husák, Gustáv, 171n
Hyperion, 29

Idel, Moshe, *Old Worlds, New Mirrors,* 111
I. G. Farben, Offenbach, 104
Ionescu, Eugène, 115
Isak, Haim, 107n
Israel:
  Archives Law (1955), 200
  and Balfour Declaration, 87
  cultural legacy of, 7, 11, 13, 40, 44–46,
    77, 78–79, 82, 83–84, 88–90, 101–5,
    108, 118–19, 162, 184, 223–24; *see also*
    National Library of Israel
  Declaration of Independence, 82n, 182
  and Diaspora, 66, 101, 102, 105, 110–17,
    119, 147, 224
  emigration to, 4, 5, 6, 45, 62n, 142–44,
    145–49
  and German language, 108–10, 117, 174,
    184–85
  and German reparations, 108
  Gift Law in, 76n
  and Holocaust, 78, 83, 108–9, 115, 117
  and Jewish identity, 52, 53, 105–6, 111–19
  and Kafka's works, 108–10, 117–19, 216
  lawsuit for possession of Kafka manu-
    scripts, 9–10, 13–14, 40–41, 42, 47,

162, 165, 198; *see also* Supreme Court of Israel; Tel Aviv District Court; Tel Aviv Family Court

and Mecelle law, 76

Six-Day War (1967), 5–6

State Archives of, 72

Succession Law (1965), 32–33, 77, 200

War of Independence (1948), 5, 102, 182–83

James, Henry, 37

Janáček, Leoš, 44

Jelinek, Elfriede, 106

Jesenská, Milena, 23, 41n, 67, 78, 107n, 118, 122, 123, 144, 161, 170, 205, 225

Jewish National Council, 52

Jílovská, Staša, 23

JNUL, *see* National Library of Israel

Job, Book of, 89, 237–38n

Joel, Issachar, 106

Johst, Hanns, 132

Jokl, Anna Maria, 230n

Jonson, Ben, 144

Joubran, Salim, 217

Joyce, James, 86, 230n

Judaism:
    and Zionism, 181; *see also* Zionism

Jüdische Verlag, 59

Kadishman, Menashe, 7

Kafka (film), 126–27n

Kafka, Elli [sister], 78, 153n, 171

Kafka, Franz, *31, 69*
    aging and illness of, 64–65, 66–67, 121–23, 125–26
    Amschel (Yiddish name), 68
    and anti-Semitism, 60–62
    and Brod, *see* Brod, Max
    cult of, 106
    and cultural legacy, 8, 11, 40, 43–44, 47–48, 82, 84, 85, 88–90, 102, 137n, 161, 165, 171n, 177, 198, 216, 219, 224, 227
    death of, 9, 79, 81, 105, 123, 128, 166
    diaries of, 67, 72, 73n, 88, 95, 98, 101, 107n, 112, 121, 123, 125, 136, 140, 151, 196

elegy for, 63

family background of, 91–93

family members killed by Nazis, 44, 78–79, 224, 234n

and German language and culture, 98–100, 116, 156–58, 166–68, 170, 172, 227

in Germany, 66–67, 170

Hebrew studies of, 62–64, 66, 67, 83, 85, 151, 156, 237n

and his father, 90–98, 225

influence of, 26, 115–17, 225–27, 241–42n, 246n

influences on, 156–57

and Jesenská, *see* Jesenská, Milena

and Jewishness/Zionism, 11, 13, 40, 48, 49, 55–57, 58–60, 62–66, 79, 82, 85–100, 105–8, 110–17, 134, 166, 168–70, 171n, 180, 181, 224, 227, 235n, 236n, 238n, 243n

last wish of, 4, 9, 34, 43, 61, 80n, 81, 84, 121–31, 132–37, 213, 223, 234n, 241n

library of, 155–56

living heirs of, 42, 75, 80, 151–53, 211, 215

on music, 21–22

papers of, 4, 7, 9–10, 34–35, 41–43, 46–47, 70, 75–77, 78, 79–80, 81, 117–18, 123, 124–28, 150–53, 194, 195–96, 198–201, 202–6, 209, 213–16, 218

personal traits of, 20–21, 22, 57, 65, 67–68, 91, 94, 111–13, 122, 123, 129, 219, 225, 226–27

poor self-image of, 26, 28, 29, 65–66, 92, 94, 111–13, 122–23, 125–26, 128, 167, 225

in Prague, 16–19, 60–62, 95, 170, 191

qualities in work of, 115–16, 133–34, 137, 138, 139, 144–45

reputation of, 133–34, 137, 139, 140n, 152, 170n, 171

will of, 80n, 127, 234n

and women, 22, 23–24, 55–56, 57–58, 61, 66, 67, 73

and Yiddish theater, 95–100

Kafka, Franz, works:
    Amerika, 21–22, 107n, 136, 146, 151, 170n, 222, 244n

Kafka, Franz, works (*continued*)
"Before the Law," 65n, 212, 221–22
Beim Bau der chinesischen Mauer (*The Great Wall of China*), 136
The Blue Octavo Notebooks, 85, 151
"Blumfeld," 151
"The Burrow" ("Der Bau"), 57, 87, 88n, 112, 151
"The Cares of a Family Man" ("Die Sorge des Hausvaters"), 226
The Castle, 87, 107n, 112, 136, 151, 170n, 173, 186, 189, 222, 236n, 237n
Collected Works, 244n
A Country Doctor, 91, 123, 125
"Description of a Struggle," 25, 38, 76, 136, 137, 151, 195
"The Giant Mole," 88n
A Hunger Artist, 122, 125, 151
"An Imperial Message," 222
"In the Penal Colony," 125, 222
"Investigations of a Dog," 22, 87, 88n
"Jackals and Arabs," 65, 87
"Josephine the Singer, or the Mouse Folk," 52–53, 87–88, 151
"The Judgment," 30, 56, 107n, 112, 125
Letters to Milena (*Briefe an Milena*), 107n
letter to his father, 41n, 72, 90–94, 97–98, 137, 151, 196, 213, 223
"A Little Woman," 151
Meditation (*Betrachtung*), 3, 29, 54, 230n
"The Metamorphosis" (*Die Verwandlung*), 21, 87, 97, 107n, 114, 125, 133, 153n, 240n
obscure character types in, 86, 94, 112, 118, 122, 144, 180, 221–23, 224, 225–27
ownership of, 5, 117–19, 133, 151–53, 163, 202–4, 210, 215, 219, 224
posthumous publication of, 124–29, 138–40, 203–4, 205–6
"The Problem of Our Laws" (parable), 211
"Prometheus," 137
"The Rejection," 41n
"A Report to an Academy," 65, 87, 165
Sämtliche Erzählungen (Raabe, ed.), 169
sketches and doodles, 73, 203–4, 234n

"Speech on the Yiddish Language," 99–100, 238n
"The Stoker," 41n, 125, 170n, 222
translations of, 107–8, 140n, 170–71n
The Trial, 7, 8, 24, 25, 38, 41n, 75, 76, 101n, 107n, 114, 117, 126, 134n, 136, 151, 161, 170n, 180, 195, 202–6, 212, 213, 216, 221, 233n, 237–38n, 244n
"The Village Schoolmaster," 41n, 161, 205
"Wedding Preparations in the Country," 25, 73, 76, 195, 203
Kafka, Hermann [father], 91–94, 95, 96, 97–98, 100, 124
Kafka, Ottla [sister], 41n, 78, 127, 162, 234n
Kafka, Siegfried [uncle], 78
Kafka, Valli [sister], 78
"Kafkaesque," 224n
"Kafka's Last Story" (film), 165
Kallen, Horace, 105
Kant, Immanuel, 165
Kaufman, Gerti, 153n
Kepler, Johannes, 27–28
Keren Ha-Yesod, 59
Kern, Christian, 83
Keshet, Yeshurun, 107n
Kiepenheuer, Gustav, 138
Kierkegaard, Søren, 24, 225
Kilcher, Andreas, 46
Kisch, Egon Erwin, 25, 51
Kittl, Julius, 140
Klausner, Joseph, 111
Kleist, Heinrich von, 24, 140, 156, 159, 186
Klíma, Ivan, 106, 170n
Klopstock, Robert, 66
Klossowski, Pierre, 107n
Koch, Hans-Gerd, 39
Kohn, Hans, 49
Kolár, František J., 171n
Kollek, Teddy, 175
Kopelevitz, Jakob, 107n
Kopelman Pardo, Talia, 34–36, 41, 43, 46, 71, 73, 74–77
Koralnik, Eva, 204
Kornfeld, Edna, 107, 107n
Kostrouchová Davidová, Helena, 80
Kracauer, Siegfried, 41n
Kraft, Werner, 174, 240n

Kraus, Karl, 43, 229n
Krauss, Nicole, *Forest Dark*, 68, 110–11
Krüger, Michael, 203–4
Kruk, Herman, 239n
Krupp, Alfried, 163
Kuehn, Heinz, 135
Kulka, Otto Dov, 44, 106
Kundera, Milan, 171n, 180
    Testaments Betrayed, 137
Kurzweil, Baruch, 180

Lachower, Fischel, 175n
Lamdan, Yitzhak, 134
Langer, Georg (Jiří) Mordechai,
    62–63, 135
Larkin, Philip, 127
Lasker-Schüler, Else, 41n, 71, 230n
Lavry, Marc, 176
law:
    on acquisition of papers from living
        authors, 11, 80, 210
    cultural heritage protection, 12, 83–84
    on gifts vs. inheritance, 47, 75, 76, 80,
        195–96, 199–200, 207, 213, 217
    and judicial violence, 144
    Kafka's motif of, 223, 225
    Mecelle law, 76
    and ownership of art, 219
    posthumous handling of literary estates,
        11, 37–38, 40, 42–43, 70–74, 80, 127–
        29, 137, 199–200, 210–11
    and private property rights vs. public
        interest, 4, 14, 75
    on "successive heirs," 32–33, 77, 200
Lehár, Franz, 21
Lenz, Siegfried, 246n
Lepper, Marcel, 41
Lessing, Doris, 12n, 140
Lev-Ari, Shimon, 179
Levi, Primo, 107n
Levi-Korem, Yaniv, 218
Lewin, Rabbi Joshua Heshel, 59
Lewy, Tom, 179
Leyris, Pierre, 107n
Liblice conference, 171n
Lichtheim, Richard, 56, 156
Lieger, Leopold, 23

Liepman Literary Agency, 204
Lindström, Carl, 55
Lintdberg, Leopold, 178, 186
Liska, Vivian, 65
Litt, Stefan, 82, 217–18
Lowell, Robert, 174
Löwy, Juliet, 94, 124, 138
Löwy, Yitzhak, 78–79, 96–97, 99–100
Lozowick, Yaacov, 83
Luther, Martin, 98, 159
Lydenberg, H. M., 148–49

Maariv, 67, 76, 185, 187
Magnes, Judah, 104
Maimonides, teachings of, 85
Malek, Nayrouz, *Kafka's Flowers*, 235n
Mandelstamm, Max, 165n
Mann, Heinrich, 25, 41n, 43, 159
Mann, Klaus, 139
Mann, Thomas, 23n, 25, 133, 148–49, 156,
    230n
Maor, Zohar, 231n
Marbach, German Literature Archive:
    accessibility of materials in, 13, 215
    and Brod's estate, 4, 13, 40–43, 48, 164,
        179, 206, 208, 215
    formation of, 160–64
    German-Jewish papers in, 42, 43, 168, 215
    and Kafka's papers, 13, 41, 43, 77, 105–7,
        158, 203, 205–6, 215–16
    and lawsuits, 8, 42
    manuscripts purchased by, 79
    mission of, 158–60
    and National Library of Israel, 162, 163,
        215
    technical facilities in, 40–41
Marcuse, Herbert, 148
Masaryk, Tomáš, 52, 147n, 242n
Maurer, Paul, 218
McEwan, Ian, 12n
Megged, Aharon, 174
Melcer, Hanan, 84
Mendes-Flohr, Paul, 233n
Meyer, Eduard, 165
Michaeli, Lali, 216
Michalski, Jakob, 236
Miłosz, Czesław, 176

Miron, Dan, 112, 214
Moked, Gabriel, 240n
Montefiore, Sir Moses, 59
Moser, Mibi, 204
Moses, teachings of, 85
Mossad Bialik, 175n
Motono, Koichi, 107n
Muir, Willa and Edwin, 107, 136, 140n
Munich Agreement, 143
Murakami, Haruki, 106
Museum of Modern Literature (LiMo),
    Marbach, 161
Muzicant, Ariel, 83

Nabokov, Dmitri, 127
Nabokov, Vladimir, 127, 133
Nadav, Mordechai, 35, 44
National Library of Israel:
    accessibility of materials in, 10, 11, 35, 211,
        215–16
    Bergmann as director of, 59
    and Brod's estate, 4, 10, 34–37, 43–44,
        47–48, 179, 208, 210, 213, 217
    Committee for the Salvage of Diaspora
        Treasures, 104
    establishment of, 59, 83, 102–3, 217
    and Esther Hoffe's will, 33–34
    and first judgment, 79, 82
    German-Jewish writers' works in, 34, 42,
        44, 46, 218, 230n
    and German literature, 10
    and Jewish cultural treasures, 77, 78–79,
        83–84, 90, 102–5, 118–19
    and Kafka's papers, 7, 10, 11, 35, 46–48,
        64, 70, 74, 77, 105–6, 108, 117–19, 152,
        199, 200–201, 209, 214–16, 217
    and last appeal, 8, 209–11, 213
    and Marbach archive, 162, 163, 215
    private property nationalized in, 46
    and Vienna Jewish library, 83
Nazi Party:
    authors persecuted by, 41
    authors blacklisted by, 132, 139, 140, 145,
        148
    concentration camps, 78, 97, 115, 145, 182,
        191, 234n, 242n
    escape from, 4, 5, 6, 142–44, 146–49, 155

    and Holocaust, see Holocaust
    and looted Jewish property, 83, 103–5,
        120, 132, 139, 140, 145, 186n, 203, 239–
        40n, 242n
    postwar attitudes toward, 167, 182,
        185–86
    rise to power, 132, 138–39, 142, 145, 149
    and Schiller, 247n
Netanyahu, Benjamin, 83, 159n
Neugroschel, Joachim, 97n
New York Times, 28n, 44, 137n, 183n
Nierad, Jonathan, 107n
Nietzsche, Friedrich, 18, 138
Novalis, 139–40

Offenbach Archival Depot, Germany, 105,
    120
Olmert, Ehud, 9
Ott, Ulrich, 205–6
Ottoman Empire, civil code of, 76
Oxford Kafka Research Centre, 134
Oxford University, Bodleian Library, 41,
    153, 162, 205, 215
Oz, Amos, 106, 112
Ozick, Cynthia, 137, 157–58

Pagi, Nurit, 45–46
Palästina, 55, 59
Palestine:
    and Balfour Declaration, 87
    British Mandatory Palestine, 140, 147n
    as Israel, see Israel
    Jewish colonies in, 59
Pasley, Sir Malcolm, 38, 39, 153, 205, 206,
    244n
Pawel, Ernst, 190
Pazi, Margarita, 39
Peretz, I. L., 96
Phillips, William, 134
Pinès, Meyer Isser, 98
Plath, Sylvia, 38
Plato, 18
Plinner, Sa'ar, 13, 42, 162, 163, 164, 210
Pohl, Johannes, 239n
Pollak, Ernst, 23
Pollak, Oskar, 157
Porat, Orna, 184, 186

Prager Abendblatt; Prager Tagblatt, 135, 149
Prague:
  anti-Semitism in, 60–62, 143, 171n, 191
  Bar Kochba Association in, 51–52
  escape to Palestine from, 4, 5, 6, 45, 62n,
    67, 142–49
  Franz Kafka Monument in, 171n
  German Jews in, 51, 60–61, 63, 91, 143,
    170
  Kafka's books banned in, 170n
  Tolerance Charter in, 90–91
Prague Circle, 24, 34, 35, 145
Prague Spring (1968), 171n
Preece, Julian, *Representative Man,* 86
Primor, Avi, 109
Prinz, Joachim, 249n
Proust, Marcel, 86

Raabe, Paul, 36–38, 169
Rabin, Yitzhak, 159n
Rashi, 13
Rath, Moses, 62, 83, 156
Rathenau, Walther, 61, 230n
Raulff, Ulrich, 13, 40–41, 161–64, 165
Ravensbrück concentration camp, 78,
    170
Reich, Hedwig, 193
Reich, Marion, 192n
Reuss, Roland, 153
Richter, Sandra, 162
Rilke, Rainer Maria, 25, 43, 50, 133, 140
Robert, Marthe, 100, 107, 156
Robertson, Ritchie, 96, 134
Robina, Hanna, 176
Rokem, Freddie, 178
Róna, Jaroslav, 171n
Rosen, Lia, 50
Rosenthal, Yemima, 71
Rosenzweig, Franz, 166, 236n
Roth, Joseph, 41n, 190
Roth, Philip, 106, 114, 116, 170, 224n, 226
Rothschild, Dorothy de, 8
Rowohlt Verlag, 29, 41n
Rubin, Abraham A., 236
Rubinstein, Elyakim, 8, 10, 13, 83, 209–11,
    217
Ruppin, Arthur, 60

Sachs, Nelly, 41n
Sadan, Dov, 175, 184–85
Salten, Felix, 59
Salveter, Emmy (later Aenne Markgraf), 190
Samuelson, Arthur, 138
Sandbank, Shimon, 107n, 118, 226
Saudková, Věra, 80
Schenhar, Yitzhak (Schönberg), 107n
Schiller, Friedrich, 21, 140, 156, 159, 160, 161,
    165, 190, 247n
Schiller Museum, Marbach, 161
Schirrmacher, Frank, 206
Schlaffer, Heinz, 167n
Schlesinger, Josef, 139
Schmückle, Georg, 247n
Schneider, Lambert, 138
Schneller, Isaiah, 78, 79
Schnitzler, Arthur, 20, 41n, 43
Schocken, Salman, 59, 65, 88, 107, 138, 139–
    40, *141*, 150–52, 179, 205, 210n
Schocken Books, New York, 138, 140n
Schocken family, 64, 153n, 245n
Schocken Verlag, 132, 138, 139–40, 152, 182,
    244n
Schoeps, Hans-Joachim, 181–82, 205, 232n,
    249n
Scholem, Gershom, 51, 109–10, 145, 246n
  on Brod's biography of Kafka, 180–81
  estate of, 71, 213, 230n
  and Kafka's influence, 117
  and Kafka's writings, 88–89, 106, 107n,
    140, 213, 237–38n, 249n
  and National Library of Israel, 104–5
  and rescue of looted books, 104–5
Schopenhauer, Arthur, 16, 18, 140, 156
Schreiber, Adolf, 21
Schubert, Franz, 140
Schulz, Bruno, 101–2n, 107n
Sebald, W. G., 41n
Seitmann, Rabbi Hoschut, 103n
Selbstwehr, 53, 61, 85, 95, 98
Selee, Yosef, 187n
S. Fischer Verlag, 38, 39, 41n, 107, 140n,
    153n, 244n
Shaked, Gershon, 117
Shakespeare, William, 12, 144, 156, 177, 178,
    225, 226

Shalev, Mordechai, 240n
Shalom, Shin, 174, 175, 176, 195, 248n
Shaphir, A. D., 186
Sharett, Moshe, 108
Sharon, Ariel, 6
Shedletzky, Itta, 71–73, 218
Shilo, Michael, 186
Shilo, Yitzhak, 10, 46, 75, 79, 152, 198–201
Shimoni, David, 112, 184–85
Shlonsky, Avraham, 175
Shmueli, Ilana, 174, 240n
Shoah, see Holocaust
Shumsky, Dmitry, 231n
Singer, Isaac Bashevis, 97
Slíva, Jiří:
    "Franz Kafka in the Waves," 69
    "Science Fiction: F. K. in Tel Aviv 1957,"
        69
Smilansky, Naomi, 5
Soderbergh, Steven, 126n
Sokolovsky, Noah, 60
Sokolow, Nahum, 60
Sol, Ehud, 47–48, 72, 218
Sophocles, 178
Sotheby's London, 202–6
Sotheby's New York, 230n
Spaini, Alberto, 107n
Spitzer, Moritz, 138, 139, 140
Stach, Reiner:
    on Brod and women, 22
    on Brod-Kafka relationship, 19, 20,
        133–34
    on Brod's estate, 38–39, 43–44, 197–98
    on Brod's literary output, 25, 73n
    as Kafka biographer, 19, 22, 27, 38–39, 59,
        140n, 215, 219
    on Kafka's papers, 42–44, 73n, 216
Staengle, Peter, 153n
Starobinski, Jean, 93
Steiner, George, 114, 132, 238n
Steiner, Marianna, 75, 80, 151, 153n, 198–99,
    206
Steiner, Michael, 42, 43, 151–52, 196, 198–
    99, 215
Steiner, Rudolf, 90
Stern, Tania and James, 136
Stifter, Adalbert, 139n

Stoffman, Judith, 74
Stollman, Aviad, 77, 213
Stopford, Robert J., 143
Strauss, Leo, 148
Strauss, Ludwig, 174, 230n
Stroemfeld Verlag, 153n
Sudaka-Bénazéraf, Jacqueline, 234n
Suhrkamp Verlag, 38, 213
Supreme Court of Israel:
    case regarding Vienna Jewish commu-
        nity, 82–84
    last appeal in (2016), 3–5, 7–10, 13–14, 82,
        84, 163, 164, 209–19, 223–24
Susman, Margarete, 89, 109
Szelińska, Józefina, 101n
Szubin, Zvi Henri, 137n

Tagesspiegel, 43–44
Tarshish Books, 244n
Tasso, 5
Taussig, Elsa, 24, 25
Tchernichovsky, Shaul, 173
Tel Aviv District Court:
    and Eva Hoffe's finances, 74
    first appeal in (2012–2015), 4, 77–78, 202
    judgment in (June 2015), 79–82, 151
    1974 lawsuit in, 10, 46, 75, 198–201
Tel Aviv Family Court:
    first judgment (October 2012), 74–77, 79
    first trial in (2007–2012), 4, 32–48,
        70–77
Teller, Judd, 111
Temkin, Mordechai, 147
Tenschert, Heribert, 206
Thatcher, Margaret, 205
Thieberger, Friedrich, 62, 230n
Tisza affair, 61
Torberg, Friedrich, 134n, 243n
Treblinka concentration camp, 78–79, 97
Tshissik, Millie, 96
Tucholsky, Kurt, 30n
Turgenev, Ivan, 87

UBS, Zürich, 71–73
Ullmann, Fritz, 143
Unseld, Joachim, 39
Unseld, Siegfried, 38, 39

Ussishkin, Menachem, 60
Uyttersprot, Herman, 244n

Valéry, Paul, 230n
Vardi, Kobi, 78, 79, 81
Vassogne, Gaëlle, *Max Brod in Prague: Identity and Mediation,* 144, 149
Vialette, Alexandre, 107n
Vienna Jewish community, 82–84
Vigée, Claude, 175
Virgil, *Aeneid,* 127
Vogelmann, David, 108
Volkswagen Foundation, 110
Voltaire, 176
von Schönerer, Georg Ritter, 191
Vrchlický, Jaroslav, 51n

Wagenbach, Klaus, 41, 70, 76, 106, 134, 203
Wagner, Richard, 21, 143
    "Judaism in Music," 165
Wágnerová, Alena, 167
Waldes, Jindřich, 192
Walser, Martin, 160
Walser, Robert, 30n, 71, 166, 204
Walsh, Robert, 104, 156
Wedekind, Frank, 43
Weigel, Sigrid, 97n, 160
Weinreich, Max, 105
Weiser, Rafi (Raphael), 11n, 64
Weltsch, Felix, 7, 41n, 45, 49, 146, 187, 230n, 231n, 232n
    Kafka obituary by, 85–86
Weltsch, Robert, 50–51, 54, 93n, 197
Werfel, Franz, 30n, 51, 187
Wiesel, Elie, 114–15
Wiesenthal, Simon, 103n
Wilson, Edmund, 225
Wilson, Woodrow, 142
Winkler, Manfred, 240n

Wohryzek, Julie, 57–58, 67, 78
Wolff, Kurt, 27, 29, 30n, 123, 136, 243n
    Helen and Kurt Wolff Archive, 41
Wortsman, Peter, 175n
Wyllie, David, 97n

Yad Vashem (Holocaust museum), 101–2n
Yehoshua, A. B., 115–16, 213
Yevseev, Yevgeni, 171n
YIVO library, Vilna, 104, 213
Yonatan, Natan, 11n
Yourgrau, Wolfgang, 108

Zach, Natan, 7
Zeit Foundation, 110
Zeller, Bernhard, 205
Zfat, Uri, 9, 46–47, 74
Zimmermann, Hans Dieter, 65, 169
Zionism:
    and Bar Kochba, 49, 51–52, 58–59
    and Brod, *see* Brod, Max
    and Buber, 49–50
    coining of term, 59
    and cultural treasures, 102, 105
    and diaspora, 189–90
    and Ha-Poel Ha-Tzair, 138
    Herzl as founding father of, 52
    and ingathering of exiles, 102, 105
    and Judaism, 181
    and Kafka, 55–57, 58–60, 62–66, 85–100, 110–17, 171n, 224n, 235n, 236n
    World Zionist Organization, 59–60
Zohar, Eli, 9–10, 13, 216
Zola, Émile, 214
Zunz, Leopold, 230n
Zweig, Arnold, 61, 108, 176
Zweig, Stefan, 17, 21, 41n, 134, 189, 190, 230n
Zylberberg, Hélène, 80n
Zylbertal, Zvi, 8, 10

BENJAMIN BALINT, a library fellow at the
Van Leer Institute, taught literature at the Bard College
humanities programme at Al-Quds University in
Jerusalem. He is the author of *Running Commentary*
(published by PublicAffairs in 2010) and co-author of
Jerusalem: City of the Book (forthcoming from Yale
University Press). He has written for the *Wall Street Journal*,
the *Weekly Standard*, and *Die Zeit*, and his translations
from the Hebrew have appeared in the *New Yorker*.